Sexually
Exploited Children

Sexually Exploited Children

Working to Protect and Heal

Phyllis Kilbourn
and
Marjorie McDermid
editors

800 West Chestnut Avenue, Monrovia, California 91016-3198 USA

Sexually Exploited Children
Working to Protect and Heal
Phyllis Kilbourn and Marjorie McDermid, editors

ISBN 1-887983-09-0

Published by MARC, a division of World Vision, 800 West Chestnut
Avenue, Monrovia, California 91016-3198 U.S.A.

Printed in the United States of America. Editor and typesetter: Joan
Weber Laflamme. Cover design: Richard Sears. Cover photo: Mikel
Flamm.

"Ten Steps to Recovery." ©1983 Jan Frank. Free to Care Ministries,
Placentia, California. U.S.A.

All Scripture quotations, unless otherwise indicated, are taken from
the HOLY BIBLE, NEW INTERNATIONAL VERSION©. Copyright,
1973, 1978, 1984 by International Bible Society. Used by permission of
Zondervan Publishing House. All rights reserved.

Contents

v

CONTENTS

Foreword

It was only a few years ago that my mind and heart awakened to the huge needs of children in our world. Phyllis Kilbourn's book *Children in Crisis*, shook me to the core of my soul. Of all the scenarios portrayed in that haunting book, the saddest are those of children who have been exploited sexually.

The United Nations reports that one million children are forced into child prostitution every year. Worldwide, an estimated 10 million children are victims of today's sex industry. Many are removed from their homes and sent into alien situations. How vastly opposed this is to God's plan that children be sheltered and safe within healthy families!

Can there really be hope for children so damaged? Yes!

> There is a Redeemer, Jesus God's own Son,
> Precious Lamb of God, Messiah,
> Holy one.
>
> Thank you, O my Father,
> For giving us your Son,
> and leaving Your Spirit
> 'Till the work on earth is done.[1]

Like the other books in this series, *Sexually Exploited Children: Working to Protect and Heal*, is a hands-on, practical resource. This book outlines helpful strategies and specific actions for addressing the needs of exploited children. It also describes effective programs that focus on prevention and healing. We need to give our most creative energy and thinking to address the needs of today's children. But let's never forget that the most loving thing we can do for abused children is to bring them to Jesus. He is the One who can restore and redeem.

And while we focus on the enormous needs of children, let's not forget their potential. Children—even children in crisis—have the potential to change the world. Remember the little slave girl who served Naaman's wife? I wonder what horrors she experienced in that land far from her home. Yet God used her to pierce the darkness of that godless culture and bring Naaman to God.

May God's will be done on earth, among children, as it is in heaven.

CAROL PLUEDDEMANN
SIM International

Acknowledgments

We traveled to many Asian countries to conduct the initial research for this book. In every city across Asia we were overwhelmed with the magnitude—and evilness—of the sexual exploitation of children. Often we struggled to keep our own hope alive—hope that these precious children, created in the image of God, could be healed and restored to wholeness physically, emotionally and spiritually. And through their restoration, comprehend the Father's great love and worth he has so lavishly bestowed on them.

We are deeply grateful for everyone who assisted us in our research efforts. Many administrators, pastors and caregivers took time from their busy schedules to give tours, answer countless questions and discuss their projects with us. They also provided us with opportunities to talk with the children in their care. The expressed needs of these front-line workers, along with the children's voiced concerns, formed the framework of this book.

The contributing authors have compassionately and sensitively added "flesh and bone" to the book's framework. Because of their commitment to the world's suffering children, they freely gave of their time and expertise to provide this resource as their gift to them. Together they have sought to provide a more hopeful future for sexually exploited children through more informed and effective caregivers. They, too, have had more than their share of struggles in addressing the compelling prevention and intervention needs of these deeply wounded and scarred children. Together they present a wealth of expertise from a variety of disciplines vital to holistic care of sexually abused and exploited children: medical, educational, psychological, spiritual development, advocacy, compassionate caregiving and community development. The contributing authors' deep compassion for these special children spurred them on to complete their arduous tasks. We express our deep gratitude to each one.

Besides the editors and contributing authors, there have been many others assisting in various supporting roles. We are especially grateful to those who have supported us with their prayers, encouraging us on to the finish line. Gratitude must also be expressed to my sister, Sharon Minor, for the many hours she spent typing and inserting corrections into the manuscripts. I have not been blessed with her patience! Please know, whatever your God-chosen role in this task, we are deeply grateful for your part in producing this resource, which prayerfully will enable caregivers to be more effective in caring for "God's best gifts."

Note

[1] "There Is a Redeemer" by Melody Green © 1982 Birdwing Music/ BMG Songs, Inc./Ears to Hear Music. All rights reserved. Used by permission.

Introduction

We had just spent time together discussing a previous handbook in this series, *Healing the Children of War*. "I may do one more handbook—for the street children," Phyllis said in parting. Marjorie had no idea that a book would result when she replied quietly, "Don't forget the child prostitutes."

A major contributing factor to Marjorie's desire had come as a result of multi-weekly rides to her church in Philadelphia. Travel on an avenue formerly known for its fashionable shops and family-oriented living now had young prostitutes on parade day and night. A church visitation program gave contact with a woman, her daughter and small grandchildren who, though not confessed sex workers, bore telling marks of that lifestyle. Their lives and their subsequent disappearance from the neighborhood made a great impact and influenced Marjorie's decision to help tackle this book.

Our trip across several Asian countries to research the needs of sexually exploited children provided countless opportunities to witness the destruction of precious children's lives. Not far into our research we realized that we had to widen our scope to take in more than the child prostitute. The millions of children assaulted, abused and exploited through incest, rape and pornography must also have our attention and care. Our goal in this book, though, isn't simply to recount the tragic circumstances of sexually exploited children. Knowing about their situations is vital to responding to their needs. Our ultimate goal, however, is reflected in a story John A. Huffman recounts from the Bosnian war:

> A small artist's shop stood amid the rubble in Mostar, over-looking what used to be the Friendship Bridge. Through an interpreter, I talked with the artist who had a number of paintings for sale of the bridge before it was destroyed. On

one wall was another painting, a painting of devastation. It showed coffee houses and artists' shops in rubble, with a gaping, empty space where the Friendship Bridge used to be. He painted the saddened face of the Muslim architect who had built the bridge hundreds of years before looking down on the devastation. In the same painting off in the distance, he painted the reconstructed bridge with the rebuilt coffee houses and shops. Above it, he painted the dove of peace. He looked me in the eyes and, through an interpreter said, "I could not paint devastation without also painting an envisioned hope for the future."[1]

We, too, do not wish simply to paint a picture of the devastation that sexual abuse has wreaked in the children's lives without also painting an envisioned hope for their future. That hope ultimately comes through Christ's loving, transforming touch upon broken lives. We, however, are called to be instruments that facilitate Christ's healing: to apply the balm of Gilead and to give practical demonstrations of Jesus' love. This book is intended to equip you to be an effective instrument in ministry to sexually exploited children.

Part 1 sets the global scene and realities of sexual exploitation of children. Through a case study from Thailand, root causes for such exploitation are explored. A profile of the perpetrator provides warning signs in how to spot a child abuser. The review of the impact of sexual exploitation on children lays the groundwork for those areas that need to be addressed in intervention programs. Please note that there are several authors throughout this book whose experiences are grounded in their work in Thailand. By including their learnings we do not mean to focus exclusively on Thailand. Thailand has acknowledged that the problem of child sexual exploitation exists within its borders, and it has been open to research and assistance in dealing with this problem.

Part 2 emphasizes the importance of families, churches, communities and child workers actively focusing on prevention of child abuse. Various prevention methods are provided, including empowering families and communities to care adequately for the needs of their children.

Part 3 looks at issues involved in holistic intervention planning for those already ensnared in sexual exploitation. The strategies and models provided are based on sound principles of child development. Vital elements of rehabilitation include providing a healing environment, counseling, spiritual healing and involving families and communities in the healing process. Our philosophy in regard to children in crisis situations is that we must include the family in our strategy for intervention. Nowhere is this conviction more vital than in dealing with the sexually exploited child, for in a large percentage of cases abuse begins in the home. To help you implement the principles of intervention planning, we include several models of successful programs. Part 4 addresses problem areas of special concern in caring for sexually exploited children: bonding and attachment, HIV/AIDS, pregnancy and abortion, with special emphasis on placing children in families and protecting them from sexual abuse.

Part 5 discusses two areas that are special concerns for caregivers of abused children. First is acquiring knowledge about the technical skills needed to enable caregivers accurately to record a child's history. Such histories enable caregivers to develop effective strategies and interventions. Second is providing an understanding of the dynamics of secondary stress and trauma that those working with sexually exploited children experience. Vital prevention and treatment techniques are also provided.

In the concluding part, Viju Abraham helps us reflect on the church's role in responding to social problems such as sexually exploited children and the poor. Poverty is often the root cause of child abuse and exploitation. Only as the church takes up the challenge of ministry to these broken children will they enjoy the hope and future promised to them by their loving heavenly Father.

Our prayer is that this book will equip you effectively to minister Christ's healing and restoring love to exploited and rejected children—those with little hope for acceptance and healing—helping them encounter Jesus, who alone can turn their mourning into dancing and clothe them with garments of joy.

Note

[1] John A. Huffman, *Bridges of Reconciliation: A Reader on the Conflict in Bosnia* (Monrovia, Calif.: World Vision, 1997), p. 57.

Contributing Authors

VIJU ABRAHAM. Pastor of the Love of Christ Fellowship in Mumbai (Bombay), India. Helps direct the Association for Christian Thoughtfulness (ACT), an urban mission and training center that helps resource the city's churches and ministries.

RENITA BOYLE. B.A. (Hons) in theology from Glasgow Bible College. Freelance journalist and associate editor of *Reaching Children at Risk: The Journal for Christians Ministering to Children at Risk* (Viva Network). Facilitates the recovery of women who have suffered childhood sexual abuse through the context of Christian faith. Currently researching children at risk in Scripture and how childhood sexual abuse affects the development of the God concept.

BRUCE BRADSHAW. Director of transformational development research at World Vision International. Author of *Bridging the Gap: Evangelism, Development and Shalom* and several articles on transformational development.

DAN BREWSTER. Doctorate in missiology from Fuller School of World Mission. Compassion International's director for advocacy and education. Involved in child and family development ministries for 18 years, mostly overseas. Visited or supervised child and family development or relief projects in more than 50 countries.

JOYCE BUNDELLU. Postgraduate degree in social work from the University of Mumbai (Bombay), India. Serves as a child welfare officer for Inter Mission in Mumbai. Is involved in caring for the dying destitute on Mumbai's streets, functional literacy for the children of the pavement dwellers, a day-care center providing educational services, relief and medical help to slum children and a residential center for orphaned children and children of sex workers.

Foster W. Cline. A psychiatrist and physician, author of eight books on parenting and dealing with difficult children and their families. *Parenting with Love and Logic* and *Parenting Teens with Love and Logic*, co-authored with Jim Fay, are best-selling parenting books. His newest book from Love and Logic Press is *Conscienceless Acts and Societal Mayhem*. In addition to presenting workshops around the world for teachers and parents, Dr. Cline and his wife, Hermie, have been conducting couples' seminars for more than 25 years. Dr. Cline founded Evergreen Consultants, a multidisciplinary clinic located in Evergreen, Colorado.

Janey L. DeMeo. A missionary pastor's wife in southern France, Janey is a writer and founder of the suffering children's association, *Sauver les Enfants*. She ministers to children worldwide. Her association has a small orphanage in Guntur, India, and works with needy children in Africa, Romania, Albania, Bosnia and France.

Geoff Foster. A British pediatrician working in Zimbabwe, Geoff established Family AIDS Caring Trust (FACT), a Christian AIDS service organization in 1987. FACT, well-known for its pioneering programs, works especially with local churches, mission hospitals and Christian organizations to implement AIDS prevention, care, training and support programs. He has published research on orphan numbers, their situation and community responses. He also is editor of *The Orphaned Generation: The Global Legacy of the AIDS Epidemic*, to be published in 1999.

Laurence Gray. B.A. in youth affairs and a graduate diploma in management from RMIT University in Melbourne, Australia. More than 10 years' experience working with youth at risk in a variety of roles in Australia. Joined World Vision International–Cambodia in 1995 as the manager of street children ministries; currently serves as manager of programs to children in especially difficult circumstances.

PATRICIA GREEN. Master's degree in social science from Waikato University, New Zealand. Director of Rahab Ministries. Green has worked with prostitutes in Bangkok for many years. In 1989 she helped found Rahab Ministries, which seeks to share the love of Christ, offer social help and support and alternative employment to prostitutes working in Patpong, a tourist brothel area.

CHRIS AND PHILEENA HEUERTZ. Directors of Word Made Flesh, an organization working among the poorest of the poor. They have traveled in more than 30 countries working among the destitute, gypsies, children with AIDS, prostitutes and recovering drug addicts. In 1994 they helped establish the first pediatric AIDS care home in South India. Chris serves as an adjunct professor for the Madras College of Evangelism, teaching on poverty issues and the church.

WANJIKU KAIME-ATTERHÖG. Postgraduate degrees in sociology from the University of Nairobi in Kenya and Primary Health Care Management from Mahidol University in Thailand. Researcher at the Unit for International Child Health at Uppsala University in Sweden. Kaime-Atterhög has worked with street and sexually exploited children in Kenya and Thailand and is particularly concerned with their health issues.

PAM KERR. R.N. from New Zealand and M.P.H. from Loma Linda University, California. Kerr had served as an international recruiter, human resources manager, program officer for international child survival and HIV/AIDS programs. Currently Kerr serves as coordinator for protection of children for World Vision International.

PHYLLIS KILBOURN. Ph.D. from Trinity International University, Deerfield, Illinois. Missionary with WEC International since 1967, serving in Kenya and Liberia. Currently director of WEC's program for children in crisis, Rainbows of Hope. Editor of *Healing the Children of War: A Handbook for Ministry to Children Who Have Suffered Deep Trauma; Children in Crisis: A New Commitment;* and *Street Children: A Guide to Effective Ministry*, all published by MARC.

CONTRIBUTING AUTHORS

ROBERT C. LINTHICUM. Executive director of Partners in Urban Transformation, a ministry focused on empowering the urban poor, the urban church and urban people's organizations. Linthicum provides consultancy services, workshops, training events and the implementation of urban ministry laboratories globally. He is former director of the Office of Urban Advance of World Vision International and author of ten books, including *City of God, City of Satan* and *Empowering the Poor*.

MARJORIE MCDERMID. Graduate of the Full Gospel Bible Institute, Eston, Saskatchewan, Canada. A former missionary to Equatorial Guinea, West Africa, with WEC International, McDermid served as editor of *Worldwide Thrust*, WEC's bimonthly communique in the U.S.A. and worked in various children's ministries. She currently serves as media director for Rainbows of Hope, along with speaking, traveling and conducting research on behalf of children in crisis.

ANN NOONAN. Has a private practice, Kainos Counseling Services, in Charlotte, North Carolina. Noonan is experienced in working with abused adults and adolescents. She holds a master's degree in special education and a master's in counselor education. Noonan is a licensed professional counselor in the state of North Carolina and is a nationally certified counselor.

DANIEL SWEENEY. Professor at George Fox University in Portland, Oregon. Former assistant director of the Center for Play Therapy at the University of North Texas. Sweeney is a licensed psychotherapist, consultant and a registered play therapist and supervisor. He has presented at many conferences on the topics of play therapy, filial therapy and sandplay. He has authored numerous book chapters and articles on child counseling, play therapy issues and parenting and is co-author of *Play Therapy Interventions with Children's Problems* (Jason Aronson Inc.) and the author of *Counseling Children Through the World of Play* (Tyndale House Publishers).

JANITH WILLIAMS, RNC, ARNP. Holds a bachelor's degree in nursing. Williams's graduate work has focused on parish nursing, natural medicine and health care management. Certified as a women's health care nurse practitioner, she has provided health care for the underserved for more than 15 years. Williams is currently employed as a clinician and manager at a community health center in Washington state.

JENNIE WOODS. President of Alliance for Children Everywhere. Woods has been a missionary to children for over 30 years; she was responsible for the establishment of an emergency crisis care home for children in Guatemala and later in Peru. She speaks and writes to encourage Christians to become involved in ministry to the world's children.

Sexually
Exploited Children

PART ONE:

Sexual Exploitation
of Children

1

Setting the Global Scene: A Sordid Picture

Marjorie McDermid

It's no shame to be poor," I remember my parents saying. We were poor, poor farmers on Canada's drought-ridden prairies in the 1930s. We didn't face starvation, but I remember a day when my brother had only bread in his school lunch box. Thankfully, Mother knew how to make hand-me-downs into acceptable wearing apparel, if not brand-name clothes. She also often put us to bed and washed our only "decent" clothes and mended them as needed, ready for school the next day.

At the age of 14 I became "mother" for two younger siblings when Mother died of TB, probably contracted partly because of hard work and poor nutrition. Two older siblings, of their own choice, had left school at 14 and 15 to work as hired hands. But would anyone have sold a child or hired him or her out for pornography or prostitution? Whoever heard of such a thing? Probably my father would have gone after anyone with a buggy whip who even suggested touching one of us . It took me many years to appreciate how blessed we were in light of the way hosts of children are treated today.

SEXUALLY EXPLOITED CHILDREN

As I began to write this chapter, I wondered about the history of child sexual abuse and exploitation. I looked first in the Bible. There I found warnings in the law against parents prostituting their children.

> Do not degrade your daughter by making her a prostitute, or the land will turn to prostitution and be filled with wickedness (Lev. 19:29).

I found evidence that children were sexually exploited:

> They cast lots for my people and traded boys for prostitutes; they sold girls for wine that they might drink (Joel 3:3).

> The fatherless child is snatched from the breast; the infant of the poor is seized for a debt. Lacking clothes, they go about naked; they carry the sheaves, but still go hungry. They crush olives among the terraces; they tread the winepresses, yet suffer thirst (Job 24:9–11).

Although exploiting children is not a new phenomenon, three factors, at least, make the children in today's society especially vulnerable: the multi-million dollar pornography industry, popular and lucrative sex tourism and the worldwide trafficking of children across borders for sexual purposes. Combined with the great numbers of children (nearly one half the world's population is under 18 years of age, and in many developing countries that age drops to 15), these conditions leave defenseless children with little hope (for the path of child sexual exploitation, see figure 1).

When I titled this chapter, I checked the American Heritage dictionary to be sure I was using sordid suitably. I found it very apropos to my subject.

> SORDID: Filthy or dirty; foul. Depressingly squalid; wretched. Morally degraded; base. Exceedingly mercenary; grasping.

These words are not what a writer normally uses to encourage readers to keep reading but, let me warn you, they do describe the picture I am about to paint.

4

Model 1
The Path of Child Sexual Exploitation

Causes of Abuse

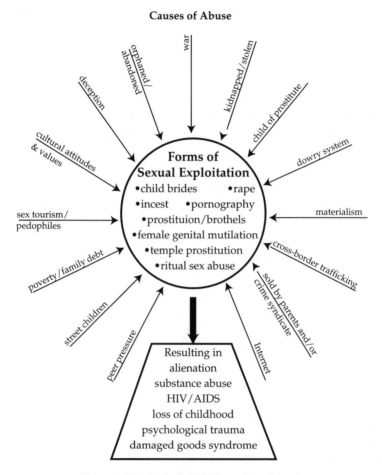

Figure 1: The Path of Child Sexual Exploitation

The sexual exploitation and abuse of children is perhaps the most wretchedly depressing subject one can contemplate. The reading I did in preparation for writing this book came vividly to life as I visited several Asian countries. Some of the scenes are indelibly etched in my mind and heart.

In a resort town south of Colombo, Sri Lanka, I watched a Caucasian man lead six young boys, ages possibly 8 to 12 years, from the exquisite beach off the Gulf of Mannar in the Indian Ocean into the walled rear grounds of a fashionable hotel. Apparently accustomed to the procedure, the boys showered off and walked through a foot-cleansing pool before proceeding into the back of the hotel. One boy who didn't stay in line merited a kick from the tall, muscular adult.

Later, as we walked to our residence, we noted a pudgy, white-haired European male of about 60 years leading a Sri Lankan boy of 8 or 9 years into one of the handsome beach homes that lined the street. Both man and boy were clad in swim shorts.

Doubtless we had witnessed so-called beach boys being herded into a night of sexual abuse and exploitation. What pain and emotional scars would these boys receive before morning just to satiate another's lust? What indignity and shame would they endure in exchange for some food and a pittance of pay or a few gifts? Perhaps they would be used to make "blue films" for distribution throughout the city and the world. Or cruelly forced into deviant sex acts.

We went to our apartment feeling anger and shame: anger at the treatment of the boys, at the parents who didn't care and at the authorities who allowed it. Shame that members of our race could treat these children as commodities, things to be bought, abused, used, terrorized.

FORMS OF SEXUAL EXPLOITATION AND ABUSE

During a total of 11 weeks in Asia, we found many forms of sexual exploitation being used against both boys and girls. Sex with children is used for entertainment and profit, for perverted enjoyment and comfort, to exert power and establish dominance. The reasons are complex and disputable, but the effects on the children are irrefutable and long lasting. Without intervention the trauma and resulting behavior will last a lifetime.

Incest and rape

Incest and rape may be thought of in terms of abuse rather than exploitation. However, when we think of exploitation as making unethical use of a child for one's own advantage or selfishly turning the act to one's own account, calling incest and rape exploitation is not unreasonable. "One's own account" may relate to lust or need for power, domination or control. Rape and forced incest used as weapons of war break down the morale and fabric of society. These tactics used regularly and mercilessly in recent wars, such as in Cambodia, Liberia and Bosnia, certainly capture the meaning of exploitation.

Often incest and rape are first steps to prostitution, especially in the case of street children. Rape and sexual abuse are sometimes rewarded with money or gifts following the deed as a means of coercing the child into prostitution.

Child brides

Men, young and old, barter for brides of very young ages. Some girls are sold as brides before they are born. This practice is well known in countries, especially in Africa, where polygamy is a way of life. The child almost always becomes a slave of the household and the other wives. Although the husband may promise no sexual activity with the child until after puberty, she is highly vulnerable to sexual abuse by him, his friends or other male members of the family.

Lesser known, perhaps, is the marriage of young girls for trafficking purposes. Travel documents are easily obtained in this way, and sale of the child takes place in the foreign country.

Female genital mutilation

Every year some two million girls undergo female genital mutilation. Girls in the Middle East, Indonesia and Africa suffer the indignity, pain and dangers of the traditional practice. Often performed under unsterile conditions and with no anesthesia, the operation cuts away some or all of the genitalia and sometimes sews the vulva closed, leaving only a small orifice for blood and urine to pass. Although ages of the girls involved vary, to avoid resistance the operation is often performed on very young children.

Having no health benefits, but many risks, the intent of the mutilation is control: control of sexual behavior and preservation of virginity.

The practice may result in excessive bleeding, urinary and pelvic infection, infertility, serious complications at childbirth and

7

even death. And it may not accomplish the desired control of the victim's sexual life.

Pornography

Asian children began to be used systematically to produce pornographic materials during the Vietnam war. Children were easy targets for pornographic films, which were made available to American troops on R&R in Thailand and the Philippines. Today, a large percentage of the world's pornographic material is produced in Asia using children. Films bringing the highest price are those in which children suffer most and the ultimate "pleasure" is to see the child die.

The death of a child for pornographic reasons makes us recoil with horror. Remember, however, that most victims live, and they live their lives deeply—perhaps irreparably—scarred spiritually, mentally and physically by the devastation of their experiences.

In recent years pornography has gone high-tech. "Surfing the web" can provide still images, movie clips and even live video conferencing. The thousand-plus new images added weekly include children, in an estimated annual $20 billion industry. The Internet is also used for solicitation of minors for sexual activities and pornography.

Prostitution, sexual slavery

Dr. Gracy Fernandes[1] of the Bombay School of Social Work recently surveyed a group of girl children in prostitution in Kamathipura, Bombay. Based on her results, this is the profile of the average girl prostitute:

- ◆ comes from a poor, dysfunctional family with many children
- ◆ is illiterate
- ◆ entered prostitution at age 16
- ◆ was deceived into the work by the promise of a good job or marriage
- ◆ receives between two and seven clients per night
- ◆ does not have direct access to her earnings
- ◆ is heavily in debt to the brothel keeper
- ◆ lives in crowded unhygienic conditions
- ◆ has already aborted one child

◆ does not trust the police
◆ has had STDs and will soon contract AIDS
◆ wants to get out, but doesn't know how.

Each year one million children become child prostitutes; 10–12 million children worldwide are visited by pedophiles and one-third of all child prostitutes in Asia are reported to be HIV-positive.[2]

Children are being traded and sold into the world's brothels and its tourism and trafficking industry in alarming numbers and with horrifying results. According to a 1994–95 UNICEF report, Asia has an estimated one million child prostitutes, including an estimated 300,000 in India; 200,000 in Thailand; 100,000 in the Philippines; 40,000 in Vietnam; 30,000 in Sri Lanka and many thousands in China.[3]

India, with laxer laws regarding child prostitution, is said to be overtaking Thailand in numbers of children engaged in sex tourism. Here the children of prostitutes face overwhelming odds since they are the lowest of the low caste.

In Bogota, Colombia, the number of prostitutes under 13 has quintupled since 1987. Brazil now has more than 250,000 child prostitutes.[4]

A 1994 figure puts American juvenile prostitutes at half a million.

Brothels

High-class brothels (if a brothel can be termed such) offer some protection for the child prostitute. The owner may insist on the use of condoms, give minimal health care and pay the girls a reasonable wage as well as giving them gifts. Generally, however, brothel owners require girls to service many customers per night, and they take a large chunk from the child's small pay for food and usually dismal quarters. Children unwilling to cooperate are given drugs or beaten into submission.

Not even the best conditions, however, can erase the trauma and stigma attached to the trade. Children caught up in the sex industry in notorious Pat Pong, Bangkok's largest "red light" district, reported to Christian social worker Patricia Green: "Many of us take drugs . . . or we could not dance naked and go with men we do not know."[5]

9

SEXUALLY EXPLOITED CHILDREN

Commercial sex tourism and trafficking

The commercial sexual exploitation of children results in an estimated multi-billion dollar business annually. Estimates show that as many as ten million children could be caught up in the sex industry. Children are reduced to commodities to be sold or traded for profit, entertainment and the satisfaction of lust.

Commercial sex traffic patterns show that children are sold from Burma, Laos and China as well as from northern Thailand tribes, through Bangkok to Malaysia, Singapore, Hong Kong, Japan and even the United States, Europe and Australia. "Thousands are trapped in a highly organized international web of gangs and government complicity."[6] Thousands of Nepali girls, prized for their fair skin and delicate features, as young as 10 years are sold and trafficked into the brothels of Mumbai (Bombay). Dinka and Nuba children from southern Sudan are sold into Libya where many become concubines.

Men from Europe, North America and Australia vacation regularly on the beaches of Sri Lanka, Thailand and other Asian shores where the sex industry supplies them with girls or boys of their choice. Younger, virgin children are most wanted because of the threat of AIDS among older ones, or from the ancient belief that sex with a virgin will heal venereal disease. Many pedophiles prefer pre-pubescent children for their nefarious sex acts.

The ways and means used to obtain the children vary widely: adopting the child, marriage/divorce/sale of the child, summer vacation for the child, orphanages as fronts and countless other ways. The trauma these children suffer is far-reaching with serious consequences.

They may experience stigmatization and have difficulty in developing relationships. The legacy of health problems, as a result of physical maltreatment and having many sex partners, is also very real. Some children may present very challenging behavior: aggression, violence and indiscriminate initiation of sexual contacts.[7]

Bonded labor

Especially in Asia, but also in Africa, children are forced or sold into sex labor to pay off debts for their parents. Often these debt

10

payments are so arranged that children are unable to pay off the debt and continue for years as sex slaves to their owners.

> Anastasia Santos last saw her daughter Veronica a year ago, before her child was traded to a brothel for $500 by a woman who lured the girl to the city with a vague promise of work. Veronica can't leave the brothel in Manila until she earns the $500 the owner paid the brothel agent. That day may never come. She serves an average of 10 men a day at $4 per customer, but $3 of the $4 are deducted for room, food, and cosmetics: she also must pay the brothel owner for clothes. Today, she is in debt beyond the original $500 to a pimp and has been infected with HIV. Veronica's life has ended, and she is not yet 12 years old.[8]

Temple prostitution

Notable among temple prostitutes are the *devadasi* (god's servants) of India. At 12 years of age girls given by their parents are wed to a goddess in a centuries-old tradition. Males who sleep with the devadasi or temple prostitute believe they are sleeping with the goddess. An estimated five to ten thousand Indian girls a year become temple prostitutes. When they grow old, they usually are resold as mistresses or end up in brothels.

Street children

Children living on the streets in every large urban area throughout the world are vulnerable to sexual abuse, rape and prostitution. They are often forced into prostitution as a means of making a living. Girls find this trade the most lucrative, if also the most demeaning. Sometimes they are expected to support other members of the family, serving as many men each night as necessary to provide food and clothing for siblings. Survival is the key word.

Street boys also see prostitution as an easy way to make money. Restaurants seem to be a favorite haunt for pedophiles who have lists and networks for referring boys to foreign customers. Street children may be exploited sexually by older street children who become pimps, by tourists and by adult workers such as taxi drivers.

11

Ritual sexual abuse

If all the foregoing descriptions are horrifying, ritual sexual abuse is sordid in the extreme. Often connected with religious cults or the occult, it is sometimes referred to as satanic ritual abuse. Children are subjected to repeated assaults in combination with secret ceremonies and use of ritualistic symbols. The ceremonies may include chanting and costumes, use of drugs and body excrement, animal and human sacrifices.

Dr. Lawrence Pazder, coauthor of *Michelle Remembers,* says the rituals are designed to "turn a child against itself, family, society and God."[9] The claims made that the sexual assault connected with rituals is not for sexual gratification are debatable.

Children subjected to this kind of abuse suffer trauma ranging from fear, withdrawal and nightmares to dissociative disorder (also known as multiple personality disorder).

IS THERE NO LAW AGAINST IT?

Yes, many countries have laws against the sexual abuse and exploitation of children. Many nations, although not all, have ratified the United Nations Convention on the Rights of the Child. Regarding the sexual exploitation of children, the Convention states that governments shall protect the child from all forms of sexual exploitation and sexual abuse, such as inducement and coercion of a child into unlawful sexual activity, prostitution and pornography (Article 34) and take all appropriate national, bilateral and multilateral measures to prevent the abduction of, the sale of or traffic in children for any purpose or in any form (Article 35).

In 1995 Taiwan passed a law "to prevent and eliminate the incidence of sexual transactions involving children and juveniles."[10] Among other things, the law called for administrative authorities to "act cooperatively with the competent authorities to deal with the affairs concerning sexual transactions involving children and juveniles."[11] It also required the appointment of social workers to investigate any cases of school absenteeism and take appropriate action.

In spite of measures such as the above, the sexual exploitation of children continues and tends to increase on a worldwide scale.

All of us know that, to be effective, laws must be enforced and under-the-table payoffs squelched. Children must have advocates who will speak up for them with authority in high places, particularly since children's witness is often not believed.

CONCLUSION

This chapter has not been an easy assignment for me nor pleasant reading for you. The chapters to follow will be similarly stressful. You may ask, as many people do, "What can anyone do to alleviate such an overwhelming tragedy?"

We need to remember how God deals with what we see as overwhelming universal problems. His compassion and love reach out to all the people of the entire world throughout all time. But he deals with people individually and according to the response he receives. Reclaiming the sexually abused children of the world works on exactly the same basis: embracing them globally in our hearts through informed prayer and reaching out in whatever way we can to rescue them—one by one.

Notes

[1] "Girl Prostitutes in India," *ECPAT Newsletter*, no. 15 (January 1996), p. 9.

[2] Dean R. Hirsch, "Stockholm . . . A Good First Step," *Together* (October-December 1996), inside cover.

[3] *UNICEF Facts and Figures*, 1994–95.

[4] Christopher P. Baker, "Prostitution: Child Chattel Lure Tourists for Sex," *The National Times* (August-September 1995), p. 8.

[5] Rahab Ministries, from an unpublished introductory paper by Patricia J. Green, p. 3.

[6] Mikel Flamm, "Lost Innocence in Thailand," *Together* (October-December 1996).

[7] Laurence Gray, Steve Gourley and Delia Paul, "Cambodia's Street Children Prostitutes: A Case Study," *Together* (October-December 1996), pp. 6–7.

[8] Christopher P. Baker, "Prostitution: Child Chattel Lure Tourists for Sex," *The National Times* (August-September 1995), p. 8.

[9] Quoted in *Child Abuse, Opposing Viewpoints*, ed. Katie de Koser (San Diego: Greenhaven Press, 1944), p. 152.

[10] The Law to Prevent Sexual Transactions Involving Children and Juveniles, Promulgated by the President of the Republic of China (Taiwan) on July 13, 1995, p. 2.

[11] Ibid.

2

Causes of Commercial Sexual Exploitation of Children

Wanjiku Kaime-Atterhög

One day a woman was sitting by the riverside eating her lunch. All of a sudden she heard a cry, "Hello, help, save me, I am drowning!" The woman got up and threw herself in the river to save the child. A little while later she again heard the cry for help. Once again she jumped into the river and saved another child from drowning. But while she was finishing her lunch, she heard other desperate sounds. This time she simply got up and went away. A passerby, surprised, asked her where she was going. The woman replied: "I am going to the mouth of the river to find out what is happening over there and to find a solution."
—Author unknown

Although commercial sexual exploitation of children is illegal in Thailand, it is a widespread practice. It occurs in most parts of the country, not only in the larger towns and tourist areas. One can find small brothels in rural areas and smaller towns, particularly in the northern region.

Opinions differ as to how many children are involved in the commercial sex sector of Thai society. The Ministry of Public Health estimates the number to be 13,000, while the Centre for the Protection of Children's Rights maintains there are as many as 800,000 children engaged in prostitution in the country. Researchers have given an estimate of 30,000 to 40,000. Despite the difference in the numbers of children involved, all institutions agree that the numbers are increasing and that child prostitution is a grave social problem. The current count of children exploited in child pornography cannot be estimated either, but indications are that Thailand is a major child pornography producing country.

Children are taken from within Thailand and from neighboring countries such as Burma, Southern China, Laos and Cambodia. Most of the children are kidnapped, misled into thinking they will be domestic workers or waitresses or bought directly from their parents in remote villages by organized criminal groups and individuals. They are thereafter sold into small-town or city brothels or massage parlors, where they are forced to offer sexual services to up to ten customers a day.

Another group of children enter the sex trade willingly and work in a-go-go bars where they are free to come and go as they wish. They dance topless and without clothes, performing a variety of shows on stage while clients watch. They earn money through commissions for drinks bought by customers as well as providing sexual services on the premises or in the customer's home or hotel room. The third group of children look for customers in public places, cafes, department stores and hair salons. These children may be completely on their own or under the control of pimps.

Children engaged in pornography do not work in cafes, brothels or other entertainment places. They are more likely to be "on call," sometimes handed over by their own families. They are often controlled by agents or pimps, who lure them on behalf of their customers. Street children are easily befriended and lured by the child pornographers or pedophiles themselves. Children who are engaged in pornography on a regular basis gradually become involved in prostitution, where they are passed around within pedophile rings or among local pimps.[1]

Before we examine the factors that cause a society to reduce a child to a commodity, we will first define some issues that arise in the context of commercial sexual exploitation of children and that we will refer to throughout this chapter.

WHAT IS COMMERCIAL SEXUAL EXPLOITATION?

The standard definition of commercial sexual exploitation[2] we will use is that of the United Nations, which defines it as the use of a child for sexual purposes in exchange for cash or in-kind favors between the customer, intermediary or agent and others who profit from the trade in children for these purposes (parent, family member, procurer, teacher). There are three forms of commercial sexual exploitation of children defined by the United Nations: (1) child prostitution; (2) trafficking and sale of children across borders and within countries for sexual purposes; and (3) pornography.

Child prostitution is the act of engaging or offering the services of a child to a person to perform sexual acts for money or other consideration with that person or any other person.

Trafficking and sale of children across borders and within countries for sexual purposes is the transfer of a child from one party to another for whatever purpose in exchange for financial consideration or other rewards. Sexual trafficking is the profitable business of transporting children for commercial sexual purposes. It can be across borders or within countries, across state lines, from city to city, or from rural to urban centers.

Child pornography is the visual or audio material that uses children in a sexual context. It consists of the visual depiction of a child engaged in explicit sexual conduct, real or simulated, or the lewd exhibition of the genitals intended for the sexual gratification of the user, and involves production, distribution and or use of such material.

A *child* as defined by the United Nations in Article 1 of the Convention on the Rights of the Child "means every human being below the age of eighteen years unless under the law applicable to the child, majority is attained earlier."

SOME FACTORS

It is not possible to say when the sexual exploitation of children first occurred in Thailand. However, studies show that it has a long history and has only begun to attract the attention of research-ers and policymakers in the 1990s. Boy prostitution and pornog-raphy are relatively recent phenomena in Thailand and are closely linked to sex tourism and pedophilia. We have more knowledge on the issues of girl trafficking and prostitution than on boy pros-titution and pornography, which explains why more examples are drawn from the former in this chapter.

Join me now on a journey to the mouth of this river that I call the river of death. The currents are often too strong for the chil-dren to put up a fight. The majority drown. Those who survive come out scarred—physically, psychologically, spiritually, morally and socially—often for life. The following are some of the mul-tiple causes at play.

Material poverty

In Thailand and along its borders with Burma, China, Laos and Cambodia, villagers used to depend on forest products such as charcoal, bamboo shoots, wild mushrooms, squirrels and even edible toads for a living. Small-scale subsistence farmers also re-lied on the forest to provide protection against soil erosion and flooding. But both legal and illegal logging projects have destroyed the variety and integrity of the local economies that until three decades ago sustained the local people. Most of this previously forested land is now being used for growing agricultural prod-ucts which are exported to other countries. Thailand is often taken as an example of a country whose economy has been boosted mainly by agricultural exports, some of which are grown on such land. But this is not the whole story. While progress has reached some, others have become marginalized.

As Thailand has shifted from an economy that depended al-most completely on small-scale subsistence agriculture to one that is export oriented, many poor villagers have sold their land to wealthy people and have become landless peasants. People are forced to work on the large farms as agricultural laborers or ten-ant farmers in the growing season, but they no longer have alter-native sources of income during the rest of the year. Many give up and move to the city in an attempt to find work there. Some farm-ers decide to remain in the rural areas and try to survive on small

18

strips of land, but these do not produce enough for their consumption. They have to borrow money for modern farming machinery, chemical fertilizers and pesticides, and for basic needs such as food, clothing and housing. A combination of these factors and low and changing market prices often lead to bankruptcy and the farmers are forced off the land in search of work in urban areas.

Once in the city, the rural migrants often settle in slums. Disappointment and frustration at not finding employment, in addition to poverty, often lead to the disintegration of the family soon after reaching the city. Drug abuse, quarreling and violence often become everyday occurrences and make normal family life impossible. When the father and husband cannot bear the humiliation any longer he abandons his wife and children. This is one of the reasons for the strong predominance of single women with children in these areas. In such cases both mother and children have to struggle to earn a living. Some mothers and children end up in prostitution, and some children run away from home and become street children.

In Thailand it has also become common for one or more of the children to go alone to find work in the city. Children are recruited as unskilled labor in the construction industry, which has been one of the large growth industries in Thailand over the last twenty years. However, employment conditions are not regulated and many people lose their jobs after a project has been completed. Other children find their way into factories or domestic work. Still others join the sex industry. Some parents find it impossible to refuse a cash payment in exchange for one of their children, although they are fully aware of the kind of work they will be engaged in. These parents are convinced that the children will earn more in the sex industry than in any other occupation.

There are children who realize that their parents are selling them into prostitution. As dutiful children, they sacrifice themselves to provide for the basic needs of other family members and bear the stigma throughout their lives. In this way they show gratitude for the care and protection their parents gave when raising them. Care and support are seen as gaining merit according to Buddhist principles. Children who do not comply with their parents' wishes are regarded as ungrateful and irresponsible.[3]

Spiritual poverty

In Thailand today many people regard materialism as a more important cause of prostitution than poverty. Studies show that parents allow, urge or force children to work in prostitution because they wish to have a better standard of living and not because they are really poor. It is also common that those parents who first send children to work in prostitution to repay debts return their children to the brothels and take out new loans after the debts have been repaid, to increase their comfort. Materialism and consumerism have a stronger impact where spiritual values among families are neglected. According to Vitit Muntarbhorn, "material values have overtaken those which place a premium on human life and development. [A child is] viewed as an economic asset or investment, not as a person of worth and value for who he or she is."[4]

In some communities there is no longer a community spirit; individualism and competition have crept in. In a village in Chiang Rai District in northern Thailand, for example, the headman acts as a middleman or broker for various agencies in Bangkok and other areas. Teachers are employed as agents and inform the sex brokers of the pretty girls in their schools. Close relatives and friends deceive others into prostitution for monetary rewards. Even older people, who are often entrusted with informal education in the community, do not seem to object to prostitution.[5] The lure of money and consumer goods has eroded morality. The religious institution is also part of the problem. Monks, whose goal in the past was to free themselves from material yearning, now build big temples. The money often comes from the village girls engaged in prostitution, who would like to earn religious merit. Businessmen whose profits are derived from the sex trade also give large donations to temples.

Wealth is the new symbol of respect, and people are judged by the amount of wealth they possess regardless of how the money is attained. A large number of remittances from prostitutes is spent on consumer goods or building new houses to compete with other villagers. In Muang Deng Noi village in Chiang Rai District in northern Thailand, for example, the most important event is celebrating the completion of a new house. Invitations are even

20

announced over loudspeakers to ensure that all the villagers are well informed. Food and alcohol expenses are paid by the host, whether or not the family can afford such an extravagance. The bigger the feast, the higher the prestige among fellow villagers.

Due to the high value given to material objects and the evidence of a good income many prostitutes earn, more girls have been drawn into this trade. Girls visiting their home villages do not tell of the hard life they lead, and villagers judge their good fortune by their beautiful dresses and jewelry, including the gifts they buy for their families. A survey carried out among school children in the north revealed that some children would like to work as prostitutes when they grow up.[6] Girls dream of working in Bangkok and buying beautiful clothes for themselves. Others have gradually been convinced by their friends who are already in the profession of the high economic rewards of prostitution and have changed from low paying jobs, such as waitressing.

Social values

Socialization studies show that Thai parents train girls more strictly than boys in sex role behavior. Whereas virginity before marriage is the most important value of a "decent" woman, sexual promiscuity is accepted for and practiced by men. "Culturally, Thai society flatters men for their promiscuity. . . . Women's magazines always advise women to tolerate the situation and accommodate themselves to it."[7] This sexual freedom has contributed to the growth of the sex industry in Thailand. Numerous studies have shown that 50 percent of Thai men have sex before 18 years and that their first sexual experience is with a sex worker.[8] Thai men justify sex with prostitutes as a way of protecting the virtue of "good" women. It is believed that sex crimes would increase if there were no brothels to cater to these men's needs. Because female virginity is highly valued in Thai society, girls who are raped often end up in prostitution because they feel they have lost their worth.

WHY THE NORTHERNERS?

There are variations within regions, and not all rural provinces in Thailand send their children to work in prostitution. Studies show that a large number of child prostitutes come from the north. Being a prostitute to support one's family has become an acceptable value among villagers in several northern communities. And despite the risk of beatings and disease, many girls sold by their parents or neighbors into prostitution return home with honor and then repeat the cycle by sending their own daughters or those of neighbors into prostitution.

One explanation for why northerners sell their children into prostitution is that girls from this region have fairer skin—considered a mark of beauty in Asia—compared to those from other provinces. Another reason given is the region's cultural history. While the rest of Thailand lived mainly in peace, the area in the north, the Kingdom of Lanna, was constantly being invaded and colonized by neighboring countries. It was the custom to use women from the area to placate the occupying forces.

Furthermore, a poor family with an urgent need for money had the legal right to sell the children to other people as a guarantee against a loan during the Ayuttaya period to early Rattanakosin period (A.D. thirteenth to nineteenth century) when slavery was legal.[9] Women, therefore, traditionally have been regarded as slaves, mistresses and concubines who could be traded as goods; this has increased the inhabitants' willingness to allow their young women to be recruited into prostitution.[10]

THE DEMAND FOR CHILDREN

Hom and Nee, who are 15 and 13 respectively, were sold to a brothel in Rayong Province by their mother. In exchange for the girls, their mother was offered Baht 30,000, which she used to purchase two buffaloes to plow her farmland. The girls said that they had to accept their fate because they could not forsake their mother and wanted to have enough money to raise their four younger brothers and sisters. The day after their arrival in the brothel, they were raped by the brothel owner to make them submit, like all the other girls who had come there earlier. The two girls reported that the brothel owner threatened to let the pimps in the brothel rape them if they refused to have sex with customers. The mother denies that she knowingly sent her daughters to the brothel. She said she thought that they were working in a restaurant in Rayong Province when she received the loan. "I couldn't help but let my daughters work in Rayong because my family is very poor and we needed the money to buy the buffaloes," the mother said. "And they convinced me that my girls would work as waitresses at Saithip Restaurant." She said she met a woman from Rayong who identified herself as Lek; Lek persuaded her to let the girls go with her. Not long after her daughters left, Lek called the mother and offered Baht 1,000 for each girl she could persuade to work at the restaurant in Rayong. The mother had so far convinced at least 17 girls in her village to work in Rayong. After the police raided the brothel and rescued her daughters, the mother said she was shocked to learn they were working as prostitutes. She has been forced to flee to another district to avoid the questions of many villagers who would like to know the fate of their own daughters.

While the socioeconomic and cultural factors have expanded the supply of child prostitutes, the demand for them has increased even more. And it is the demand for child prostitutes that turns vulnerable children into victims. International tourism has helped propel prostitution into an increasingly large industry. Most of the tourists visiting Thailand are male, the majority of whom come specifically for sex. Sex tourism in Thailand is not exclusive to men from the West and Japan, though these are primarily the tourists who visit the typical tourist areas. Child prostitution in the lesser-known districts is mainly for the local population, but a number of customers come from neighboring countries.

To be successful as a tourist destination, countries believe they must offer new and different experiences to travelers. Child prostitution is the newest tourist attraction offered by poor countries.[11] There are other long-existing traditions that tolerate and even encourage the sex industry among another group of travelers in Thailand. Senior officials visiting rural areas are offered "local flowers" as a sign of hospitality. This tradition has now infiltrated the university and business communities.[12] A saying among Thai men goes that one cannot say he has been to a place unless he has had a "taste" of it.

The belief that a child has less risk of carrying AIDS makes children attractive to agents advertising "AIDS-free" services and to clients afraid of being contaminated with the virus. O'Grady observes that customers at brothels have become very selective. In earlier years customers might not have objected to the age and condition of a prostitute, and would often prefer an older and experienced partner. But there has been a marked change in attitude in the last two years. Brothel workers, O'Grady further notes, claim that their customers are particularly anxious to have a prostitute who "looks healthy." Since young children usually convey a stronger sense of being healthy than older prostitutes, demand for them is increasing at all brothels. Many massage parlors in Thailand now have a separate room in back where selected customers can view girls, some as young as ten and eleven, whose health is guaranteed and whose price is accordingly higher. Involving children in prostitution is facilitating the spread of HIV and is rapidly killing the children. Younger children are more likely to contract HIV during intercourse, because their tissues are more easily torn.

The preference for virgins, particularly among Middle Eastern and Chinese clients, is another factor. These people pay large sums of money to brothel owners for an attractive young girl who can be proved to be a virgin.[13] This habit might be reinforced by the belief that "deflowering" and sleeping with a girl revitalizes the sexual potency of an old man and makes him prosper in business.

LAST WORDS

In this chapter I have discussed the multiple causes of commercial sexual exploitation of children in Thailand. While working toward improving the socioeconomic and spiritual conditions of communities, we should not neglect the factors that create a demand for these children. It is also certain that some of the sex establishments that employ children are owned by influential people in society, including law-enforcement personnel. Introducing harsher penalties for offenders will not solve the problem unless these are combined with effective measures to counter corruption and crime.

While we work at preventing more children from being sexually exploited, let us not forget the children, like Hom and Nee, who are already caught in this river of death. Our disgust at these practices and the depth of our compassion will be put to the test by our willingness to take action.

At the beginning of the chapter there is a story of a woman who rescued children from drowning in the river of death. However, no sooner had she rescued one child from drowning when she heard another one crying for help. Frustrated, she stopped the rescue operation and made her way to the other end of the river to stop the flow of children falling into the river by cutting it off at its source.

This is how most of us working with sexually exploited children reason. We become overwhelmed by the problem and decide prevention is the only way to address the issue. Although we must emphasize prevention, we must not forget those who have been caught up in this river. Every life is valuable, and the rescue operation must continue alongside prevention efforts.

Notes

Parts of this chapter were drawn from the following papers written by Wanjiku Kaime-Atterhög and Orathai Ard-An: "Child Prostitution in Thailand: A Documentary Assessment," Mahidol University, Thailand (1993); "Children in the Sex Sector of Thai Society," Mahidol University, Thailand (1993); and "Children Without Childhood: The Young Prostitutes of Thailand," Mahidol University, Thailand (1993).

[1] Centre for the Protection of Children's Rights (CPCR), "Case Study Report on Commercial Sexual Exploitation of Children in Thailand" (1996).

[2] UNICEF, ECPAT, NGO Group for the Convention on the Rights of the Child, Background Document, World Congress Against Commercial Sexual Exploitation of Children, Sweden, August 27–31, 1996.

[3] N. Naowarat, "Child Prostitutes," in *A National Seminar on Prevention and Protection of Working and Abandoned Children* (Bangkok, Thailand: National Youth Bureau, 1988), pp. 108–21.

[4] V. Muntarbhorn, "Sexual Exploitation of Children," Centre for Human Rights, United Nations (1996).

[5] Y. Santasombat, "Women Who Sell Their Bodies: Community and Commercial Sex in Thailand," Local Development Institute, Thailand (1992).

[6] Skrobanek, S., "Child Prostitution in Thailand," in *Report of the First National Assembly on Child Development* (Bangkok, Thailand: Government House, 1990).

[7] S. Hantrakul, S., "The Spirit of a Fighter—Women and Prostitution in Thailand," *Manushi* (October-November 1983), pp. 27–35.

[8] UNICEF, ECPAT, NGO Group for the Convention on the Rights of the Child, Background Document.

[9] B. Piroh, "Status and Role of Women in Thai Society," unpublished M.A. thesis, Department of Sociology, Chulalongkorn University, Bangkok, Thailand (1976).

[10] Skrobanek, "Child Prostitution in Thailand."

[11] R. O'Grady, "The Child and the Tourist: The Story Behind the Escalation of Child Prostitution in Asia" (Bangkok, Thailand: ECPAT, 1992).

[12] Thanawadee, Friends of Women Foundation, personal communication (1993).

[13] O'Grady, "The Child and the Tourist."

3

Perpetrators, Policy and Protection

Renita Boyle

Rhymes of Lost Innocence

Rock a bye baby
in your own room,
you live in a house
that feels like a tomb,
you cower in the corner
you stare at your bed,
tears on your teddy,
you wish you were dead.
   Dead.

Hush little baby,
don't say a word,
Does Momma know what's going on?
Maybe she's not sure.
Pappa plays his little games
and leaves you there confused.
You love him and you hate him
as you go on feeling used.
   Abused.

SEXUALLY EXPLOITED CHILDREN

Georgie Porgie
Pudding and pie
kissed the girls and made them cry,
touched the girls
I don't know why.
   Why?

Jack be nimble,
Jack be quick
how it makes your stomach sick.
Not a woman
but a child,
simple innocence defiled.
   Child defiled.

Ring a ring of roses,
a pocket full of fears,
wounded bruised emotions
through the countless years.
Silence is not golden,
tell your story well.
Share it to defeat it
and journey back from hell.
   Tell.
      —Renita Boyle

Although this poem is about familial sexual abuse, it is in many ways the emotional story of all victims. Whether living in wealthy Western pressure-cooker families or selling their bodies in Asian brothels, emotionally voiceless victims often want to know why they are being abused. So do those of us who care for and work with them. Who are the perpetrators? Why do they perpetrate? How can we develop policies that will protect children and provide quality care?

PERPETRATORS: WHO ARE THEY?

What do you think of when I say child sex offender? What mental image comes into focus? What qualities do you imagine such a person has? If words like *sex beast, unfeeling animal, heinous monster, scum* or *twisted pervert* trip off your tongue, you are not alone. These are common perceptions. They arise from our utter anger, revulsion, grief, helplessness and disbelief. Though understandable, they are not very helpful. Such perceptions create a myth and serve to perpetuate the climate of denial in which child sexual abuse thrives.

Which one of us truly believes that our parent, child, minister, spouse, sibling, uncle, neighbor, teacher, business partner, grandparent or self would ever be capable of sexually abusing a child? As difficult as it seems, every perpetrator is one or more of the above to someone. Obviously not everyone, or even the majority, sexually abuses children. However, it is vital to recognize that anyone can.

In *Breaking Free: Help for Survivors of Child Sexual Abuse*, Carolyn Ainscough and Kay Toon sum it up this way:

> Very few abusers fit the stereotype. Abusers may be young or old, male or female, rich or poor, kind or cruel, scruffy or smart, strong or frail. Abusers may be dominant men who rule their families or weak and ineffectual, women who keep to themselves or friendly well-liked young men. In fact they are indistinguishable from any other person. Abusers may be laborers, members of parliament, professors, unemployed, stockbrokers, housewives, bus drivers, teachers, clergy or from any other occupation. . . . It is not possible to tell abusers from non-abusive people unless you know they are abusing. People of all classes, cultures, ages and personalities abuse.[1]

WHAT DO THEY DO?

Child sexual abuse is defined as the involvement of children or adolescents in sexual activities they do not truly understand and to which they are unable to give informed consent for the sexual pleasure, gratification or profit of an adult or significantly older person. This definition acknowledges a number of important things. Victims are vulnerable and dependent, sexual abuse is an abuse of power and authority, the seeming consent of the victim is irrelevant and a definite personal motive lies behind the abuse. Child sexual abuse involves inappropriate exposure, fondling and/or penetration. It includes a broad range of sexually oriented activities from obscene telephone calls to indecent exposure, fondling or being fondled, taking pornographic photos or videos or making children watch them, incest, rape, sodomy, penetration with objects, involving or forcing children or young people into prostitution or using them in such activities. It may be a single incident or events that occur over a number of years.

Child sexual abuse excludes relationships with young people over the age of legal consent (though this is morally questionable in certain situations—teacher-pupil cases, for example) and the normal, curiosity-based sexual play that occurs between younger children. However, forced or tricked sexual contact between teenagers and much younger children is sexual abuse.[2]

WHY DO THEY DO IT?

Medical and social science, victims and perpetrators themselves continue in their attempts to find a satisfactory answer to this question. It must be emphatically stated that any supposed explanations for such behavior are never an excuse. They do not minimize the damage to the victim or the responsibility of the perpetrator.

Most of the information known about child sex abusers comes from studies done in prisons. Since relatively few offenders are caught, convicted and sent to prison, our knowledge of them is limited. Here, however, are some possible insights into why perpetrators perpetrate and some of the reasons they have given for sexually abusing children. Perpetrators act out of a combination of supposed reasons.

Obsession: "It's my nature to do it"

The word *pedophile* means "child lover." This is inappropriate and ironic considering the selfish motivation and devastating effects of pedophilic behavior. Nevertheless, *pedophilia* is the diagnostic term used to describe the condition of one who is considerably older than his or her victim(s), and whose sexual attraction and behavior is inclined to prepubescent children. These sexual urges are recurrent, intense and arousing. It has been common to classify pedophiles under three basic categories: regressed, fixated and undifferentiated. This classification is problematic in that most offenders do not neatly fit in to any one division. However, exploring these categories is useful.

Regressed pedophiles have successfully developed a primary orientation to opposite sex peers. Under stress, however, they revert to episodic child sexual contact. This contact is presented to the child as spending "special" time alone. Female children in a general age group spanning five years (aged 5–10, 6–11, etc.) are preferred. Contact with the child tends to be firmly coercive, from a base of power. The child will most often be told what to do. Oral sex is the most common, with some penetration. Pedophilic activity usually coexists with sexual involvement with a peer. The regressed pedophile is usually a family member or trusted care provider and has genuine feelings of love for the child. Secrecy is established through the hint of threat ("you will get into trouble or be hurt if you tell"). Psychologically the child is raised to an adult level.[3]

Fixated pedophiles have a compulsive primary sexual preference for children. Sexual contact with children is a life focus, an overwhelming obsessive desire. Fixated pedophiles do not have age-appropriate relationships with peers; they spend most of their time with children or finding ways of gaining access to them. They prefer male children in a specific age group spanning two years (aged 3–4, 4–6, etc.) and many children are targeted. Contact with the child tends to be gentle, from a base of manipulation. Fixated pedophiles are very patient. Their approach to the child is slow, methodical and aimed at winning approval as well as sexual gratification. This process can take months, because they must undermine the child's belief system. They are genuinely concerned about the child's well-being. Fixated pedophiles prefer playing games, touching, rubbing, kissing and avoid penetration. They are usually a trusted adult in regular contact with the child and the child's family, such as a youth leader, babysitter or teacher. Secrecy is established through the manipulation of the child's feeling for the perpetrator ("we don't want to get in trouble," "if you care about me you won't tell"). Psychologically the fixated pedophile becomes like the child in age. Photography involving children known to them is a common hobby, as this provides a backup in case of loss of access to the child.[4]

Undifferentiated pedophiles tend to be isolated loners and unknown to the child or their family. They have troubled, unsuccessful relationships with adults and children alike, and they make only the shallowest of emotional connections. Psychologically they are incapable of empathy and have no concern for the child at all. This precipi-

31

tates and enables the cruelest and most sadistic of behaviors.[5] Undifferentiated pedophiles act more from a dynamic of anger than desire and use sex as a weapon to express deep hostility.[6] They have no preferences. They will have sex with either gender and in any age group. As contact with the child has no basis in relationship, it is often perverted, violent and forced. Kidnapping, binding, enslaving, torture, injury and death are endured by the child, often during penetrative sex. Undifferentiated pedophiles are the most avid users of child pornography, prostitution and snuff movies. The undifferentiated pedophile experiences a heightened sense of sexual gratification from enforcing physical pain and merciless power.

Not all perpetrators of sexual abuse would be classed as pedophiles. The use of postpubescent teens in prostitution, for example, is still sexual abuse, even if it is engaged in only once. Offenders have abused all ages, including infants, children and youths. It is also interesting to note that a significant number of men who commit child sexual abuse also offend in other ways, sexual and nonsexual. One study reveals that 25 percent of men who targeted girls outside the family also committed rape. Of 126 rapists in this study, 44 percent had sexually abused girls outside the family, 14 percent boys, and 28 percent had engaged in exhibitionism.[7]

Studies are confirming that nearly half of all male perpetrators begin offending when they are adolescents, and some don't even reach adolescence before they begin.[8] The average age of identified juvenile sex offenders in the USA is 14 and the average number of victims prior to age 18 is seven.[9]

Though the vast majority of perpetrators are male, women do also abuse. It has been estimated that 20 percent of the abuse of boys and 5 percent of the abuse of girls is by females.[10] There are question marks as to the extent of female abuse. It is thought that fewer cases are reported than exist because women may so easily cover their abuse as nurture. It may be rare for women to be solitary abusers; they are most often brought to justice as accomplices to male perpetrators. Sexual abuse by older girls in the family may be justified by them as sexual exploration.

Networks: *"All my friends are doing it"*

Although sexual abuse has always existed, both inside and outside the family, it has traditionally been seen as unacceptable and immoral. Hence, pedophiles become experts of deception, secrecy and double standards to feed their compulsion. A rising number are joining pedophile organizations, clubs and networks. Members share an obsession for child sex but maintain a respectable facade because they rely on one another for protection, secrecy and information. Ron O'Grady, author of *The Rape of the Innocent*, explains:

> The pedophile learns early in life that his sexual desires are not acceptable to most members of the community, and he hides his sexual deviance as much as he is able. This means that he will conform to the most conservative attitudes and standards of society in order to merge into the mainstream of people. Each member [of the club] knows that if he is caught in a compromising situation with a young child he faces the loss of his employment, the hatred of the community, the tears of his family, the agony of a court trial, the embarrassment of media attention and, finally, a long prison sentence during which he will have to suffer the taunts and the physical abuse of other prisoners."[11]

There are 200 pedophile rings in the United Kingdom alone. These allow pedophiles to swap child pornography, contact magazines, addresses and even children themselves. Britain's National Criminal Intelligence Service has information on about 4,000 convicted or suspected pedophiles. Chief Superintendent Brian Mackenzie, president of the police superintendents, stated, "They operate like any other special interest group. Networks and rings form by word of mouth. Individuals will exchange pornography and quite often they will pass compliant juveniles between groups. The whole thing spreads out and it is difficult for the police to break down."[12] The Internet is playing a vital role in the increase and acceptability of child sexual abuse. Easy access to millions of users, slack censorship and encoding devices make it an ideal haven for pedophiles. Carnegie Mellon University recently carried out research that revealed that 68 American Internet servers offered 450,620 pornographic images, animation and text files that had been downloaded by consumers 6,432,297 times.[13] Experts now believe that pedophiles dominate nearly one-third of the chatlines used for direct conversation between individuals.

Availability: "It's getting easier to do it"

With the possibilities of getting caught and facing the consequences increasing at home, many pedophiles are heading for countries where child sex is made so available that deception is hardly necessary. Child sexual abuse is now a multi-billion-dollar business involving pedophile rings, child sex tourism, porn videos and abduction. The main centers for child sex tourism are Sri Lanka (an estimated 30,000 boys), Thailand (100,000, primarily girls), the Philippines (40,000–60,000, primarily girls) and Cambodia. There is no way of knowing accurately how many tourists sexually exploit children. In 1992, for example, 22 million people visited Southeast Asia, a figure doubled from 1987. Over 6 million of these were destined for child sex locations.[14] Four hundred thousand Germans are said to fly to two-thirds-world destinations for sex every year. The German Justice Ministry estimates that 5,000 of these are deliberately looking for sex with children under the age of 13.[15] It is estimated that in Thailand 60 percent of male tourists are there for sex.[16] Since 1992 ECPAT (End Child Prostitution Abuse and Trafficking) has been attempting to monitor pedophile and sex tourism activity in Asia. By 1994 the details of 160 foreign men had been documented. Of these 25 percent were American, 18 percent German, 14 percent Australian, 12 percent British and 6 percent French. Men from 21 different countries were represented.[17]

These figures represent only those foreign convictions in Asia appearing in the press. They do not give any real indication of the global scale of international child sex tourism, nor do they reveal the extent to which locals and nationals are involved in their own tourist trade. In his 1992 UN Report on the Sale of Children, V. Muntabhorn states, "Sex tourism involving local customers is often neglected in the press in favor of transnational sex tourism; numerically, however, there may well be more local people than foreigners who resort to the services of child prostitutes."[18] One local survey of Bangkok revealed that 95 percent of Thai men admitted involvement with prostitutes by the age of 21.[19]

34

Most sex tourists who abuse girls also like women. They tend to be regressed pedophiles who offend episodically. The sexual exploitation of girl children in countries where girls are already discriminated against increases devastation. Culturally, the role, value and validity of women have been and remain, in many countries, linked strongly to reproduction and motherhood. Hence female premarital virginity is of paramount importance. Compromised virginity, even when forced, stigmatizes for a lifetime, further degenerating an already low self-esteem. Men, on the other hand, are often encouraged to be sexually agile even outside marriage and praised in the boasting of it. This double standard for sexual behavior has proven fertile soil for the sexual exploitation of children, the vast majority of whom are girls.

Although there are fewer boys in the flesh trade, fixated pedophiles prefer them. A recent American survey discovered that 403 pedophiles had among them molested 67,000 children, with those abusing young boys averaging 283 victims each.[20] The open practice of child sexual exploitation in many countries, combined with the number of young boys each fixated molester may abuse, has added up to an ever-increasing market for boy children. An estimated 30,000 boys aged between 6 and 13 are being exploited by tourists and locals in Sri Lanka.[21] In July 1992 stacks of letters between pedophiles sharing descriptions of children's bodies and sex organs were found in a home in Stockholm, Sweden. Child pornography videos (300 hours worth) were also found. Most of the footage was filmed in Sri Lanka with titles such as "Boy Love in Negombo and Hikkaduwa—the Child Sex Paradise."[22] An estimated 250 million copies of child porn videos are said to be circulating globally, most filmed in the Philippines, Thailand and Sri Lanka. Mauritania and Cambodia have also reported an increased visibility of foreign pedophiles and boy prostitutes.[23] Suspicions are growing that boys from Polish orphanages are being rented out to Westerners to be sexually abused. Both Dutch and Swedish media report that boys from Eastern Europe are being "increasingly employed in gay night clubs in Amsterdam and pornographic film studies in Sweden."[24]

Pedophile rings are in the forefront of the child sex industry. In 1990 an Australian pedophile club in Melbourne was infiltrated by

35

a police officer. A number of the members were heading for a tour of pedophile centers throughout Thailand, which had been organized by an accomplice living there. One of these men had had sex with 250 children. He was questioned by police and was quite open about his practice because he knew that he could not be legally tried at that time.[25] Pedophiles have also bought guest houses to service their members or set up legitimate-looking youth clubs as a cover.

Free choice versus no choice: "The devil made me do it"

Pedophilia is gaining ground in the battle to become socially, legally and morally acceptable. Some organized groups believe in and advocate sex with children as a religious freedom and/or freedom of choice. They publicly argue with the sincerest of convictions that sex with children should be legalized and that children are capable of giving informed consent at age four. Sex with children is, therefore, a form of religious expression and sexual liberation for both the perpetrator and the child. These include the Rene Guyon Society, N.A.M.B.L.A. (North American Men and Boy Lovers Association), P.I.E. (Pedophile Information Exchange) and the Howard Nichols Society. Each one has a newsletter and shares information and ideas on how to promote its beliefs and practices. Recent American legislation intended to keep pornography and other offensive material off the Internet through the Communications Decency Act is already being challenged as unconstitutional under freedom of speech. At the same time pedophile groups are beginning to gain status as churches and claim their practices as religious freedom under the First Amendment of the U.S. Constitution.

Freedom of choice or religion is a mask. Many perpetrators of child sexual abuse have an intense need for power and control that they attempt to exercise through their sexuality. Their desires are so increasingly unconventional that sex with consenting adults becomes harder to achieve. Children become unwilling victims. "Sexual domination is high on the list of ways to be powerful over other human beings," write James J. Mead and Glenn M. Balch Jr. in *Child Abuse and the Church*. "The easiest human being to have power over is a child who doesn't understand, doesn't know how to say no and probably would not be believed if they did tell."[26]

"Some cults, witches, Satanists, devil worshipers and pagan religions have sex acts as part of their religious practice or as the main focus of these ceremonies. Children, preferably premature infants, may be sacrificed and parts of the child used as aphrodisiacs for the high priest and priestess. Children are also defiled because child sacrifice is tremendously offensive to God."[27]

Child sexual abuse and sacrifice as religious practice capture many headlines and are the focus of huge debate. So, too, is the role of demonic influence in the abuser's life. These are vital issues not deserving of the ridicule they sometimes receive. At the same time, however, panic and sensationalism in this area is unhelpful. A calm, clear-headed, systematic approach is better.

"In a world where child abuse can masquerade as 'children's lib' and adult supremacism masquerades as civil liberty," says Hilary Cashman in her book, *Christianity and Child Sexual Abuse*, "it is particularly important to have a clear idea of the evil involved in child sexual abuse and the responsibility of its perpetrators."[28] The two conflicting views on evil, one accusing individual character and personality and the other blaming social conditions and pressures, are deterministic and leave little room for perpetrators to take personal responsibility for their actions. Spiritual forces are at work in heavenly places, and the theology and practical outworking of this truth need serious consideration. However, people still have autonomy to choose to do good or evil.

This is no less true of those who choose to sexually abuse children, many of whom are Christians or have strong religious convictions. Despite the current societal revolt against morality and passing judgment, child sexual abuse must be seen for what it is and condemned as such. It is a grave sin against God, the child and all of humanity. It is sexual sin because the perpetrator acts out of lust, misusing sexuality in adultery and fornication. Many other commandments, such as those against covetousness, deceit, violence and the abuse of power, are also violated. Most of all, child sexual abuse is a sin because of its impact on vulnerable and dependent children. Jesus reserved his strongest condemnations and warnings for those who misused or failed to protect children (Matt.

37

19:14, Matt. 18:6). "What could have caused Jesus to issue such dire warnings?" asks Patrick Parkinson, author of *Child Sexual Abuse and the Churches*. "Perhaps in that moment, knowing the secrets of men's hearts, and being able to see what was so deeply hidden from the view of others, Jesus was thinking of all the children who would be caused to stumble and to lose their faith by the sexual exploitation of adults."[29]

Family Trauma: "Circumstances made me do it"

Incest is the most common form of non-prostitution related child sexual abuse (75–85 percent in Western countries). In many cases the father figure develops a loss of self-confidence or feels a loss of control over his life and family. This loss is precipitated by traumatic circumstances like a death, major illness, unemployment, divorce or financial setback. He becomes so afraid of adult rejection that he looks to his own child for emotional support or sexual gratification. He uses his absolute control to meet his own need for power.[30] Psychologically, he raises the child to his own age level, seeing himself as the victim and the child as seducer. In some homes men view their wives and daughters as property and themselves as rulers, though they would rarely admit this. In some Christian homes these views are reinforced by misunderstood teaching about Christian headship. Men use this teaching and label the domination of family members as biblical submission. Sex is seen as an entitlement for the man of the house. When the wife denies the husband it becomes his "right" to demand sexual gratification from his child. He might also use the excuse that he is fulfilling his responsibility to offer the child sexual education.

Family Background: "I was taught how to do it"

Some studies have shown that a significant number of child sexual abusers were themselves sexually abused as children. However, it is not correct to derive from this that children who are abused become abusers. This faulty assumption further damages victims by assigning an unfair label to them. It has also damned them by reducing opportunities for ministry as agencies have begun to develop policies that prohibit their involvement with children. A recent study of adult men who were sexually abused revealed that half had become perpetrators and half had not.[31] These results continue to be confirmed, not least of all by the fact that there are many more victims than abusers.[32] We should be asking why so many children who are abused do *not* become abusers and why others who have not been abused *do*.

Factors arising from family background cannot wholly be written off, however. Though it is unwise to use common characteristics as a diagnostic tool, certain factors do appear consistently among perpetrators and may put some individuals at higher risk of abusing than others. These have been helpfully highlighted by Gail Ryan[33]:

1. Non-normative sexual environment

Sexuality in the offender's childhood home and community tends to fall into one of two extremes. Attitudes are either rigid and non-permissive with little information being given and sex being viewed as bad and sinful or over-sexualized with a lot of stimuli, sexualized attention and the possibility of overt sexual abuse.

2. Sexualized models of compensation

The perpetrator has learned from his or her role models to use sex as a way to compensate for perceived inadequacies and insecurities. Sex is used to feel better, be popular, release tension and avoid problems. The media, entertainment and advertising are full of messages to support this model of problem solving.

3. Lack of a confidante

The perpetrator's childhood lacked someone with whom the offender could confide about personal matters. This role is primarily parental and familial and supported by others outside the family. For perpetrators this confidante tended to be lacking almost altogether.

4. Non-empathetic parenting

Empathy and communication skills are learned in relationship to the significant people around us. As a child, the perpetrator's needs for empathy and love have been met inconsistently or conditionally, if at all. Hence the skills and emotional intelligence to experience empathy and feel for the suffering of other human beings are damaged.

5. Inconsistent care

Family stability has been lacking for many offenders. The physical parent/child relationship has been disrupted, in many cases, through institutionalization, hospitalization, incarceration, parental disappearance, abandonment, rejection or the termination of parental rights.

6. *Emotional impoverishment*

Emotions were often masked in the offender's childhood home. Hence, the appropriate way to express feelings healthily was not learned.

7. *Secrecy*

Various forms of dysfunction, including substance abuse, eating disorders, police arrests, incarceration of relatives, mental illness and sexual, physical and verbal abuse, occurred in the family circle but were never talked about inside or outside the home.

8. *Lack of quality attachments*

The quality of the perpetrator's attachments within the family tended to be poor. Many needs went unmet through emotional instability, even if the family appeared physically stable.

Ryan noted, "Almost anyone in our culture would experience one or more of these risk factors and the majority do not become offenders. Thus none of these are adequate to explain why someone becomes a perpetrator . . . though they may increase the risk."[34]

Denial: "I don't have a problem with it"

When confronted about their behavior, perpetrators give varying responses. Closely examined, these add up to denial. Perpetrators use denial as a way to avoid responsibility for their behavior and perpetuate further abuse. In "The Excuses of Child Molesters: Behavioral Sciences and the Law," N. Pollock and J. Hashmall explore five levels of denial.[35] These are outlined as follows, supported by some of the things perpetrators say in their own defense.

1. Denial of fact: Nothing happened. I didn't touch you. I don't know what you are talking about. You are a liar. You are mentally ill. You have an active imagination.

2. Denial of responsibility: Something happened, but it wasn't my idea. You kept taking your clothes off in front of me. You asked for it. I saw the way you looked at me.

3. Denial of sexual intent: Something happened and it was my idea, but it wasn't sexual. I was only tickling you. I was only playing with you. I was only giving you a bath.

4. Denial of wrongfulness: Something happened, it was my idea, it was sexual, but it wasn't wrong. I was only teaching you the facts of life. You enjoyed it. You consented.

5. Denial of self-determination: Something happened, it was my idea, it was sexual and it was wrong, but there were extenuating factors. I couldn't help myself. I was upset, angry, needy. Your mum was sick.

Perpetrators continue to sexually abuse children because they justify, blame and minimize. Perpetrators live in a framework of denial.

HOW DO THEY DO IT?

So far in this chapter we have asked and attempted to answer some questions about the perpetrators of child sexual abuse, albeit on a fairly superficial level: Who they are, what they do and some supposed explanations for why they sexually abuse children. If we are to protect children, particularly those in our care, we must also understand something of how perpetrators gain access to the children that they sexually abuse. It is important to recognize that child sexual abuse as a behavior does not occur in isolation. It is a cyclical pattern. Situations, thoughts, feelings and behaviors precede and follow the abuse. Perpetrators, especially those for whom a relationship with the child is important, sometimes take months to seduce a child. D. Finkelhor outlines four steps that take place in the abuse process.[36] S. Lane describes the sexual assault cycle.[37] These are combined below for easier access. As most perpetrators are male, I have used masculine language.

The perpetrator is triggered internally

A situation occurs in which the perpetrator himself feels victimized—helpless, a lack of control, betrayed, fearful, worthless, useless. It is usually something reminiscent of an earlier life experience. The situation that brings these feelings to the surface is blown out of proportion and personalized. He begins to withdraw and internalize, leaving himself isolated from anyone who might help mediate.

His response to the situation continues to worsen, as does his anger. He begins to blame and act out in a variety of behaviors in a futile attempt to feel better. The perpetrator wants to abuse.

As we have seen, a variety of factors combine to produce a perpetrator. At this stage he is increasingly overwhelmed by his feelings and desires and is getting little interaction from outside. He is left with the problem of how to feel more powerful, bigger, better, stronger, sexier, smarter, loved. He begins to fantasize about what will make him feel better or will make someone else feel as bad as he does. These fantasies become sexualized. The perpetrator formulates a plan and works on creating the opportunity to act on it. He begins to target a carefully chosen victim and develop the necessary relationship and structure for the plan to succeed. The perpetrator usually has a preference as to gender and age and is often already involved regularly with children in this preference. Among those to whom he is attracted, he chooses children who are most likely to be responsive and least likely to tell. Those who are trusting, friendly and positive are less suspecting of perpetrators than those who are reserved and distrustful. He methodically begins to build trust. Note that the child does not trigger the abuse. The perpetrator wants to abuse and chooses a victim.

The perpetrator overcomes inhibitions about abusing

Before the abuse can occur, the perpetrator must deal with his conscience and remove any objections it might throw up. If he requires a measure of supposed consent from the targeted child, the perpetrator will also be working to subtly remove any objections the victim might have. The levels of denial come strongly into play. He must convince himself that the proposed sexual abuse is acceptable. For many perpetrators abuse is simply not dissonant with their worldview. The perpetrator must also objectify the victim. He must remove any trace of seeing the child he is about to abuse as a human being with feelings. Hence he will be able to abuse with little appreciation for the needs and desires of the child or the impact of his actions on the child. He dissociates himself from reality.

The perpetrator gets the child alone

The perpetrator must get the child away from protective adults. Abusers in or known to the child's family plan ahead; they know the routine. A high level of trust has been achieved, so there is little or no suspicion.

The abuse occurs

If the perpetrator has been effective in the process of preparing the child, little coercion is necessary at this point.

The perpetrator feels transitory guilt

The perpetrator may feel guilt after the abuse. This guilt is not a true sorrow for what he has done. He is afraid and sorry that he may be caught. He is also sorry that the abuse has not achieved its desired effect. The perpetrator still feels powerless, helpless, unloved, worthless and full of anxiety. At this point the perpetrator is unsuccessfully trying to convince himself that he is in control and the cycle is set up to begin again.

HOW CAN WE STOP THEM?

It is a fact that many perpetrators of child sexual abuse target Christian childcare ministries. If you are involved in Christian ministry to children, take heed! Perpetrators are counting on you to provide a conducive environment for their abusive behavior. They are telling themselves that you won't be looking for abuse, that you are too naive to believe it exists or could happen in your ministry. After all, they reason, you won't even talk about it. Perpetrators are aware that you are unlikely to report abuse when discovered or disclosed because you don't want the bad publicity. They believe that even if you did want to get involved you wouldn't know how. Perpetrators view your ministry as an easy target with minimal risk. They've seen the lax guidelines and practices you employ. Above all, perpetrators believe that your hard line on grace means a soft line on sexual abuse.

Of course, this scenario might not be true of your ministry. Sadly, it is true in many. How do we change this scenario and provide a greater degree of protection for the children in our care? Obviously the answer to this question is every bit as vast and complex as the issue of child sexual abuse itself. Political, physical, emotional and spiritual solutions spanning prevention, intervention and rehabilitation are equally necessary and daunting. Where can we start? Perhaps with the development of good volunteer and employment policy.

According to Mead and Balch, investigations conducted in churches where child sexual abuse has occurred indicate the following common factors:

1. No application for the perpetrator is on file.
2. If there is an application, it is incomplete.
3. No background information is included on the application.
4. No effort has been made to verify the background information that does exist.
5. There is no educational information.
6. There is no indication of specific training.
7. There is no indication of supervision on file.

We must ask the question: If a co-worker in our ministry was found guilty of child sexual abuse, would the same policy and procedural factors have enabled the person? Do we have a policy? If so, when was the last time it was examined, updated and practiced? Whether we are examining existing policy or developing one, the following questions are good for discussion.

◆ Should we have an established policy?
◆ Is it better to act before or react after?
◆ What are the criteria for rejecting an applicant?
◆ How much supervision is appropriate?
◆ How long must an applicant have been a church member or known to the mission agency before working with children?
◆ How much Christian education should be required?
◆ How far are we prepared to go to verify applicant information?
◆ Will anyone be exempt from screening?
◆ What does our legal counsel have to say about this issue?
◆ What does our liability insurance carrier have to say about this issue?
◆ Who will be in charge of the screening process?
◆ Who will be in charge of supervision?
◆ Who will file the required reports if an incident occurs?

◆ How will we deal with an incident?

◆ Who will tell someone that he or she can't work with children?

◆ How can we avoid making current workers feel suspected while implementing policy?

Developing a policy will not be easy. Some people don't want to talk about sensitive issues. For some, sexual abuse has been a personal reality; others feel so strongly about children being hurt that talking about the subject is difficult. Some fear that suspicion will fall on them or those whom they know, while others think developing policy is an impractical bureaucratic waste of time. Whatever the barriers to developing policy doing so is vital if we are to keep perpetrators of all forms of abuse out and bring, encourage and keep quality staff in. The following suggested strategy is summarized from *Child Abuse and the Church* by James Mead and Glenn Balch Jr.[38]

The application

All staff—elected, paid or volunteer of any age, duration of service or role—must complete an application form. This requires time and thought. Those who are unlikely to follow through on verbal commitments will be screened out here by their own lack of enthusiasm. Detailed applications also give you the information you need to check out background details and send a signal about what you expect from applicants and how seriously you take their roles. No application is acted upon until it is complete. This must be applied to everyone. Any proposed applicants who refuse are disqualified unless and until they do so.

Initially a special task force should be appointed to send out applications to those currently in positions and help them understand the necessity for the change or development in policy. Most will be happy to comply. Those who have not applied by the agreed-upon deadline are sent a reminder through the post. If they do not respond by the extended deadline, a phone reminder is given. If they still fail to apply, they must be asked to step down or resign. All information given in the applications or by referees is revealed only to the task force, who review all returned forms and, at its discretion, selectively conduct interviews, send references and place phone calls. Special emphasis should be placed on those in current high-risk positions and those in positions held for fewer than two years. Subsequently, an ongoing task force (three respected representatives who serve three-year terms, with one member's term expiring each year) should be set up to send, receive and follow up all avenues of the application forms of those indicating new interest. Requests for references should be accompanied by a return envelope marked "confidential." Confidential forms must be kept in a locked cabinet. Check all background details. Approval or denial of the selection should be by unanimous agreement of the task force. Those in current positions may remain there at the discretion of the task force. No new applicant is to start service until his or her selection is approved at every level.

The oral interview

Successful applicants will be interviewed by an oral review team comprising a few ministry members and staff with some personnel or counseling background. The applicant is being interviewed for a responsible position and the setting for the interview should reflect this. However, the purpose of the oral interview is not to intimidate, so an air of informality is appropriate. A relaxed but private setting with no interruptions is best. Those between the ages of 11 and 16 will be interviewed with a guardian present.

The purpose of this oral interview is twofold:

1. To ensure safety for the child and the worker.
2. To discover, encourage, develop and release the gifts of the applicant into ministry with children. Discussions that take place in the oral interview are confidential; they are not recorded. Selection at this stage is the team decision of the oral review board.

The following are some suggested questions specifically directed at child protection issues. (Q stands for question and L stands for what you are looking for in the answer.)

Q: What was your childhood like?
L: To reveal issues the applicant might not have dealt with.

Q: Could you tell us how you came to be a Christian?

L: To be sure the applicant is a Christian and feels strongly about it.

Q: How long have you known the Lord?
L: To track the person's record of service since salvation.

Q: How long have you attended your local church?
L: To ensure that the applicant has not been moving about looking for children.

Q: Do you prefer to work with boys or girls? Why?
L: Be alert to someone looking to meet his or her needs, not to serve the Lord's children.

Q: How is your driving record?
L: Too many tickets, a record of drunk driving indicate that this person might be unsafe with children.

Q: Have you ever been treated for a drug or alcohol problem?
L: To determine if there is an existing problem or an untreated one.

Q: Have you ever been accused of a sex crime?
L: To watch the person's reaction to the question.

These questions should be mixed with those aimed at discovering, encouraging, developing and releasing the gifts of the applicant into ministry. These questions might include:

Q: Are there issues in your life (past or present) that are unresolved or that could be relevant to the proposed ministry position?
L: To encourage the applicant to share concerns with you.

Q: How do you handle your anger?
L: To learn how the person might cope with stress.

Q: What, other than Jesus, makes you feel significant?
L: What does the person rely on when it isn't Jesus?

Q: What gifts and strengths do you think you will bring to this position?

L: Look for healthy self-perception.

Q: What do you think you might struggle with?
L: Again, look for healthy self-perception.

Q: How would this position fit into your present commitments: your relationship with God, family, yourself, your place of employment, social life, hobbies?
L: Discuss how the applicant might need to reprioritize.

Q.   How would this ministry fit into your present emotional commitments?
L: Is the person taking on too much?

Q: How does each member of your family feel about your proposed ministry involvement?
L: What obstacles might the person face and need support through?

Q: Do you have any physical conditions that the stress of this ministry might affect?
L: To determine the applicant's general health.

Q: What is your devotional life like?
L: To determine ways he or she might need support.

REQUIRED TRAINING

Minimum levels of training are essential to ensure that staff and volunteers follow procedures, understand policies and have the basic skills necessary to carry out their responsibilities. Each job or position should have a clear statement of what combination of training and education is needed and require a specified number of hours of training. Job descriptions should be clearly worded, detailing responsibilities for the protection of children and the person or persons to whom they will be accountable for their work; the person or persons whose work they will supervise, if any; a description of the work they will undertake with children; a statement of their duty to prevent the abuse of all children and young people with whom they are in contact; and reference to the action to be taken if abuse is discovered or disclosed. Required training should include information about child sexual abuse prevention, intervention and ways in which a victim's rehabilitation may be supported. It should also involve appropriate theological training about children, childhood, Jesus' attitude toward children and other biblical material. Standards of wise practice about personal conduct in the company of children and how to avoid wrongful accusation or misunderstanding are also vital.

Required training is fundamentally about good management. It provides confidence and security and minimizes liability by showing that each person has been informed and has had materials provided. Required training is also good screening, because people without good intent are not likely to complete the course. It may be felt that some people who finish this section of the procedure should still not be allowed access to children. The board might feel that the applicant would never do any harm to a child, but that he or she is simply not gifted to work with children. This position is difficult. However, it is not fair to the applicant or to the children to leave it unaddressed. The board will need to consider pastorally how to deliver the truth that the applicant is loved and cared for but that work with children is not considered advisable.

After applicants have been selected and begun ministry, they will need support. In-service training will provide new ideas, new books and new materials for review. It will inform them about changes of law and regulations. Mixed with regular quarterly or monthly supervision, it provides an avenue for workers to express concerns, joys and vision in ministry. It also provides an important structure for ongoing accountability and the success of the ministry.

How can we stop perpetrators? Good policy will go a long way. Good policy will help keep perpetrators out and keep quality staff in. It will implement good procedure, including written application, verbal interview, ongoing quality training, supervision and accountability. Good policy formalizes concern for children and supports the family in protecting them. Good policy is a deterrent to those who would use Christian childcare ministries as a screen for abuse. Good policy helps in the detection of potential problems before they happen. Good policy helps build up, encourage and strengthen ministry among children. Good policy helps to tear down, discourage and weaken those who would seek to harm children.

Notes

[1] Carolyn Ainscough and Kay Toon, eds., *Breaking Free: Help for Survivors of Child Sexual Abuse* (London: Sheldon Press, SPCK, 1993), pp. 204–5.

[2] Kidscape, "Sexual Abuse: An Issue for Youth Clubs?" *Youth Clubs with Edge* (September 1991), pp. 8–11.

[3] James Mead and Glenn Balch, *Child Abuse and the Church: A New Mission* (Costa Mesa, Calif.: HDL Publishing Co., 1987), p. 65.

[4] Ibid., p. 64.

[5] Daniel Goleman, *Emotional Intelligence: Why It Can Matter More than IQ* (London: Bloomsbury, 1995), pp. 106–10.

[6] Priscilla L. Denham, "Toward an Understanding of Child Rape," *The Journal of Pastoral Care*, vol. 36:4 (1982).

[7] Patrick Parkinson, *Child Sexual Abuse and the Churches* (London: Hodder and Stoughton, 1997), p. 35.

[8] Ibid., p. 42.

[9] Gail Ryan, "Working with Perpetrators of Sexual Abuse and Domestic Violence," *Pastoral Psychology*, vol. 41:5 (1993), p. 311.

[10] Parkinson, *Child Sexual Abuse and the Churches*, p. 42.

[11] Ron O'Grady, *The Rape of the Innocent* (Bangkok: ECPAT, 1994), pp. 34–40.

[12] Quoted in Richard Ford, "Belgian Case Throws Light on Global Scourge," *The Times*, August 19, 1996.

[13] Raymond Hammond, "Internet Censors Fight Rising Tide of Depravity," *The Sunday Times*, April 28, 1996, p. 11.

[14] Jubilee Action, *Child Prostitution: A Global Report* (Guildford: Jubilee Action, 1994), p. 3.

[15] Roger Boyes, "How Sex Tourists Evade Justice." *The Times*, August 22, 1996, p. 22.

[16] Patricia Green, "Prostitution: Children the Victims: The Effects of Prostitution and Sexual Exploitation on Children and Adolescents," unpublished work, 1994.

[17] O'Grady, *The Rape of the Innocent*, pp. 67, 136, 137.

[18] Jubilee Action, *Child Prostitution*, p. 3.

[19] Lay Bee Yeoh, "The Problem of Child Prostitution in Thailand," unpublished work, 1993.

[20] O'Grady, *The Rape of the Innocent*, p. 39.

[21] S. Rand, ed., "Rescuing Child Prostitutes," *TEAR Times* 67 (December 1994), p. 20.

[22] Jubilee Action, *Child Prostitution*, p. 25.

[23] Ibid., p. 14.

[24] Ibid., p. 18.

[25] O'Grady, *The Rape of the Innocent*, pp. 42, 43.

[26] Mead and Balch, *Child Abuse and the Church*, p. 69.

[27] Ibid., p. 67.

[28] Hilary Cashman, *Christianity and Child Sexual Abuse* (London: SPCK, 1993), pp. 91–92.

[29] Parkinson, *Child Sexual Abuse and the Churches*, pp. 27–28.

[30] Mead and Balch, *Child Abuse and the Church*, p. 64.

[31] Ryan, "Working with Perpetrators of Sexual Abuse and Domestic Violence," pp. 303–19.

[32] Ainscough and Toon, *Breaking Free*, p. 183.

[33] Ryan, "Working with Perpetrators of Sexual Abuse and Domestic Violence," pp. 303–19.

[34] Ibid., p. 303.

[35] In Parkinson, *Child Sexual Abuse and the Churches*, p. 54.

[36] In Ainscough and Toon, *Breaking Free*, pp. 38–42.

[37] Ryan, "Working with Perpetrators of Sexual Abuse and Domestic Violence," pp. 306–11.

[38] Mead and Balch, *Child Abuse and the Church*, pp. 26–30.

4

Impact of Sexual Exploitation on Children

Patricia Green

This is my virgin body
sold to you for a song
take, beat, thrust, burn . . .

An estimated one million children, the majority of them in Asia, are believed to enter the multi-billion-dollar illegal sex market each year. Children taken from their villages are sold in the cities or overseas by highly organized syndicates or individuals for prostitution or for pornographic purposes. The exact number of children involved in prostitution is unknown and unknowable. Non-government organizations (NGOs) and unofficial sources suggest that upward of two million females are engaged in prostitution in Thailand alone. The United Nations suggests that as many as ten million children may be involved globally.

General estimates of the number of Thai child prostitutes vary between 30,000 and 800,000, depending on the age criterion used to define a child. Although the UN Convention on Children's Rights defines a child as anyone under 18 years of age, local laws vary; in Thailand a child is usually considered to be someone under 15 years of age. Child prostitution includes boys and girls. In Thailand it affects a far greater number of girls. The Center for the Protection of Children's Rights estimates that in Thailand 20 percent of girls between the ages of 11 and 17 could be prostitutes (1993). Most of these girls are forced into brothels where they may be required to service up to 20 men a day.

Child prostitution and the sexual exploitation of children are not new. Literature written on these subjects suggests that prostitution and exploitation of children have a long history. In Thailand young girls have been sold or forced into prostitution from early times because of family poverty. However, child prostitution has increased dramatically in recent years and is a phenomenon spreading rapidly throughout many developing countries in Asia.

Increasing numbers of adolescent and pre-adolescent girls are being brought to Thailand from the northern hill tribe areas and across international borders from Burma, southern China and Laos. They are tricked, kidnapped and sold into small town and city brothels. On the wider scene, large numbers of Nepalese girls are sold into brothels in Indian cities and Taiwanese tribal and aboriginal girls into brothels in Taipei. Children from China, Vietnam and Laos are obtained by agents to provide sexual services for tourists and military personnel in Cambodia.

This chapter focuses on the impact of prostitution on the children. It also discusses the reasons children are forced into prostitution and sexual slavery. Reference is made to the relationship among poverty, economic development, child prostitution and tourism. The chapter has three objectives:

1. To present a general picture of the issue of prostitution and sexual exploitation of children;
2. To examine the causes and resulting physical, social and psychological effects;
3. To present a challenge to caregivers to direct their expertise at confronting these issues not only from a clinical, counseling basis as the "helper," but from a community psychology base of action, research, prevention, education and advocacy.

SOURCE OF INFORMATION

This chapter focuses on child prostitution in Thailand, where the author works with sexually exploited girls through Rahab Ministries in the Patpong area of Bangkok. Information for this chapter was gathered by the writer from personal observations, informal conversations and some structured interviews with girls rescued from forced prostitution through Rahab Ministries. Observations and conversations occurred over a period of four years with girls working voluntarily as prostitutes in the Patpong area. Discussions also were held with caregivers in homes caring for girls rescued from prostitution. A sampling of files kept on girls rescued by other organizations from brothels was also examined.

ROOT CAUSES

Child prostitution and trafficking in children are linked to poverty, economic development, industrialization, increasing materialism, international tourism and militarization. Inappropriate development policies have deprived rural people of their land and means of survival. Forced into desperate poverty or lured by materialism, thousands of Thai villagers have chosen to sell their land or, knowingly or unknowingly, even their children to agents for a few hundred dollars. Brokers have promised a better life and a good job for their children.

Traditional cultural and community values have eroded and been replaced by a greater emphasis on individualism and competitiveness. This value shift has precipitated the sale of children for increased cash to purchase material goods and thus achieve higher social status.

International tourism has helped propel prostitution into a large international industry that usually is seen as threatening to human life and dignity. The growth of third-world tourism is increasingly linked, in turn, to highly organized sex tourism that may be linked with powerful international crime syndicates.

Seventy percent of tourists visiting Thailand are males. Sources indicate up to 60 percent of these males come specifically for sex.[1] To meet the demand of sex tourists, particularly Middle Eastern and Asian men, younger and younger children are forced into sex slavery. Children of three or four years of age are purchased and used for pornographic purposes and abused by both men and women.

STUDIES ON CHILD PROSTITUTION

Recent surveys by the Thai Foundation for Women found that in nine villages in three northern provinces only five girls between 13 and 16 years of age remained in the village. An analysis[2] of why Thai girls and women enter prostitution showed that less than 10 percent of adolescents entered willingly; 90 percent entered because of family poverty. They were sold, deceived or pressured by parents into believing that they were fulfilling their obligation of gratitude to family.

Studies: root causes

Naowarat[3] found that 13 out of 19 village girls were deceived into entering prostitution. Other factors were the lack of education and alternative employment opportunities. Another study showed that in one village in Chiang Rai Province, 41 out of 170 households had sold their daughters; five of these families were acting as brokers to sell other girls in the village. A further study estimated that in one northern province 80 percent of all girls who have completed primary education are working in prostitution. School teachers are employed as agents to inform the sex brokers of the prettiest girls.

In some northern villages girls grow up with the expectation of being sold at the age of 12 or 13. A 1990 survey of northern villages reported that of the girls under 16 years of age who had been sold into prostitution, 63 percent were sold directly by parents, 21 percent by neighbors or friends and 16 percent by agents. Of these families 42 percent had an annual income above the poverty village level. Thus, desire for material goods and the good life, rather than true poverty, also may be reasons why parents sell their children. Selling children was viewed by some helpers and researchers as 70 percent greed and 30 percent poverty.

Studies: psychological trauma

Studies show that sexual abuse and prostitution have a devastating effect on children and adolescents. In one study in which 1,012 Thai adolescent and young-adult prostitutes were interviewed, 90 percent disapproved of prostitution and what they were doing; 50 percent felt society showed contempt for them; 43 percent felt hopeless, disappointed in themselves and trapped; and 26 percent said that they would commit suicide if they knew they had contracted AIDS.[4]

A Canadian study of 229 juvenile male and female prostitutes suggested an association between poor mental health and gross childhood sexual trauma. This study indicated that 80 percent of the juvenile prostitutes suffered serious depression, 71 percent had a sense of devastated self-esteem, and the subjects were three times more likely to have suicidal tendencies than the control group.

Kraipatsapong[5] lists the following psychological symptoms experienced by child prostitutes: negative opinion of self, lack of self-confidence, low self-esteem and thinking of oneself as stupid and dirty. These findings are consistent with other research findings on the effects of sexual abuse of children and adolescents.

IMPACT OF PROSTITUTION ON CHILDREN

Wan is not sure how old she is but thinks she was 13 when her mother knowingly sold her into prostitution some years ago. Her life is spent in one small room. She is provided with food, clothing and some medical care. Every three months her father comes to visit her and arranges with the brothel owner to raise a further loan against payment for her services. Wan has no idea how many men she has serviced but says she often has between five and ten per day. If she refuses to work, she is beaten. She has not been told if she has AIDS, but she has many diseases and is often sick and in pain. The impact of prostitution on children like Wan is devastating for them in every area of their development.

Physical effects

Many victims suffer severe physical damage and sexually transmitted diseases, including AIDS. Of the sample the author interviewed, 63 percent had gonorrhea or syphilis. Most had been tested for HIV but said they had not been told whether they had AIDS or not. In some areas up to 87 percent of low-class prostitutes, mostly children and adolescents, are HIV-infected. The Centre for the Protection of Children's Rights states that 80 percent of girls under 17 years of age rescued from brothels are HIV-positive.[6] The younger the girl, the more susceptible she is to damage and infection. Some girls complained of being forced to continue to service customers in spite of severe internal damage and consistent bleeding and pain.

Living conditions in the brothels are frequently unsanitary and cramped, and there is inadequate food and medical care. Girls spoke of being beaten or jumped on when pregnant to force miscarriage. Repeated forced or self-induced abortions with no medical follow-up care contributed to internal physical damage and sometimes death. Two girls related how they were knocked unconscious when they refused to work while menstruating. Severe physical damage contributes to health problems, trauma and poor mental health. A depressed self-image correlated with the nature, frequency and severity of sexual abuse.

Psychological effects

Many girls were traumatized and raped into submission. They expressed fear of repeated beatings, starvation or torture if they refused to comply with customer demands. Stories of young teenagers beaten to death by pimps for refusing to comply with customers' demands or trying to escape frightened them. Such stories have been substantiated by police and press reports. Sometimes children were subdued with drugs and consequently developed drug or alcohol dependency.

Most of the children expressed attitudes of self-rejection and self-hatred for what they had become. They felt rejected by other people. Ninety percent of the girls exhibited very low self-esteem, feelings of inadequacy and confusion. They felt humiliated and expressed feelings of self-blame and being unclean because what they were doing was "bad." Associated with this were feelings of deep guilt and shame, with comments such as, "I must have been bad or they wouldn't have sold me."

Some girls felt they were broken to a point where they could never regain self-respect and dignity. Three or four years later they were still tearful when relating their experiences. A common observation made to the author was, "Although I smile on the outside, on the inside I am still crying."

Severe depression and high suicidal tendencies were also evident. More than 50 percent stated that while in the brothel they wanted to kill themselves. Suicide was not uncommon. Most girls had strong feelings of hate toward those who had tricked, sold and abused them. They wished they could punish them.

Values and family relationships were confused. Most children showed strong feelings of denial and inner conflict about their families. They experienced difficulty in reconciling the facts that their parents loved them yet sold them "into hell." A frequent comment was, "If my parents really loved me, how could they have sold me into this life?"

Children expressed many fears concerning further violation, being sold again, men's actions and violence. Others feared returning home without money and being subjected to beating or resale. Fear of new caregivers or helpers and authority figures was also evident. Fear of being resold contributed to difficulties in building trust and self-disclosure.

Most of the girls interviewed held distorted perceptions of sex. They viewed sexual intercourse as disgusting and associated it with deception, pain and violence. Few could equate sexual activity with loving or caring; they saw it simply as a means of economic exchange. This contributed to a sense of loss of personhood. Children and adolescents seldom gain financially in the sex industry, so there is an added sense of loss, sacrifice and suffering no gain. Several girls said that they became desensitized: "I no longer care what happens to me, nothing more bad can happen to me now."

Desensitization blanks out the children's minds, enabling them to cope with the constant trauma of abuse and loss. Dissociation and only talking about what had happened to others were evident as coping mechanisms. When interviewed two or three years later, some girls were unable to recall their life in prostitution or any other significant life events at that time.

Thai cultural patterns such as smiling, conflict avoidance and being *jai yen* (cool-hearted) provide the psychological ability to repress emotion and detach oneself from the reality of the situation. This may be a means of stress reduction and coping for some.

Impaired development and psychological damage are unlikely to be noticed or understood by the family if the girl returns home. Her trauma is likely to be compounded by her being resold or continuing in sexual service. If help and the opportunity for a new life are not available, a high percentage return to prostitution.

Meo, at 14, was forced by her mother to sleep with an old man to earn money to pay her mother's gambling debts in order to keep her out of prison. From this experience and the constant pressure from her family to make money Meo drifted into the city and prostitution. Now 19, she is addicted to marijuana, alcohol and other drugs to keep her high, enabling her to continue in this work. Meo perceives herself as "a person no good for anyone or anything now."

Girls who have been sold into and continued in prostitution in later years tend to imitate parental child-rearing behaviors. Like their parents, they sell or coerce their own daughters into prostitution. Sixty-two percent of the interviewees who had been sold into prostitution had been trafficked from Burma. Seventy-five percent were tribal, Burmese and Thai. They spoke of confusion in not knowing the Thai language and thus not understanding what was being said to or about them. Some had no idea of their location in Thailand because they could not read names and road signs. One stated: "It was cruel. There was no one who could tell me where I was or anything about disease." Several girls commented that they felt that they had lost their innocence, their body, their sense of self—had lost everything and had no future. Ah Sor commented, "I feel that my heart has gone from me."

Dreams and nightmares were frequent among some of the girls—dreams such as being resold, chased by a tiger and suffocated.

Social behaviors

Some girls exhibited excessive emotional attachment and attention-seeking behaviors. For a large majority learning ability was affected, and attention and memory span were short. They were forgetful and seemed to find difficulty in applying themselves to even simple tasks. They tended to escape into sleep or fantasy. Many of the adolescent girls appeared to have a "sense of floating." Unable to ground themselves in reality, they lacked motivation to consider alternatives or to make decisions.

They spoke of wanting to study and to have a vocation, but they were unable to apply themselves to planning a future or making decisions. There appeared to be a strong present-time orientation and little sense of past or future. This could be a form of escapism and the result of severe trauma.

Some of the girls who had been placed by rescue organizations in rehabilitation homes were able to accept help, counsel and adapt to a new life. The tribal girls, especially the Akka girls, seemed more able to adjust and put their experiences behind them than the Thai or Burmese girls.

Few behavioral differences were noticed between girls who had been sold and those who had entered prostitution voluntarily under 17 years of age. Caregivers and social workers commented on some behavioral differences between girls who had been rescued from prostitution and other village girls of the same age. These differences were greater social and sexual awareness, smart talk and boldness in their approaches to males, both their peers in age and older men. They also noted difficulties in concentration; they were easily distracted. Although many of the girls wanted education and vocational training, they were unable to accept the reality of consistent study.

In spite of their fears and negative experiences, some girls did not want to leave prostitution. They saw prostitution as a replacement for family love, acceptance and affection. Others, although offered alternatives, tended to drift back into prostitution voluntarily, as it was something known and did not make demands on them mentally. Change of values also affected their desire to leave. If money had become their highest value, they were more likely to remain. For older adolescents who had voluntarily entered prostitution, the "Cinderella Syndrome," the fantasy that some man would come and take them away and offer them a life of ease and happiness ever after also appeared to prohibit them from leaving or contemplating alternatives. However, most considered that their lives were waking nightmares in which they were subjected to inhumane conditions and treatment.

Attitudes

Attitudes toward prostitution vary across cultures. Thai family socialization processes teach female children to adhere to values where submissive behavior is considered noble and respectful. *Bun khun* or "attitude of gratitude" toward parents for raising, feeding and educating them is a prime value. Thus, willing entry into prostitution is viewed by some parents and children as a sacrifice for the family and is also perceived as "gaining merit" according to Buddhist beliefs and principles.

TOWARD A SOLUTION

Prostitution, sexual exploitation and sex slavery of children and adolescents are increasing social problems in many developing countries. Child prostitution is linked to poverty and economic development and is escalated by international tourism. Child prostitution is destructive to life and an affront to human dignity.

Caregivers are encouraged to direct their expertise into tackling these issues at the levels of prevention as well as cure, as child prostitution will continue to increase throughout the world, hand in hand with increased tourism and economic development. Action and care must lead to social change: the change of attitudes toward women and female children; increased education on family values; and a new valuing of the dignity of life. Community awareness and viable alternatives for employment must also be considered.

Caregivers also need to have an understanding of the psychology of the pedophile, the abuser, the exploiter and the family members who are willing to sell their children to provide a better house, a television or other material goods. It is hoped that in the process of development in other Third World and Asian nations this gross violation of the dignity of the rights of children can be avoided.

Notes

[1] Wanjiku Kaime-Atterhög and O. Ard-am, *Children Without Childhood*, unpublished paper, Bangkok, Institute for Population and Social Research, Mahidol University, 1993.

[2] S. Skrobanek, *Report of Kamla Project* (Bangkok: Foundation for Women, 1988).

[3] N. Naowarat, "Child Prostitutes," *National Seminar on Prevention and Protection of Working and Abandoned Children* (Bangkok: National Youth Bureau, 1988), pp. 108–21.

[4] Unpublished studies presented at the Thailand World Bank Conference (Bangkok, 1991).

[5] D. Kraipatsapong, in *The Cry of My Appeal*, video produced by the Catholic Commission on Peace and Violence (Bangkok, 1994).

[6] International Centre for the Protection of Children's Rights, "AIDS: Children Too," *Children Worldwide*, vol. 3:23, International Catholic Child Bureau (1993).

PART TWO:

Prevention

5

Empowering Communities
to Enhance Survival Strategies

Bruce Bradshaw

*And his master commended the dishonest manager because he had
acted shrewdly; for the children of this age are more shrewd in
dealing with their own generation than are the children of light
(Luke 16:8, NRSV).*

Agents of the sex tourism industry throughout the world export thousands of young girls from their impoverished third-world rural villages to sleazy urban brothels every month of the year. Some of these girls are as young as 9 years of age; too many of them become diseased and die before their sixteenth birthday. All of them are antiques before they turn 21. One woman, at that seasoned age, lamented that she became professionally obsolete because of the belief that having sexual intercourse with a virgin cures AIDS. This belief lowered both the entry age and the retirement age in the industry, putting her out of business. She said: "I'm like a damaged egg; nobody wants me."[1]

This trafficking of humanity is a vital concern for Christian missions, for it insults a central tenet of our faith: that all people are created in the image of God. Our struggle, though, is to discern how the Good News of Jesus Christ transforms the conditions that rob these girls of any realization that they do, in fact, bear God's image. This struggle is complex. We are prone to approach it by condemning its immorality. For good reason, we become disgusted by stories about parents who sell their daughters into prostitution. We also grieve over other stories about children who flee from their families and communities with hopes of finding lucrative jobs and a better life in the cities. These hopes are shattered when they learn that their bodies are their only economic assets.

While the immorality of child exploitation is a major issue, child exploitation is not simply a moral problem. Condemning the immorality of the practice does not solve it; instead, condemnation masks the nature of the problem by simplifying it. The immorality of child exploitation is a symptom of greater economic and social problems. Child exploitation results when the survival strategies in rural communities lose their ability to support the social and economic welfare of a community.

In this chapter we explore the role of Christian development ministries in addressing child exploitation by enhancing the survival strategies of rural villages. While realizing that child exploitation is a complex issue with many strands of causation, we address the economic dimension of survival strategies as one salient strand. In that context we offer an interpretation of the parable of the shrewd manager that illustrates the centrality of development ministries to Christian missions, particularly in the effort to empower people to transform the economic conditions that victimize them. We conclude with a story to illustrate how a revolving loan fund in a rural Asian village made a difference in the lives of children who might have been exploited without it.

WHAT ARE SURVIVAL STRATEGIES?

All communities have survival strategies, a combination of activities that keep villages functioning. They include, among other things, systems for reconciliation and justice, social harmony, health and medical care, land and water management, sanitation and economics. They embody the matrix of beliefs and values that people hold concerning what they view as important. The customs, practices and habits in a culture are integrated into the community's survival strategies. Survival strategies provide order in a community; they shape the character of the community and of the people who live in the community.

The survival strategy is the medium through which development practitioners work. When community development facilitators do an assessment of a community, they are trying to understand that community's survival strategy. Any development intervention improves one or more aspects of the community's survival strategy. When a village is not functioning well, development practitioners, in partnership with the community, seek to identify the strengths and weaknesses in the village survival strategy. Together they design innovations to enhance the strengths and overcome the weaknesses.

Churches, as stewards of a community's values, traditions and beliefs, have the ministry of interpreting how the survival strategy of the community participates in the reconciling work of God in creation. The biblical foundation of this ministry is Colossians 1:15–20. The passage affirms that God reconciles all elements of creation, the seen and unseen, through Christ. The result is peace through the blood of Christ.

The seen and unseen elements of creation that God reconciles through Christ are embodied in the various aspects of the survival strategy. The image of peace that results from the reconciling work of God is described in Isaiah 65:17–25. This image communicates a survival strategy that is fully functioning. It addresses social harmony, justice, long life and a satisfying spirituality. This passage serves as the inspiration for development practitioners who are enhancing survival strategies.

The survival strategies of a healthy village reflect characteristics of Isaiah 65:17–25. They foster a sense of interdependence among its residents. Each family and individual participates in the village survival strategy by making some contributions to the community that ensure its own well-being and continued existence. Typical survival strategies divide various activities among men, women and children. They also create relationships with other communities to provide goods and services that might otherwise be unavailable.

No community has a self-sufficient survival strategy. All communities, regardless of their location and size, ensure their survival by participating in the global economy. They depend on importing and exporting products and services locally and abroad. Many people in Asian villages, for example, produce baskets that are sold in America and Europe. Also, Coca Cola is not produced in any rural villages, but we can find it virtually anywhere. For better or worse, it is the most common indicator of a rural community's participation in the global economy.

While many rural villages do not have products or services to export, child prostitution is one service that impoverished rural communities do provide to the global economy. When the viability of a community's survival strategy is jeopardized, parents often cannot meet the economic demands of caring for themselves or their child. The parents are tempted to abandon their children; they sell them into prostitution, or the children leave the villages and are lured into the sex industry. There is no shortage of demand for their services.

Christians must address the economic aspects of child exploitation if we are going to make any contribution to transforming the conditions that cultivate it. This effort to transform survival strategies is central to Christian development ministries. Survival strategies, embodying the beliefs and values of communities, are the media through which communities express their spiritual convictions; people normally express their beliefs and values by the decisions they make in daily life.

However, because survival is a central value to all of us, people who live in impoverished conditions struggle with the dilemma of compromising their values to ensure their survival. They find themselves making bad decisions to deal with difficult problems for the hope of survival. For example, parents, for the most part, do not value the idea of selling their daughters into prostitution. However, when their very survival is threatened, they succumb to this practice as a way of navigating through the moral dilemmas with which survival confronts them.

When Christians work to transform survival strategies, they are working to empower people to resolve the dilemmas central to their survival. The ultimate purpose of this work is to make Christ, rather than secular or non-Christian beliefs and values, the foundation of the village survival strategy. This purpose is met first by offering Christian beliefs and values as alternatives to the prevailing beliefs and values in the communities. Second, it is met by empowering communities to integrate these Christian beliefs and values into their survival strategies. In the example of child exploitation, development innovations in the survival strategy empower people to express the conviction that the lives of their daughters are more valuable than the monetary exchanges they receive in the sex industry.

This effort to make Christ the foundation of a community's survival strategy is one expression of the creative, reconciling and sustaining work of God through Christ in creation. The apostle Paul wrote that God was pleased to reconcile all things to himself through the blood of Christ, bringing peace to a fallen creation (see Col. 1:15–20). The amelioration of child exploitation is a profound expression of this peace.

A BIBLICAL NARRATIVE
THAT DEFEATS ECONOMIC EXPLOITATION

The parable of the shrewd manager[2] (Luke 16:1–13) may help us understand the dynamics of economic exploitation in a rural Asian village. The conditions in the parable are somewhat analogous to the economic conditions in rural villages that supply young girls to the sex industry.

The parable has three main characters and three main sections. The characters include a rich man, a manager and the debtors. The first section of the parable tells about the rich man, who is threatening to fire the manager. The manager, fearing unemployment, has to preserve his job or find an alternative means of survival. He eliminates some obvious employment alternatives because he is too weak to dig and too proud to beg.

The second section of the parable tells about the manager planning a scheme that he expects to endear him to his master's debtors. He summons the debtors and reduces their loans. He reduces a debt of 100 jugs of olive oil to 50 jugs, and a debt of 100 containers of wheat is reduced to 80 containers.

In the third section of the parable Jesus tells the audience that the manager's master was impressed by this shrewd scheme. The rich man commends the manager and reinstates him. Jesus comments on the parable with some teachings on how the children of this age are more shrewd in dealing with their own generation than are the children of light. He continues the parable by telling his audience to make friends for themselves by means of dishonest wealth. He bases this statement on the expectation that their friends may still prove useful in acquiring an eternal home even when the wealth is gone. Finally, Jesus teaches that whoever is faithful with very little is also faithful in much. Conversely, whoever is dishonest in little is dishonest in much. He reinforces this teaching in the verses that follow and closes by reminding the people that they cannot serve both God and wealth.

The parable is spiced with irony and humor, some derision and a little mockery, making it difficult to interpret. However, it gives us some insights to address unjust economic patterns in rural villages. Today many rural villagers, like the people in the parable, live in desperately impoverished, cash-poor, subsistence economies. They always need money, particularly for major purchases, such as livestock. They do not have credit ratings and collateral to enable them to qualify for bank loans. Therefore, they must accept loans from moneylenders at interest rates that can exceed 20 percent per week.

At these rates, interest payments escalate. If the villagers borrow $50, they must pay $10 per week interest. These payments can easily represent their entire income. The villagers cannot make the payments, and they find their $50 debt escalating to amounts beyond their imagination. The villagers inevitably find themselves in a spiraling cycle of debt that they cannot get out of. They pay all their income to the moneylenders, and many become bankrupt.

Before we address the fate of bankrupt villagers, let's examine the role of the money managers in the village economy. Money managers are middle managers; they work for the rich people and exploit the villagers. They live as an endangered species; they are always under the threat of termination. This threat is based on two conditions of their employment. The first condition is that they must create new loans to generate revenue for their bosses. The second condition is that they must collect money from existing loans. Their bosses readily fire them when they cannot meet either condition adequately.

The bosses constantly threaten the money managers with termination by suggesting that the money managers will have to live with the villagers if they do not produce. The money managers are not going to live with the villagers; they and the villagers hate each other. Also, the villagers are too poor to support themselves; they cannot provide support for fired money managers.

The managers are always under threat of termination because their bosses know that the success of any manager lasts for only a short time. These threats of termination are necessary because moneylending is a competitive business; the villages are full of moneylenders who are generating new loans. The bosses also know that the villagers tend to pay new debts and neglect old ones. Therefore, the bosses' revenues will decline without new loans. The bosses must terminate managers to generate new business. They have to replace old managers with new ones to generate new loans to replace old loans. New managers generate new loans, and new loans generate new money.[3]

The money managers soon find themselves in the quandary of not collecting adequate payments from the old debts and not generating enough new loans to maintain their jobs. The only way out of the quandary is to build loyalty from the existing debtors. The shrewd managers build this loyalty by pruning loans like fruit farmers prune trees; they stimulate new growth by cutting old growth. The managers reduce loans, giving the villagers the illusion that they are reducing the debts.

Reducing debts, because it sounds generous, endears the managers to the debtors, but it fulfills the purposes of the money managers by ensnaring the villagers into more debt. The money managers don't care about the money they are losing by reducing debts; they have already lost that money. Their concern is enticing the villagers to borrow more money. The villagers will borrow money if they believe the old debts are reduced. Also, the villagers will borrow that money from the moneylenders who they believe reduced their old debts. The money managers, by reducing the debts of the villagers, appear to advocate the welfare of the villagers.

The money managers, though, are *not* advocating the welfare of the villagers; the new debts of the villagers will eventually become as unpayable as old ones, and the villagers will become hopelessly mired in more debt. Eventually, the money managers will run out of schemes to keep their jobs. Before they go, though, they will use their last option to milk the villagers of their dearest assets. They offer the villagers' daughters employment in the city. The moneylenders promise that the girls will be employed as waitresses, but the girls become fodder for the sex industry.

The parable tells us that the poor lose even when they appear to be winning. Jesus condemned the scheme of the moneylenders who violated the laws of God for the benefits of money. Christians, in turn, should work to confront the poverty that jeopardizes village survival strategies, particularly when it generates child exploitation. Above all else, we need to be shrewd enough to unmask the schemes that victimize people and provide economic alternatives to empower people to avoid these exploitative schemes. The final result of these alternatives is making Christ the foundation of community survival strategies.

TRANSFORMATION THROUGH SMALL-ENTERPRISE DEVELOPMENT

Small-enterprise development and revolving loans are two related methods that are effective in empowering people to enhance the economic aspects of their survival strategies. Small-enterprise and revolving loan programs (hereafter called SED) are effective means of creating employment. SED projects are successful for two reasons. First, they enhance community survival strategies by transforming local economics in ways that are socially acceptable. The second reason is related to the first. They fit E. F. Shumacher's definition of good work: "They give people opportunities to utilize and develop their faculties . . . and they bring forth the goods and services needed by all of us for a decent existence."[4] These two reasons, by reflecting Christian values, integrate Christ into this aspect of the community survival strategy.

72

Examples of this integration abound throughout the many places in the world where Christians have executed transformational development projects. A good example took place in a rural Asian village. The residents of this village overcame the economic exploitation that dehumanized them when World Vision facilitated a SED project with them. The village people avoided getting trapped in a downward spiral of poverty by borrowing money from the project at reasonable rates of interest to purchase livestock and to start cottage businesses.

The project was successful, to some extent, because it was based in the community's seedling church. This arrangement inspired the few Christians in the community to work for its success and empowered the Christians to make a tangible contribution to the welfare of the community. In doing so, it displayed how Christ, and Christian beliefs and values, can transform the prevailing beliefs and values of the community survival strategy. It demonstrated the truth that the reconciliation of Christ addresses the economic struggles of the villages.

I visited one project in this community: schoolchildren raising chickens. The children used the money from the sale of the chickens to purchase uniforms and school supplies. The money made a valuable contribution to their survival strategy by enabling them to get an education and by preventing them from suffering the social and economic alienation of child exploitation.

Another project in the community empowered women by lending money to them to purchase piglets. They raised the piglets for slaughter. Many of these women were widows or divorcees who were mothers of young daughters. Before the project they had to borrow money from the moneylenders at exorbitant interest rates. They were caught in a spiral of debt that could only be broken by selling their daughters into prostitution. The project, by lending money at rates that would keep the project sustainable, enabled these women to maintain viable household economies, and it protected their daughters from resorting to "work in the city."

A missionary who worked in an East Asian country for several years told me that prostitution is common in that country and that it had lost any moral stigma that it might have once had. I asked whether this statement implies that the people in that country do not perceive child or adult prostitution as a problem. He said yes. If he is correct, I would venture to say that the people in that country have lost some basic human values. They are living in a dehumanized world.

This dehumanization makes the gospel more relevant in that country than it has ever been. Ignatius Loyola is credited with saying: "The glory of God is a human being fully alive." The people in that country are losing the ability to define what being fully alive means. Christian development practitioners have ample opportunity to minister to communities in that country by integrating some basic Christian values into the villagers' survival strategy. One expression of this effort is delivering young women from the snares of the sex industry, and empowering them, their families and their communities to glorify God by being fully alive.

Notes

[1] Global Evangelization Movement, http://www.gem-werc.org→Reality Check→1997 index→no. 9, "Sex: A Stronghold of Sin."

[2] My analysis of this parable is based on William R. Herzog II, *Parables as Subversive Speech* (Louisville, Ky.: Westminster/John Knox Press, 1994).

[3] Terminating managers causes the bosses to cancel existing loans, but they accept this loss because the money they have collected on existing loans far exceeds the original balance and a reasonable interest rate on that money. The money they make on new loans far exceeds any money they can collect on old ones.

[4] E. F. Schumacher, *Good Work* (New York: Harper & Row, 1979), p. 118.

6

Rescuing Children of Sex Workers

Joyce Bundellu

Three-and-a-half-year-old Ashok was missing.[1] His mother, a prostitute, searched in all the neighboring brothels for three days but could not find her son. Between her alcoholism and her customers, she had not had time for Ashok. Now the child had disappeared. Finally she asked at the Government Children's Home and found that the police had picked up Ashok as a vagrant.

Mahesh, at one-and-a-half years, was a problem to his mother. She did not have a safe place to leave him while she served her clients, so she thought of another way. She tied one end of a rope to Mahesh's ankle and the other end to the foot of the bed. On the bed above him, his mother earned money to feed him and herself.

Two-year-old Vinay's mother doped him and left him alone in a room. Throughout the day Vinay was dull and sleepy, only to be doped again at night.

Young Lazmi was sold into prostitution. While she was under the control of the brothel keeper, she became pregnant twice. The forced abortions left her sick and in mental and emotional anguish.

Kasibai accumulated a lot of debt because of her two young children. She had admitted them into an institution where they could be safe. But because the children were a guarantee that the mother would pay the debts of the brothel keeper, she was beaten, threatened and forced to bring the children back into the atmosphere of fear, neglect and hopelessness.

Shantabai found another alternative to her situation. She sold her three-year-old to someone who wanted to adopt the child and paid some of her debts—only to fall into more debt.

Ruckshana's mother was dying of AIDS. The brothel keeper was keeping a sharp eye on the child's whereabouts. When her mother died, Ruckshana would be needed to service clients in place of her mother. She was almost thirteen and would bring in a thriving business.

Despite deep-rooted social prejudice against their children, 70 percent of prostitutes in India are mothers. While a majority of the male children become criminals, daughters are inducted into the trade as early as age 10, very often by their own mothers, who have lost their market value and want to boost their fortunes. Studies show almost 30 percent of prostitutes in India are minors between the ages of 16 and 18 and close to 20 percent are under age 15.[2]

THE STRATEGY

Scores of the sex workers' children live on the streets of the red light areas of Mumbai.[3] They play in the dirt, unkempt, uncared for, learning to survive, growing up to take their mothers' places at an early age. These children are destined for a life of shame and poverty. Under the powerful Hindu doctrine of karma, actions of the previous life govern those of the present and future. Children of prostitutes are born cursed and forced to languish in shame for a past life they never knew and a future in which they have no hope. In real life that means a life of poverty and destitution, with no hope of escape.

What do they look for? Just their next meal! Is that all life has to offer them? Can anyone make a difference in their lives before they, like their mothers, end up on the streets? Some people feel sorry for these children. Many feel repelled by them—children born of immorality. But some work to make a difference in their lives, these children of prostitution.

In the city of Mumbai some night shelters run from 6 P.M. to 8 A.M. for these children. The mothers can leave their young ones for the night and then at a day-care center until noon. In this way some children get care for more than half the day. However, this service is more relief than rescue. The children are still exposed to the immoral, oppressive and dangerous environment.

Some of the children are able to find admission to boarding schools through sponsorship. Continuation in school largely depends on the academic performance of the child.

Some mothers leave their children in the village with their parents. This arrangement is often temporary. As the child becomes older the grandparents are no longer able to manage, and the child is brought back to Mumbai, soon to be absorbed into the same activities as the mothers.

INTERVENTION STRATEGY

Inter Mission has opened a home for children of prostitutes in Mumbai. Thirty-eight children, rescued from these kinds of circumstances, are being cared for in a family setting. Currently four couples care for the children, who relate as brothers and sisters to the couples' own children. They all live together in a family home rather than a traditional dormitory arrangement. In these homes the children are learning to live normal lives, experiencing respect and acceptance.

These homes are located away from the city of Mumbai. The children live in clean, open surroundings. They go to the local government-run schools and are nurtured in an atmosphere of Christian love and security.

BELONGING TO A FAMILY

The life of most children of sex workers is one of neglect, violence, hunger and instability. The children are exposed to physical violence from their mothers as well as from neighbors and brothel customers. They are also in danger of road accidents, kidnapping and drug abuse. Yet, used to the freedom to do what they please, they learn to be tough.

In the Inter Mission family setting the children learn to adjust to normal family life under the loving care of home parents. They learn from the children of our home parents. They learn how to control their bowel movements, how to control their tempers, how to give as well as receive and how to respond in love to the parents in the home.

Five-year-old Chintu narrated: "I was naughty, so Uncle (the home parent) scolded me, but when my mother was angry with me she used to beat me and sometimes burned me with a hot spoon." He showed the marks on his head to prove his statement. The same child responded positively when the home parents expressed their sadness about his misbehavior. In various ways the children learn to appreciate the loving discipline of the home.

Children as young as four pick up influences from their surroundings. Home parents are always challenged to help the children change. We found some children played "Love," acting out sexual behavior as ordinary children would play with a doll house when pretending to be a family. Without expressing astonishment or horror, the home parents helped these children play in a normal way.

The real mothers have a love-hate relationship with their children. They often blame the children for the state they are in. The children become scapegoats at the receiving end of their mothers' anger.

At the same time, the children are all these mothers can call their own. Their families have rejected them, brothel keepers only use them and society at large ignores them. On their children alone can they bestow love and in them find hope and security.

This dichotomy often confuses the child, who, as a result, becomes indifferent to the mother. When admitted in the Inter Mission home, the child has the same indifference toward the home parents, but the clear responses of the home parents soon help him or her adjust and respond.

In the Inter Mission home these children live with other semi-orphaned children. This living situation is very important because it gives them a new identity. No longer are they "children of sex workers" but children of the Inter Mission home. They are accepted in the home, at school and in society.

The mothers visit the home periodically. They enjoy coming because they find acceptance and respect and are treated as human beings, not objects. The mothers even stay overnight with their children. This time together helps strengthen the bond between mother and child.

THE CHANGE

Patu was just four years old when his mother admitted him to the Inter Mission home. A withdrawn child, he refused to utter a word. Only his eyes showed his sharp mind. He was prompt at meal times, very possessive about his toys but totally unresponsive to anything else. It has taken a lot of expressed love by the home parents to give him the security that has enabled him to come out of his shell and blossom. Today Patu is a happy, active, hopeful ten year old.

Neelam's mother knew she was suffering from AIDS and wanted her daughter out of the brothels. She approached the Inter Mission in Mumbai for admission for her daughter. While the formalities of admission were being completed, Neelam's mother died. However, a friend had promised that she would rescue Neelam and admit her to our home. Today Neelam is a happy child at six years old, goes to school regularly and finds her place in the Inter Mission home.

Rita, another infant dying of diarrhea, was placed into the hands of the Inter Mission staff. By God's grace she survived but was soon diagnosed as HIV-positive. This happened in 1991 when there was very little knowledge about HIV infection in India and many myths about its spread. No institution catering to infants was willing to admit Rita, but Inter Mission accepted her. Today, at seven, Rita is blossoming. Although she has health difficulties and the future is uncertain for her, we rejoice to see her growing. We've seen God's hand in her life, and she is a blessing to many.

THE CHALLENGE

Today, the numbers of sex workers' children in the city of Mumbai alone continue to increase. Very few people will love and care for them.

The rapid growth of HIV infection among the prostitutes leads to a growing number of orphaned children. This group will continue to increase in the coming years. The number of HIV-infected infants is also on the rise, presenting a need for more homes in this field. Inter Mission home now has two HIV-infected children and is preparing to care for more.

The workers at Inter Mission have been challenged greatly through working with the children and their mothers. We have seen attitudes entirely changed, and some of the mothers have given up their profession.

As we see the children growing in stature, doing well in school, growing to love God and committing their lives to Jesus, our hearts are filled with gratitude to God who has called us and entrusted us with such precious jewels. These children will grow up with alternatives for making a livelihood. The vicious cycle of following Mother into a life of prostitution has been broken.

INTERVENTIONS FOR CHILDREN OF SEX WORKERS

To help children marked by societies as castoffs be restored to wholeness will require active involvement on their behalf by local churches and communities. Only by direct, active involvement in rescuing them from their plight can these children be provided with both daily needs and long-term hope for their futures. Research is a vital key to understanding the felt and perceived needs of prostituted women and their children.

The church

One of the most vital needs for churches is information on the real situation of children of sex workers. Without information the churches cannot be mobilized to action. Exposure to the needs of these children perhaps can best be achieved through field trips where the church can witness firsthand the children's plight. Talking to project caregivers for these children will help the church grasp the vast needs they are confronted with on a day-by-day basis.

Responding to the children's plight will require practical, concrete demonstrations of Christ's love and compassion. Only as these children experience human love and acceptance will they be able, in time, to understand the Savior's unconditional love for them. The Lord exhorts his people through the prophet Isaiah to share food with the hungry, to bring right into your homes those who are helpless, poor and destitute. He promises his blessings on those who do so (Isa. 58).

The church must also understand the biblical commands to engage in advocacy for these children who have no voice. Speaking out against prevailing, damaging attitudes is vital to church and community acceptance of these children and involvement in their rehabilitation.

The community

The local community, along with the church, needs to respond to the challenge of helping these children. Tapping into community resources for holistic care for them, however, is not easy. Prostitutes are often seen as a health issue only. Their business is seen as a necessary evil. The prevailing attitude can cover the following range:

- ◆ Give them something to help them cope.
- ◆ Don't put their children in school with ours—they will be a bad influence on our children.
- ◆ Social work for prostitutes? Ridiculous!

The results of these attitudes? The children are "recycled": the girls into prostitution; the boys into the underground.

RESEARCHING THE PROBLEM

1. Study the community for six months before you begin a project there. Find out what the issues are. For example, what do the mothers and children need? Health care? Education? Water supply?
2. List the different issues and set priorities.
   - ◆ What diseases are prevalent among the women and children?
   - ◆ What is the need for immunization?
   - ◆ What medical facilities are available to these particular women and their children? Are they affordable? (If setting up a clinic, makes its focus wider than an STD (sexually transmitted diseases) clinic. Include other gynecological problems to avoid the stigma.)

◆ Do the women have "ration" cards (food stamps)?

3. Build rapport with the women. Addressing the needs of her child is a non-threatening approach. Encourage the mother to save money and to leave prostitution as a means of livelihood.

4. Know legislation and government policies that address the problem.

5. Study your own capacities and count the cost before you begin. You can easily lose people's trust. Remember, you have to be there for the community 24 hours a day.

Taking time for adequate research will enable you to plan a holistic program that targets the deep needs of these children and their mothers. Research will also provide vital information for church and community education and advocacy.

Notes

[1] All names have been changed.

[2] India's Accursed Children, *The Boston Sunday Globe* January 28, 1996, p. A-25.

[3] Mumbai is perhaps better known in the West as Bombay.

7

Living and Responding to Heal and Transform

Chris and Phileena Heuertz

We had decided to show our visiting friends the beautiful side of Calcutta, away from the noise, pollution and poverty that plague the city streets. Monsoon season had brought heavy rain that day. Between showers we saw the Victoria Monument, one of the last reminders of the British Raj and English rule in India. Typical of the streets of Calcutta, people were everywhere.

As we left the monument, a small boy, no more than nine or ten, followed our group. A sweet child, he retained the untarnished look of innocence amid the cruelty and hostility of Calcutta. His big, dark eyes looked up at us as he walked. His tattered red shorts and T-shirt spoke of a hard life on the streets. He wore no shoes, his hair was tousled and his skin was darker than most Bengalis.

He went from one person to the next, telling us, in broken English, his sad story and asking for a couple of rupees. His mother and father had died, he said, and he was very hungry. We weren't sure whether to believe him or not. The boy is one of thousands of beggars in India.

The issue of beggars in India has always been a personal dilemma. They all seem to have the same needs, but many of them fabricate stories to prey on the emotions of rich foreigners. Seeing far more of them than we had money to help, the arguments for giving and not giving to beggars constantly tear through our minds.

On one hand, giving to a beggar encourages a lifestyle of pathetic dependency. It is a challenge to determine whether the man, woman or child is being forced to beg by the black market. The black market in India is cruel. It has been known to kidnap children and intentionally cripple them, gouge out their eyes or otherwise maim them, placing them in strategic locations to earn money for their handlers.

On the other hand, the man, woman or child begging from you may literally be dying before your eyes. How can you not give? Scripture says, "Give to the one who asks you" (Matt. 5:42). But does that mean giving exactly what they ask? What about our attitude and motivation for giving? Are we performing an act of kindness to get that beggar to leave us alone? Can we give only a handful of change and feel good about it? What about the lingering question, Will we be held accountable for not giving to that child? The Scriptures also say, "I was hungry and you gave me nothing to eat" (Matt. 25:42).

As our group walked on, the little boy followed for almost a mile. A few of us struck up a conversation with him. Sadly, for the most part, we ignored him.

Later that afternoon one of our friends told us he had to get something off his chest. He asked if we remembered the child who followed us earlier that afternoon. We did. Then our friend said that this little boy had sexually propositioned him. We listened in disbelief and horror. That boy seemed so innocent and naive. Our friend wept as he told the details of his encounter.

Suddenly I was convicted and my heart broken. That boy had asked for a couple of rupees (not even a dime in U.S. currency) for something to eat, and we had walked on by. That night we kept wondering in what dark room that child would be sexually abused so he could earn enough money to buy the food we had refused to give him.

This story illustrates how giving can be a preventive measure in the fight for the purity of children. When we give our resources, our time, our love and ourselves, we contribute to winning the battle to preserve the innocence and purity of children's sexuality.

IDENTIFY THE PROBLEM

All over the world hundreds of thousands of children are forced into lives of sexual slavery, compelled against their will to perform acts that many of us could never imagine. The statistics, because they are more than we can bear, scarcely faze us. But the truth remains—these statistics represent more than numbers. They are boys and girls who want to grow up and live normal lives just like our children. How do they become entangled in this flesh trade?

Economic, cultural, religious, social and emotional reasons all contribute to the crime of child sexual exploitation. Some children are forced into it against their will. Many are promised lucrative jobs that never materialize, and others are actually "married" to middlemen who look for bodies to fill brothels.

Some children are born into the sex trade. Others voluntarily drink this bitter cup as a solution to the crippling poverty of their families. Many children are abducted and sold into the commercial sex industry. Those who are forced resist as long as they can, but eventually rapes—including violent gang rapes—forced starvation, threats against the children's families and emotional abuse and manipulation are pressures too great to overcome.

The tragedy can happen to anyone, and it has. Primarily, brothels look for the most vulnerable. They find children who are isolated, abused and impoverished, and who need community and identity. Though the commercial sex trade may not be a good identity or community, it is often the only evident option. Children who have been sexually abused deal with tremendous emotional scars and, at times, respond by finding some twisted form of solace in this cursed work force. The desperate poor may even go as far as selling their children into this brutal and abusive profession just to find money to make it through one more day.

WHY SHOULD WE RESPOND?

Why get involved? After all, we reason, we have the care of our families and our own often seemingly unsolvable problems.

We need to be involved because if we, the church, will not stand up for these boys and girls, who will? Our stand will be our message. Here are some reasons for getting involved.

It's not their fault

Most of the boys and girls involved in the commercial sex industry are not there because they volunteered. Nepali village girls do not dream of spending their adolescent years sleeping with seven to ten strange men each day in a foreign land, often incurring permanent internal damage as a consequence. The children used in child prostitution and child pornography have been forced, many times violently, into these cruel and humiliating circumstances.

It's not fair that eight-year-old girls all over Asia will be sexually abused tonight while we tuck our children into their beds. It's not fair that nine-year-old boys are forced to perform acts that our children would be punished for if they even described them at their Christian elementary schools. It's not fair, and it's not their fault.

We are responsible for their suffering

This may sound extreme, but we firmly believe the children's suffering is our fault in many ways. In the culture of the kingdom of God, justice has a broader definition in terms of corporate responsibility than many of us are willing to acknowledge.

We play a part in their suffering when we sit back and allow the culture of lust to pervade Western entertainment and art. The repercussions of these sensual pleasures are felt on the other side of the world inside the torn and used bodies of sexually exploited children. We permit the media to degrade women in advertisements and movies, and these media have a larger impact than we can begin to imagine. Our apathy and compromise have effects on the rest of the world.

The materialism and consumerism esteemed by the developed world—including many inside the church—also contribute to the suffering of the sexually exploited. People in the developing world learn from their neighbors in the developed world to value things rather than people. If the church does not take a stand against overconsumption and affluence, it is then responsible for those children who are sold into the flesh trade by parents trying to keep up with the elusive material standards set by the West.

God, in Scripture, actively engages in the lives of people. God defends the oppressed and makes provision for those literally dependent on others and on society. We can no longer hide from the wickedness. We must engage it, confront it, stand up to it and show the world a better way.

Love warrants a response

The way we love ourselves and the way we love our neighbors are often very different. We make sure we eat and dress well; we see to it that our basic need for clothing, housing and food are met. But when we see a beggar, do we want all of that for him? We will see to it that our children receive the best education we can afford, but are we burdened because the boys and girls living as slaves in brothels all over Asia are not in school?

> This is how we know what love is: Jesus laid down his life for us. And we ought to lay down our lives for our brothers. If anyone has material possessions and sees his brother in need but has no pity on him, how can the love of God be in him? Dear children, let us not love with words or tongue but with actions and in truth (1 John 3:16–18).

RESPONDING PREVENTIVELY

It is to be hoped that the vast majority of us will never be sexually propositioned by a child. Many of us may never cross the threshold of a brothel in North America, much less Asia. Many of us may never be confronted by child pornographers. So, how can we respond preventively? How can we live lives that make a difference in the battle to preserve the purity and dignity of the world's children?

Value the child

Our future is in the children, and unless we are good stewards of this precious resource, we will contribute to the downfall of society.

We find it hard to imagine a father or mother who willingly and deliberately sells his or her child for a TV, but are we any different? We sell the dignity of our own children to feed our reputations, to hide our insecurities, to excuse our own shortcomings and to indulge our appetites for control. The consequences may be different, but the spirit of the matter is nearly identical.

At times we misplace admiration and praise. We focus on the earned prestige and achievements of our children—the academic successes, the athletic triumphs, the spiritual maturity. We must learn to celebrate our children because they are children and appreciate and enjoy them as a gift from God. We must relearn to value the child.

Valuing the child is essential because sexual exploitation is an issue concerning the image of God. Every man, woman and child has been created in the image of our Lord. To degrade that individual in any way is to show contempt for our Maker. Because we are created in God's image, we all possess an intrinsic and essential form of dignity that must be preserved. Boys and girls in Sri Lanka, Thailand, Nepal and India, sold today for television sets, send a message of how an unredeemed world values the image of God.

Protect the family

Much of the sexual exploitation of children today happens because of a breakdown in the family structure. In our preventive response to preserve the purity and dignity of children we must begin at home.

The way we protect our families will be a message. The example of a family set apart and dedicated to the Lord will stand as a challenge to those families still searching for meaning and identity.

Eight weeks before Mother Teresa passed away, we had the opportunity to visit with her for a few moments. As we shared with her the details concerning our ministry among children with AIDS, she asked us whether or not we had any children of our own. We replied, "Not yet."

"When you do," she said, "you must remember that loving your child will be your most important ministry." If everyone understood that truth, imagine how different our world would be.

Become aware of the crisis

As active and deliberate kingdom persons, we must increase our knowledge and awareness of the needs of the world. Our tendency is to run from the reality of the sexual exploitation of children and other related issues. It depresses us and makes us feel guilty. Exposure demands a response. In our ongoing discipleship we are exposed to the suffering of the world for a redemptive purpose. Embrace the pain and become an agent of healing and transformation. Become informed and get involved. God, who feels the pain and suffers with the afflicted, desires that all be made whole. That healing can happen only through his hands and his feet—the church. If we refuse to embrace God's heart, we fall short of God's calling on each of our lives.

Respond to the poor, the isolated, the abused

The flesh trade exists among children in a large part because of poverty. The Bible is clear—the poor are poor because of our disobedience (Deut. 15:4–11). Scripture is full of references regarding our responsibility to the poor. Nearly 300 verses in the Old Testament and more than 100 verses in the New Testament deal with the poor, the orphaned, the fatherless, the widowed, the oppressed, the alienated and the disadvantaged.

God identifies with the poor and the needy (Prov. 19:17, Isa. 3:15, Matt. 25:34–45). The prophet Jeremiah equates knowing God with having compassion for the poor (Jeremiah 22:16). How do we measure up?

For too long the church in the West has spiritualized the poor in Scripture, but the Good News is good news because it was preached to the poor. We challenge you to reinterpret your reading of the Bible. Read it as the peasants of first-century Palestine might have read it. You will find answers you never saw before.

Preserving the dignity of the poor is also our responsibility. The church of the West has held very negative views of the poor. We have made unjust assumptions as to what causes poverty, and we have judged those on the margins of society, adding to their marginalization. Unless we assume the poor have intrinsic value, they may continue to feel that their daughters are only worth a new TV or can be sold for $200.

As a preventive measure in combating the flesh trade and the trafficking of young boys and girls we must respond to the poor, the isolated and the abused. We must reread Scriptures through new eyes, identify ourselves with the poor and disadvantaged and become a voice for the voiceless.

Reinterpret spirituality in the context of a dying world

Our faith has become very exclusive. If someone does not fit the social and economic mold of our churches, they may have a tough time being accepted by Christians. We must learn new ways to celebrate our faith inclusively so that those on the margins of society will feel welcome in our churches and in our communities.

How many of us belong to a congregation that wouldn't stare at a prostitute if he or she walked into the sanctuary on Sunday morning? One that would not wonder why he was there? One that would not judge and criticize her in our hearts and minds? The prostitutes of first-century Palestine felt as if they could spend time with Jesus—why can't they feel the same way with his followers?

If the world did not need redemption, we would not need to discuss the sexual exploitation of children. The cries and moans of children in pain, children begging for rest, children screaming "Stop! You're hurting me!" continue to fall on the deaf ears of a world in urgent need of redemption.

Sexual slavery exists on two levels. The first is for those held as slaves in brothels who need to be freed. The second is for the captors, bound in sexual slavery—the brothel owners, the brothel customers, and the lost who find their fulfillment in sensual pleasures and financial gain. The world must be set free from these forms of slavery through redemption in Christ.

Finally, the answer lies in love

We have been asked to love our neighbors as ourselves. The sacrifice of the King of Kings became the supreme example of love. Ask God for an unstoppable love for the world's children. Pray that God would give you his heart for these boys and girls who have no hope. If you begin to taste the pain our Father feels for these little ones, there is no telling what you will do to help them.

Jeremiah the prophet condemned child sacrifice, yet child sacrifice still happens today. It happens in the dark and sultry brothels all across Asia, in the homes of child pornographers across Europe and the U.S.A., as well as in the hearts of men and women who lust after the purity of boys and girls.

Tonight, a small boy in Asia, desperate for his next meal, will look for an older man who will abuse and sexually defile him. May the church stand up against this injustice and cry "Enough!" May our lives and our faith be made relevant to a world in need, and may we stand and be counted with the boys and girls who are looking for a way out of this cruel and painful life.

PART THREE:

Strategies
and Interventions

8

Child Development and Intervention Planning

Phyllis Kilbourn

To facilitate healing in traumatized children, an effective caregiver must be knowledgeable about what children need for healthy development. What we know about how children grow, learn and adapt to the world around them is critical to their care. This knowledge allows a greater understanding of children's behavior during a crisis. Such knowledge also provides an understanding of what results when children's developmental processes are affected by trauma.

Early child development focuses on language acquisition, intellectual development and the process of attachment to others. Development also involves a series of cognitive, physical, emotional, spiritual and social changes. Usually we distinguish children by their physical characteristics, the most obvious difference. Observing children carefully will help us know when they are sad, angry, distressed or hurt. The observant caregiver, however, must learn to "read" children for evidence in other areas of developmental growth. Children quite naturally express these characteristics with their whole body; each child's response is unique.

The concept of the "whole child" is based on the accepted principle that all areas of human growth and development are interrelated—intertwined and mutually supportive. Normal physical development, for example, depends on meeting not only the child's physical needs (food, clothing, shelter) but psychological needs (nurturing caregivers or parents) and social needs (adequate play and exploration) as well. Social development is aided by the ability to communicate verbally; a well-developed attention span helps a child develop fine motor skills; and relating to others is more successful if intellectual problem-solving skills are already mature.

Understanding how a child's development in one area of growth affects other areas is vital in understanding the impact of traumatizing sexual abuse on children. This understanding also is helpful in planning effective interventions. Sexual assault is an expression of power and control that damages the very basis of a child's sense of self. It inflicts psychological, emotional, social and physical damage and leaves long-term effects.

PSYCHOSOCIAL DEVELOPMENT

Early childhood education draws from several fields of study. Much of what we know about children comes from child development and child psychology research. Understanding how psychological processes begin, change and develop is foundational to intervention planning.

Child development is a broad field of study with many differences of opinion. No one set of principles encompasses all developmental and learning theories. However, I have found Erik Erikson's theory of human development a helpful way to evaluate the impact of trauma on childhood development. Using this frame of reference, caregivers can compare expectations, children's needs and developmental tasks.

Erikson[1] states that life is a series of stages through which each person passes, with each stage growing from the previous ones. He proposes eight stages of psychosocial development from infancy through old age. A stage is a period during which certain changes take place. What one achieves in each stage is based on the developments of the previous stages, and each stage presents certain kinds of problems to be solved. When children succeed, they go on to attack new problems, and they grow through solving them.

According to Erikson, everyone has certain biological, social and psychological needs that must be satisfied in order to grow in a healthy manner. There also are basic intellectual, social and emotional needs that must be met for a person to be healthy. Whether these needs are met or left unfulfilled will affect development.

The first five stages of Erikson's theory of human development are discussed below. These stages cover the ages from birth through adolescence.

Stage one: infancy (birth to one year)
Developmental task: trust versus mistrust

The first stage of a child's life involves being or becoming, learning what it is to be alive. Theodore Lidz, chairman of the Department of Psychiatry at Yale University School of Medicine, states emphatically that "during no other period of life is the person so transformed both physically and developmentally as during infancy."[2] He further affirms that "no part of his life experience will be as solidly incorporated in the individual, become so irrevocably a part of him, as his infancy."

When babies cry out, they are expressing needs. Infants' needs are basic: love, touch, social interaction and stimulation, adequate rest, food, cleanliness, shelter, warmth and safety. How those needs are met determines whether they can accomplish their first developmental task—learning how to trust and in whom to place that trust.

Children need to develop trust in their environment and in their parents and caregivers. Through their trust children learn that their world is a safe, predictable, interesting and friendly place. Initially parents help an infant develop a basic sense of trust in self and an ability to trust other people. They give affection, provide a predictable environment, ensure emotional security and provide for physical needs. Infants develop trust particularly in the area of interpersonal relationships.

Trust allows children to explore, thus learning about their environment. Babies who have learned to trust well will feel safe in exploring and touching their world; they will also develop hope.

With love and adequate nurturing they will be better equipped to navigate successfully and cope with future stages of life and with developmental crises.

Inconsistent or inadequate care, however, prevents infants from trusting their world. Infants are totally dependent on adults to meet their needs; they are particularly vulnerable to difficulties because they have few skills for coping with discomfort and stress. It is critical, therefore, that they bond to warm, caring adults who are sensitive and respond affectionately to an infant's needs when they arise. In this way the very young begin to develop trust in the world that will support their growth into the next stage.

Trust and Maturity

For maturity, this basic trust acquired in infancy needs to continue to grow and develop and requires warm, loving and stable home environments. Children need healthy relationships with the adults in their world—adults who have been given special positions of authority and trust. When such a person sexually assaults a child, the assault is an abuse of that trust. This betrayal, often by a family member, is one of the worst things about child sexual assault. It produces ever-present fear in the children that if they trust they will only suffer abuse and rejection again.

Many abused children, such as those on the street or in brothels, have no family members near to give them support. The safety net of the extended family has disintegrated in many societies, leaving the child vulnerable and without adult support.

Stage two: early childhood (two to three years)
Developmental task: autonomy versus shame and doubt

Children's characteristics in this stage include assertiveness, forming a separate identity from their parents and seeking independent control over their actions. They are testing their limits, pushing boundaries and learning to think for themselves. The child must learn to manage and control impulses, and to use both motor and mental skills. Children need to gain a sense of self-control as well as control over their environment. This is a critical time of development because so much can go wrong.

Children can be severely disciplined for accidental breakage or potty-training accidents. Parents can become exasperated at their slow or seemingly irrational behavior. At this stage children need to experiment, be free to explore with all their senses, make mistakes and test limits within a safe environment. Gerald Corey, psychologist and author, states:

> It is important at this stage that children begin to acquire a sense of their own power. If parents do too much for their children, the message transmitted is, "Here, let me do thus-and-thus for you, because you are too weak or helpless to do these things for yourself." During this time children need to experiment, to make mistakes and feel that they are still acceptable persons, and to recognize some of their own power as separate and distinct individuals. So many clients are in counseling precisely because they have lost touch with their potential for power; they are struggling to define who they are and what they are capable of doing.[3]

Toddlers need permission to make mistakes while experiencing success in doing things for themselves: expressing themselves, feeding, developing toilet habits and performing various other motor tasks with hands and feet. They need assurance that no one is perfect; mistakes are part of the learning process. Children must learn to apologize, take responsibility for cleaning up their messes and get on with life.

A child needs help in developing a healthy balance between autonomy and shame. Restrictive or compulsive caregivers may give the child a feeling of shame and doubt, causing a sense of insecurity. Successful growth in this stage gives a child the strength of will.

Stage three: preschool (three to five or six years)
Developmental task: initiative versus guilt

Out of a sense of autonomy grows a sense of initiative as opposed to feelings of guilt about never doing anything right. In this stage of development the healthy child achieves a sense of competence and learns to initiate action over his or her environment and to overcome feelings of powerlessness.

Preschoolers are aware of their bodies and the sexual differences between boys and girls. They begin to discover their roles and levels of power in relationships with adults and peers.

Erikson suggests that if children are allowed to select activities that are personal and meaningful to them, they tend to develop a positive view of themselves. They also follow through with their projects. Not being allowed to make their own decisions or to take the initiative can produce guilt. Then, rather than taking an active stance, they may become passive, allowing others to make decisions and choices for them.

The child is now ready to plan and carry out thoughts and ideas. Children must be given enough freedom to develop their own ways to deal with one another and still develop a sense of fairness and conscience.

Stage four: school age (six to twelve years)
Developmental task: industry versus inferiority

Industry in this stage refers to the ability to set and to attain personal goals. The major theme is mastery of life, primarily by adapting to laws of society and things. Failure to navigate this task successfully can lead to inferiority or a sense of inadequacy.

School age children are ready to apply themselves to skills and tasks and to receive systematic instruction in the culture. They now begin to handle new tools of learning, such as books, school supplies and sports equipment. They need large doses of encouragement and praise as they experience both achievement and disappointment. Academic, physical, social and work skills are important in developing healthy self-esteem. Children need nurturing adults to help them discover and develop their special talents and abilities.

The danger for children in this stage lies in feeling inadequate and inferior, especially when their mistakes are emphasized. At the same time adults must encourage children to work toward excellence, not letting children restrict their own horizons by doing only what they already know. Particularly in social situations it is essential for children to learn to do things *with* others, as difficult and unfair as this may sometimes be.

Corey[4] lists several emotional problems thought to originate during this time of middle childhood. These emotional problems are compounded through sexual abuse:

◆ a negative self-concept;
◆ feelings of inadequacy related to learning;
◆ feelings of inferiority in establishing social relationships;
◆ conflict over values;
◆ a confused sex-role identity;
◆ unwillingness to face new challenges;
◆ a lack of initiative;
◆ dependency.

The negative self-concept that all sexually abused children experience must be counteracted. Interventions must include help in overcoming feelings of worthlessness—the "damaged goods syndrome"—and guilt. Methods for building self-esteem must be incorporated. Emotional, social and creative development are related to the child's self-concept and self-esteem.

Self-esteem is an individual's sense of personal worth and an acceptance of who one is. Children's self-esteem (the way they feel about themselves) is expressed through their behavior. They make judgments about themselves as they confront the world. To the extent that children feel worthy and capable, they are ready to succeed. If children disapprove of themselves, they may feel like failures and expect to do poorly.

Self-esteem develops as a reflection of experiences. The way people respond to you suggests your importance and value. When children are thought of simply as commodities to be bought and sold, they cannot have a sense of self-worth and respect for themselves. (The commercial sexual exploitation of children turns them into sex objects and pieces of merchandise.) A child who has positive experiences with others, however, will more likely have a higher sense of self-esteem than one who has felt unloved, abused and abandoned.

Early in life self-esteem is tied to family, friends and other important people. Four components of self-esteem have been identified[5]:

1. a sense of one's own identity;
2. a sense of belonging;

3. a sense that one's uniqueness is recognized and respected;

4. a sense of self through the power of self-definition.

Children having these characteristics are ready to meet the emotional, social and creative challenges of the early years. They will have the self-confidence to deal with the reality of their emotions, the adaptability of their social learning and the risk of creativity.

Stage five: adolescence (twelve to eighteen years)
Developmental task: identity versus role confusion

Adolescence is a time of transition. Again, as for toddlers, it is a time to test limits. To establish a new adult identity, dependency ties must be broken. Parents and adolescents experience conflict as children try to clarify their identity and life goals, figure out the meaning of life and discover where they fit into that life. Failure to achieve a sense of identity can lead to role confusion.

The adolescent has the task of integrating a system of values that will give his or her life direction. In the formation of a personal philosophy of life, adolescents must make key decisions relating to religious beliefs, sexual ethics, values and such. In this search for identity, role models are especially important.[6]

Accomplishing the developmental tasks at each stage is vital to a child's emotional well-being. How well children accomplish them will determine how well they can cope with difficult situations, trauma or crises at all stages of life. Children's behaviors are highly individual; they show their own personal responses to life. Their responses to sexual abuse also are singular. The way children experience abuse largely depends on their state of development and their personality. The duration and intensity of the abuse are also decisive. Yet all victims speak of a complete loss of trust, feelings of guilt and shame, fear and a withdrawal to themselves.

EMOTIONAL DEVELOPMENT

Emotions are the feelings a person experiences: joy and sorrow, love and hate, confidence and fear, loneliness and belonging, anger and contentment, frustration and satisfaction. Emotions are responses to events, people and circumstances. Feelings are outgrowths of what a person perceives is happening. Emotionally healthy people learn to give expression to their feelings in appropriate ways. They do not allow their feelings to overshadow the rest of their behavior. The optimal time to learn these skills is in the early years.

Children need to be encouraged to identify and to express their emotional nature so they can learn to live with these powerful forces. When a child begins to understand and express feelings, the emotions are no longer in control of the child; the child is becoming the master of the emotions.

Sexually abused children are especially affected in the area of social-emotional development. This includes the children's relationships with themselves and others, self-concept, self-esteem and negative feelings concerning what they have experienced. Victims of sexual exploitation have voiced their feelings in statements such as:

"I felt dirty, ashamed and unworthy of human love."

"It is impossible to exaggerate the sense of shame and revulsion that those acts brought to my soul."

"After the abuse I hated myself, my name, and the very breath I took. By age five, I didn't want to live anymore."

Browne and Finkelhor[7] suggest that emotional symptoms for the sexually abused child may include anger, denial, repression, fear, self-blame, self-doubts, helplessness, low self-esteem, guilt, dejection and apathy; inappropriate behavioral symptoms may include acting out, withdrawal, somatic symptoms, nightmares and phobias; and the child's belief system may be affected to make the world seem unpredictable and hostile.

Dealing with feelings involves four steps. Each builds upon the earlier ones so that they follow a developmental sequence; the learning that takes place at one level affects the development that follows. The steps are:

1. *Noticing and labeling feelings.*
2. *Accepting feelings.* Children can feel overwhelmed by the very strength and intensity of a feeling, whether it is of anger or of love. As children come to accept feelings, they learn how to handle the depth of the feeling and not let it overpower

them. The changing nature of feelings is also part of accepting the feeling. It can be a source of comfort and relief for children to discover that the strong emotion they now experience will pass. Caregivers need to help children work through their feelings safely.

3. *Expressing feelings in an appropriate way.* This is a two-part process. First, children must feel free to express their feelings; second, they must learn ways of expression that are suitable to the situation.

4. *Dealing with the feelings of others.* Helping children to tolerate and appreciate how different people express their emotions leads to understanding and cooperation.

To summarize, sexually abused children have learned not to trust themselves, other people or their environment. The world and the people in it are viewed as inconsistent and hurtful. Withdrawal from this painful world is safer than chancing relationships. Often they have been deeply hurt by those they love, such as when a parent sells them into a life of prostitution or sexual abuse. Caregivers will have a difficult time developing the relationship of trust needed to effectively help a child. A trusting relationship is possible; it just requires much time and patience.

Sexually exploited children are also vulnerable to forced adaptations for vital needs. This prevents them from achieving vital developmental tasks. Normal developmental tasks that get stymied include achieving independence, learning to relate to peers, developing confidence in self, coping with an ever-changing body, forming basic values and mastering new ways of thinking and processing new information.

SPIRITUAL DEVELOPMENT

A key element that is tragically missing from most developmental charts is the spiritual growth and development of the child. Children are born with a strong spiritual awareness that needs to be nurtured and developed. According to Scripture, God knows us intimately; he has written his word on our hearts (see Jer. 1:5, 31:33, and Heb. 8:10). Scripture also teaches that we are responsible for the spiritual training of our children.

> All your children shall be taught by the LORD,
>> and great shall be the prosperity of your children
>> (Isa. 54:13, *NRSV*).

In *Stages of Faith* James Fowler[8] builds on the development theories of Piaget (cognitive), Erikson (psychosocial) and Kohlberg (moral) to present six stages of faith development. Fowler believes these six stages emerge in working out the meaning of our lives.

Space does not permit examining these stages, which range from the intuitive (infancy), imitative faith of childhood through conventional (adolescence) and then more independent faith (young adulthood) to the universalizing, self-transcending faith of full maturity. Fowler also discusses the issue of conversion and the stages of faith.

Understanding children's spiritual development helps caregivers relate trauma issues (such as injustice, loss of trust or an abusive parent) to the impact of such on a child's spiritual development. Children who have been treated unfairly find it difficult to discern right from wrong. Similarly, children's image of God usually directly corresponds to the image of those who are in authority over them; this will be a false image if the child's parent is abusive. The results can be devastating to a child's spiritual development. Instead of peace and joy, the child experiences shame, confusion, fear and misplaced loyalty.

Our task in helping children grow will be to present them with a Christlike role model. As we encourage children to grow and develop through each phase of their lives, we will want to be especially careful to include healthy spiritual training. We must not deny the children we care for the spiritual food needed to nourish and maintain healthy souls.

CHILDREN'S BASIC NEEDS

Maslow,[9] like Erikson, believed we all have certain basic needs that must be met for us to reach our potential in all areas of development. He believed if our lower level basic needs are not met, we will be unable to meet higher order needs. His hierarchy of needs suggests reasons why we cannot motivate children to escape the vicious cycle of sexual exploitation without a holistic approach to their care.

Level one: physiological needs

The first level of Maslow's hierarchy consists of physiological needs for food, shelter, water and warmth. Abandoned and street children often enter prostitution to provide these basic needs for themselves and for their younger siblings. If alternate provisions for these basic needs are left unmet, the children must remain in this lifestyle.

Level two: safety

The second level is the need for safety. Because family, community and society no longer provide adequate safety nets for children, they are left vulnerable to every form of sexual abuse.

Level three: love and belonging

The first higher order need that emerges, according to Maslow, is seen in level three, the need to feel loved and to belong. Humans are social beings who want to feel part of a group. This need often is fulfilled in sexually exploited children by "sticking together." These children often hide their feelings of rejection or compensate for the rejection with antisocial behavior.

Love and acceptance are two of the deepest needs and longings of childhood. The following quotes from adult survivors of sexual abuse prove this:

> "A child growing up needs a lap to cuddle up in. That never happened to me. Never. It's a . . . tragic hurt, wanting to be wanted so bad."

> "Do you know what I am going to do when I get to heaven? I'm going to sit on Jesus' lap and ask him to just hug me until it doesn't hurt anymore."

Level four: self-esteem

Sexually exploited children have the most trouble satisfying their need for self-esteem. Sexual exploitation leads to feelings of anger, being "damaged goods" and loss of self-respect. All children need to be respected as worthwhile individuals, capable of feeling, thinking and behaving responsibly.

Level five: self-actualization

The satisfaction of needs at the first four levels contributes to achievement of the fifth need in Maslow's hierarchy—self-actualization. Maslow stated that a self-actualized person is moving toward the fulfillment of his or her inherent potential. Fulfilling this need implies that the child is not blocked by hunger, fear, lack of love or feelings of belonging or self-esteem. The child is not problem-free but has learned problem-solving skills and can move forward to becoming all that he or she can be.

RESILIENCY

Many children pass successfully through the developmental stages of childhood and adolescence and become fully functioning adults. Some children even seem to be able to overcome the adversities of their childhoods and go on to lead productive and meaningful lives. These children have the resilience to carry them through neglect, abuse, poverty and other unfavorable home conditions. Beardslee[10] defined *resiliency* as unusually good adaptation in the face of severe stress; resilient children have learned to expect and cope with difficulties in their lives. Werner[11] wrote that resilient children play vigorously, seek out new experiences, lack fear and are self-reliant. They can find help from adults and seek refuge when they need it.

Flack[12] identified several traits of the resilient person:

◆ a strong sense of self-esteem;
◆ independence of thought and action;
◆ ability to give and take in personal interactions;
◆ a high level of personal discipline and a sense of responsibility;
◆ open-mindedness;
◆ flexibility;
◆ insight into one's own feelings and those of others;
◆ ability to communicate feelings to others;
◆ a high tolerance for distress;
◆ a philosophical framework that gives meaning to life's experiences.

Flack also suggested that faith in a higher power to which a person can turn in times of crisis can give a sense of purpose to life and therefore encourage survival. This is a key element to spiritually nurturing sexually exploited children who do not feel it is worthwhile to survive. Since caregivers will be working with children in need of adult support in their lives, Flack encouraged all who work with children to instill resilience. This can be accomplished by providing predictable and supportive structures.

Some children do have the resiliency to survive some kinds of abusive situations. Most children who have been sexually abused, however, have emotional, behavioral, social and other problems. For these children, understanding what is healthy and normal is essential in intervention planning that restores vital aspects of childhood development.

Notes

[1] E. H. Erikson, *Childhood and Society*, 2d ed. (New York: W. W. Norton, 1993).

[2] Theodore Lidz, *The Person* (New York: Basic Books, 1968), p. 117.

[3] Gerald Corey, *Theory and Practice of Counseling and Psychotherapy*, 3d ed. (Pacific Grove, Calif.: Brooks/Cole Publishing Company, 1977), p. 21.

[4] Ibid, p. 24.

[5] Harris Clemes and Reynold Bean, *How to Raise Children's Self-Esteem* (San Jose, Calif.: Enrich, 1981).

[6] Corey, *Theory and Practice of Counseling and Psychotherapy*, p. 25.

[7] A. Browne and D. Finkelhor, "Impact of Child Abuse: A Review of the Research," *Journal of Counseling and Development* 67 (1986): 66–77.

[8] James W. Fowler, *Stages of Faith: The Psychology of Human Development and the Quest for Meaning* (San Francisco: Harper & Row, 1981).

[9] A. Maslow, *Motivation and Personality*, 2d ed. (New York: Harper & Row, 1987).

[10] W. Beardslee, "The Role of Self-understanding in Resilient Individuals: The Development of a Perspective," *American Journal of Orthopsychiatry* 59 (1989): 266–78.

[11] E. Werner, "Resilient Children," *Young Children* 40 (1984): 68–72.

[12] F. Flack, *Resilience: Discovering a New Strength at Times of Stress* (New York: Fawcett Columbine, 1988).

9

Counseling
Sexually Exploited Children

Daniel Sweeney

Tragically, it is all too common an experience for those in the helping fields. A little boy walks into your office, hiding behind the legs of his parent. A little girl awkwardly strolls into the classroom, refusing to look at the teacher or her classmates. They are terrified. They have experienced the trauma of sexual exploitation. You know that they need a place of safety and a place to process the pain of their experience and that the counseling process may be slow. Where do you begin?

Many counselors would say that these children need to *talk* about what happened to them, that they must verbalize their pain as part of the healing process. My experience, as a psychotherapist, as a child advocate, and as a play therapist, does not support this conclusion. Also an increasing body of research literature points to a different approach.[1]

I would like to discuss counseling sexually exploited children from a play therapy perspective. I am confident that the reader already recognizes the importance of children to the very heart of God, and I am also confident that many of the core issues of sexual

109

exploitation have been excellently discussed in other chapters. There is no need for me to provide an apologetic on these matters. What the sexually exploited child needs in the counseling experience is not the application of complex therapeutic techniques. He or she needs a representative of God to build a therapeutic relationship in the child's natural world—the world of play.

ENTERING THE CHILD'S WORLD

A fundamental truth about children is that they do not communicate in the same way adults do. Adult communication requires both verbal abilities and abstract thinking skills. Children do not communicate this way. Children communicate through play. It is their natural medium of communication. The basis, therefore, for doing play therapy is to honor children through entering their world of communication rather than forcing children to enter our adult world of verbalization. This is empathy (the core counseling skill) in action. The greatest act of empathy in the history of the world was modeled for us by the Creator himself through the Incarnation. I would argue that if it was not below God to humble himself and enter our world of humanity through Christ, perhaps it should not be below those of us who work with children to enter their world.

But don't people need to talk about their issues in order to process them? Yes, people need to. Children, however, *talk* through play—the toys become their words. Is this the same as verbalization? No. When I am conducting training on play therapy, I often ask for a volunteer to stand up and share with us his or her most embarrassing and traumatizing sexual experience. After the nervous laughter has subsided, I point out: "Isn't this what we do to children who have been molested when we ask: 'Tell me what happened to you.'" This is unfair at the least and potentially retraumatizing.

We need to rethink as a community of helpers how we approach the sexually traumatized child. I attended a conference several years ago where the keynote presenter stated that he requires his sexually abused child clients to draw a picture of the perpetrator on the first visit. *Requires?* Hasn't the child already been *required* to participate in enough trauma? Other therapists suggest using

110

toys and play as a means of leading children to talk about what happened to them. The idea is to use the toys as a way to build rapport so that the sexual trauma might be discussed. We should be careful about this. Doesn't a common pattern of molesting involve the offender using games, candy and toys to build up some trust with the potential victim before abuse begins? Do we want the therapeutic process to follow the same pattern? Perhaps not.

I am not suggesting that talking to children is wrong. It is an essential part of the investigatory process when dealing with sexually abused children. It has been my experience that play therapy with traumatized children often leads to verbalization of the events. This is, however, not my requirement (which is not fair to the child), nor my expectation (which will cause me to control the healing process rather than letting the child lead).

SEXUAL EXPLOITATION AND TRAUMA

Children who have experienced sexual trauma have suffered blows to their physical, psychological and spiritual self. Victimization not only damages children's bodies and emotions but also wounds their souls. Shengold uses the graphic and appropriate term *soul murder*:

> The dramatic term for circumstances that eventuate in crime—the deliberate attempt to eradicate or compromise the separate identity of another person . . . sexual abuse, emotional deprivation, physical and mental torture can eventuate in *soul murder*. . . . Children are the usual victims. For the child's almost complete physical and emotional dependence on adults easily makes for possible tyranny and therefore child abuse.[2]

The child who has been sexually abused has a view of self which is often far from the self image intended by the Lord. We know that the "thief comes only to steal and kill and destroy" (John 10:10, NRSV). When children are stolen from and destroyed by sexual abuse, the enemy not only robs children of their childhood but potentially steals from their adulthood, thus weakening the effectiveness of the church. It is part of our job as Christian counselors to be spoilers of the enemy's plan.

It is important to recognize that children view trauma quite differently from the way adults do. Adults generally have stronger coping mechanisms (as well as established defense mechanisms) with which to defend against and process traumatizing experiences, even sexual exploitation. Children are no different from adults when it comes to fearing and being adversely affected by exploitation. The limited understanding and developmental immaturity of a child, however, simply make for a decreased ability to deal with pain and trauma. Understanding the child's world and the child's perspective becomes all the more important when dealing with traumatic issues.

How should trauma and sexual exploitation be defined for the child counselor? Trauma refers to overwhelming, uncontrollable experiences that psychologically affect victims by creating in them feelings of helplessness, vulnerability, loss of safety and loss of control. Sexual exploitation has been defined in a number of ways. The important point is that *any* sexual contact between an adult and a child is by definition exploitative and traumatic. A continuum of sexual activity may be considered abusive, including genital exposure, fondling, masturbation, oral-genital contact, as well as digital, object or penile penetration of the vagina and anus.

In her extensive research on childhood trauma, psychiatrist Lenore Terr suggests that children, regardless of their age, exhibit four primary characteristics following the exposure to trauma: (1) strongly visualized or otherwise repeatedly perceived memories of the trauma; (2) repetitive behaviors; (3) trauma-specific fears; and (4) changed attitudes about people, aspects of life and the future.[3] Unlike adults, who may reexperience memories of a traumatic event in an abrupt and intrusive manner, children tend to reexperience memories during times of relaxation such as while watching television, before falling asleep and while playing. The child who experiences post-traumatic visualizations or memories may do so while daydreaming in a class or while playing in the counseling session. Traumatized children generally do not find themselves suddenly interrupted with dysphoric sensorium (unpleasant input to the sensory apparatus), in contrast to adults who experience trauma. Repetitive behaviors usually take the form of either reenactment or post-traumatic play.

112

Several authors have identified various traumagenic states or conditions in the evaluation and treatment of traumatized children. James's categorizations of traumagenic states vividly apply to the trauma of sexual exploitation: self-blame, powerlessness, loss and betrayal, fragmentation of bodily experience, stigmatization, eroticization, destructiveness, dissociative/multiple personality disorder and attachment disorder.[4]

Self-blame is a common characteristic for children who have been sexually traumatized. When children experience the trauma of sexual exploitation, their inherent egocentrism leads them to believe that they are to blame. Young children simply tend to believe that the sun rises and sets because of them. So when trauma occurs, they instinctively think that they are the cause. It becomes crucial, therefore, that children believe that the traumatic event is not their fault.

Sexually abused children feel a strong sense of *powerlessness*. Although the word *empowerment* is probably overused in modern psychology and counseling, it is a primary therapeutic goal for children who have been traumatized. They must regain a sense of power and control in their lives. Trauma is overpowering, and the physiological and psychological immaturity of children exacerbates the effect. Many children hold on to the powerlessness they experienced when they were traumatized. As a result, they develop significantly impaired self-images.

Loss and betrayal surround children who have been sexually exploited. Perhaps the most notable loss is the loss of dignity and a sense of safety. In addition, they may feel the loss of security because people didn't protect them from trauma. Betrayal, which is essentially a loss of trust, shakes the very foundation of childhood development. Children who experience betrayal view the world as an unsafe and threatening place and often believe that they do not deserve any better than the traumatizing experience.

The *fragmentation of bodily experience* is a very real experience for child sexual abuse victims. Children who have experienced physical and sexual trauma often appear to have encoded the traumatic event through sensory and muscular memory as well as affective memory. These children do not trust, respect or feel mastery over their bodies. One of the reasons that play therapy is helpful

113

in treating this element of trauma is that, in play, children have the opportunity to engage all of the body's senses in the therapeutic process and can express themselves nonverbally and actively.

Stigmatization also marks children who have endured such trauma. They feel an internal sense of shame as well as an external categorization and labeling. These children experience pronounced shame and alienation from others because of the traumatizing experience. It is not uncommon to encounter children who have an inordinate portion of their identity based on the sexual trauma. Despite their own efforts to compensate, such children are often stuck in a relentless pursuit of acceptance. Group therapy, both for stigmatized children and the parents of these children, can greatly facilitate the abatement of shame and alienation.

Sexually traumatized children may experience *eroticization*, which can be quite disturbing to parents, teachers and even counselors. Through the experience of molestation and rape, children may perceive that their value is centered on being sexual; thus they often become eroticized. The child's entire personality may be wrapped up in the perspective of being valued only for his or her sexuality. Without a doubt, children who carry these messages into adulthood are at risk of entering inappropriate sexual situations. Social-skills training about appropriate and inappropriate touching may be an important adjunct intervention.

Destructiveness is another hallmark of traumatized children. Many children lose their impulse control, establishing a self-defeating cycle of aggression and destructiveness. This cycle may lead to frightening displays of temper and release of rage. This destructive behavior often causes people to dislike or punish the traumatized child. The punishment can, in turn, cause the hurting child who is acting out to internalize shame and anger even further, which leads to greater displays of destructive behavior. It is important for parents and counselors to work together on behavioral strategies and to provide a play therapy experience for the child.

Dissociative disorders can provide an efficient way for a child to cope with traumatic events. Although defense mechanisms such as denial, repression and dissociation are seen as dysfunctional, they realistically serve a very valid function for the child experiencing sexual trauma. It may be that the only way for a child to cope with an uncontrollable situation is to dissociate; fragmentation and depersonalization can help protect the child from the overwhelming emotions from traumatizing experiences. The problem is that while these defenses help the child in the midst of trauma, they do not serve well in terms of daily functioning. Children need to be free to explore all feelings and feeling states in counseling. Although counselors should not reinforce dissociation, they should accept it so that the child may integrate within the counseling process.

Attachment disorders are additional ways children may respond to trauma. Attachment is vital for survival, so it is understandable that threats to attachment are life-and-death issues for children. Children may experience attachment disorders from repeated traumatizing events that prevent a secure attachment from forming or from a single event such as parental abandonment, death of a parent or removal from the home. The crucially important relationship that is established in play therapy forms a primary foundation for the development of positive attachments.

PLAY AND PLAY THERAPY

Play is the most important and most natural activity of childhood. Children have played through history, and children in all cultures play. For children, play is not just what they do, but an expression of *who they are*. Scripture recognizes play as a natural activity for children—"And the streets of the city shall be full of boys and girls playing in its streets" (Zech. 8:5). Landreth notes:

> Children's play can be more fully appreciated when recognized as their natural medium of communication. Children express themselves more fully and more directly through self-initiated spontaneous play than they do verbally because they are more comfortable with play. For children to "play out" their experiences and feelings is the most natural dynamic and self-healing process in which children can engage.[5]

Play, and play therapy, are fundamentally preoperational. Adult "talk" therapy is, essentially, characterized by formal operations in terms of Piagetian development. Adult communication is by its nature abstract, whereas children are by their very nature concrete. Play and language are essentially relative opposites, as they are contrasting forms of representation. With cognitive verbalization children must translate thoughts into the accepted medium (talk). The inherent limitation is that children must fit their world into this existing medium. Play and fantasy, however, do not carry this limitation. Children can create without the restriction of making their creation understandable. Play and children, therefore, do not lend themselves to operationalism—they are preoperational.

So, what is play therapy? This is an important question, as many who work with children describe their work as play therapy when it is little more than adult cognitive therapy that includes the presence of toys. Landreth defines play therapy as

> a dynamic interpersonal relationship between a child and a therapist trained in play therapy procedures who provides selected play materials and facilitates the development of a safe relationship for the child to fully express and explore self (feelings, thoughts, experiences and behaviors) through the child's natural medium of communication, play.[6]

Crucial elements are contained within this definition. Play therapy involves a dynamic interpersonal *relationship*. It is relationship with Christ that brings us into spiritual healing—it is relationship that is the basis for therapeutic healing. It should be without question that therapeutic relationships be dynamic and interpersonal. The play therapist should be *trained in play therapy procedures*. Providing play media and using talk therapy does not make the process into play therapy. Attending a brief workshop or reading a book about play therapy does not make a play therapist. Training is essential. *Selected play materials* should be provided—not a random collection of toys. In play therapy the play is the child's language and the toys are the child's words. The *development of a safe relationship* is *facilitated* by the play therapist. This does not involve following the agenda of the therapist. The sexually abused child already feels disempowered and out of control. The child needs to be given the opportunity *fully to express and explore self*. Healthy self-exploration enables the client to discover a proper self-image, which is a process that should lead a person to the Creator. And, as already noted, play therapy allows the children to use their *natural medium of communication, play.*

There are a number of theoretical approaches in the use of play therapy with children. I take a primarily child-centered play-therapy approach to working with hurting children. While all approaches to play therapy generally recognize that play is the natural medium of communication for children, this does not mean that all approaches are child focused. The focus of all child counselors, regardless of their theoretical approach, should be on the child rather than on the nature of the problem. Taking a prescriptive approach with children, even children who have experienced sexual trauma, makes the problem the spotlight in the treatment process instead of the child.

Since play therapy focuses on the person of the child rather than the nature of the child's problem, the therapeutic *relationship* becomes the key to healing. The alliance between the child and the therapist is the single most creative force in the healing process. Just as the Christian life is all about relationship, it is our relationship with the Son of God that brings redemption and wholeness, and we are called as Christians to be in relationship with each other. The counseling techniques and the play materials, as well as other related issues, are important—but should be considered summarily subordinate to the therapist-child relationship.

The scope of this chapter precludes extensive exploration of play-therapy procedures, techniques or materials. I would encourage the reader to seek appropriate training and consider the reading recommendations at the conclusion of this chapter.

When we are willing to enter the world of the children, especially the world of abused children, we are honoring them. And we are also honoring their Creator. Since Scripture reminds us to be like little children to enter the kingdom of God, perhaps we learn more about God by entering the "kingdoms" of our child clients as "little children." We must remember that although we as adults may have "put away childish ways" our child clients have not. Our child clients "talk like children, think like children, reason like children." Let's let them continue to do this in counseling.

COUNSELING SEXUALLY EXPLOITED CHILDREN

Children who have been sexually traumatized have a need for a therapeutic experience that is safe and empowering. It needs to touch their senses and provide them with an opportunity to gain the mastery and control that have been stripped away by the traumatizing event of sexual exploitation. I believe that the sensory and kinesthetic quality of play is key in this regard.

For those readers who use the DSM-IV,[7] you may notice that the diagnostic criteria for Post-traumatic Stress Disorder—one of the most common diagnoses given in cases of sexual trauma—is largely sensory based. This makes sense because trauma is sensory-based. Trauma overwhelms the senses, both psychologically and physiologically. In fact, many researchers believe that trauma memories are encoded not only in the brain but also within the body. It would seem to make sense, therefore, for the treatment to be sensory based. "Talk-based" counseling approaches do not meet this need:

> Psychological trauma is an extremely stressful event or happening that is usually atypical in the life experiences of the child and is remarkably distressing to the child to the point of being overwhelming and causing the child to be unable to cope. Young children should not be expected to verbally describe such experiences because they do not have the verbal facility required to do so, and such experiences are usually too threatening for the child to consciously describe. The natural reaction of children is to reenact or play out the traumatic experience in an unconscious effort to comprehend, overcome, develop a sense of control or assimilate the experience. This repetitive playing out of the experience is the child's natural self-healing process.[8]

Randy's experience illustrates this dynamic of repetitive playing out of a traumatic experience. Eight-year-old Randy had been severely sexually abused; the injuries were so severe that Randy needed corrective surgery. His behavior in the foster home ranged from depression and isolation to aggression and delinquent behavior. His play in the counseling sessions moved from being occasionally controlling to being very aggressive. Randy began to play "cops and robbers"; he took on both roles. He would give me the play money and then rob me of it; then he would suddenly switch roles and arrest me for robbery. This play moved to a prevalent and repetitive theme. He would stab the bop bag in the lower part of the back and then would attempt to do the same with me. Although I set a limit on this latter activity, Randy needed to express himself through this play. It was an effort to "comprehend, overcome, develop a sense of control, [and] assimilate" his experience. It was also his way of telling me as his therapist: "This is what I experienced. I want you to know how I was hurt, and I need to know whether or not you will still accept me." As he worked through these issues in the play therapy, Randy's behavior in the foster home and at school significantly improved. Randy moved from long-term residential treatment to "adoptable" status. Traumatized children need to have special places like these to play out and process their experiences.

It is crucial to remember that sexual abuse is extraordinarily intrusive. Therapeutic interventions, therefore, should not only be nonintrusive but also provide great levels of safety for the sexually abused child. One of the primary advantages of using a play approach to treat children who have been sexually abused is the safety the play-therapy environment provides. People of any age will not grow where they do not feel safe. A large part of this process in psychotherapy involves the appropriate use of boundaries and structure. When the structure of therapy requires verbal disclosure, intrusion may continue. In play therapy the child has the opportunity to project emotionally charged issues onto the play media, rather than having to verbalize them.

For children who have been traumatized, it is yet another disempowering experience to be placed in a room with a strange adult who is asking questions about the trauma. Since questions inherently cause a person to think, and thus remain in a cognitive realm, could it be that the issues of the heart—for the heart is "the wellspring of life"(Prov. 4:23)—might not be adequately dealt with? Allowing children to "talk" on their terms and at their level provides a forum for the issues of the heart to be safely addressed. Through play, the traumatized child can process intrapsychic pain in a safe and therapeutically distant way.

The therapeutic distance of play therapy provides children with the opportunity to bring memories of trauma to the surface with a corresponding release of emotion. This helps sexual abuse victims resolve the trauma experience. Schaefer suggests several properties that allow play to provide the sense of distance and resultant sense of safety that children experience: (1) *symbolization*—children can use a toy (for example, a predatory animal) to represent an abuser; (2) *"as if" quality*—children can use the pretend quality of play to act out events as if they are not real life; (3) *projection*—children can project intense emotions onto puppets or toy animals, who can then safely act out these feelings; and (4) *displacement*—children can displace negative feelings onto dolls and other toys rather than expressing them toward family members.[9]

I generally do not take any more of a prescriptive approach with sexually traumatized children than I do with any other presenting problem. I may stock the playroom with additional toys that children might relate to their trauma. For instance, I may provide a blindfold for the child whose abuse involved blindfolding, a toy video camera for the child involved in child pornography, or a toy workshop tool that represents what was used as a penetration device. I will not, however, direct a child to play with any particular toy provided; I will simply make the toys available. It is difficult to list or categorize types of play to look for with traumatized children. Most of these children will play out the trauma, but the therapist may not always recognize the process. A child who vigorously cleans toys in the sink may be dealing with a sense of being dirty from having experienced sexual trauma, or may be acting out life in the home of an obsessive-compulsive parent, or may be dealing with enuresis. Other possibilities certainly may exist as well. The point is that it is more important for children to have the opportunity to express themselves and to feel the acceptance and understanding of the therapist than it is for the therapist to be able to interpret the play themes.

This brings me to a related point. I do not believe that interpretation of the play behavior is essential to the healing process. I often need to remind myself that when I interpret, I do so with an adult's mind and experience, not a child's. We need to be careful in interpreting a client's expression of an experience that the

120

sharing of the interpretation is meant to serve the client's need and not the therapist's. The therapeutic progress for abused children does not come through the therapist's interpretation of the play, but the *process* of the play.

I would expect that traumatized children will experience regression and emotional release in the play. The child who was sexually abused at age four and enters therapy at age seven will often regress to age four in the play while acting out the trauma. It is also possible that this child will regress to an age earlier than the age of the trauma to experience within the fantasy of the play what life was like before the trauma. It is not uncommon for the traumatized child to regress a little bit in the play to test the therapist's level of acceptance. When children find that it is safe to regress a little bit, they will feel safe to go further and further, until they are able to bring the play back to the trauma itself. Following this regression, traumatized children often will further test limits in the play (which, in fact, is testing the relationship) and will be able to gain the impulse control that is a problem for many traumatized children. Often traumatized children will be experiencing some level of developmental arrest. As the children have the opportunity to process the trauma in the play, they will be able to progress to the appropriate developmental level. Quite simply, after the regression comes progression.

Play is children's way of making sense of the traumatic event. In children's efforts to make sense of what happened to them, they often "act out" after a traumatic event. Post-trauma reactions can be seen in their behavior, their affect and certainly through their play. Children's wounds begin to heal as they build a relationship with a counselor who understands and accepts them, as they experience the therapeutic distance of the play therapy setting, and as they process issues in their natural medium of communication. Piers and Landau assert:

> Children actually heal themselves of emotional injuries
> through play, coping with and mastering potentially devas-
> tating occurrences. . . . Without the chance to experience the
> natural healing power of imaginative play, the emotional
> wounds caused by such events might never close, leaving

the child with a lifelong residue of anxiety and insecurity. If children did not play, they could not thrive, and they might not survive.[10]

There are many lists of behaviors and symptoms related to children who have experienced the trauma of sexual exploitation. One simple inventory that I have used suggests twelve possible indicators of child sexual abuse; it appropriately cautions that none of these behaviors alone necessarily means that sexual abuse has occurred, but a combination of these behaviors indicates that further evaluation is necessary.[11]

- Excessive masturbation;
- Excessive sexual acting-out toward adults;
- Simulation of sophisticated sexual activity with younger children;
- Fear of being alone with an adult, either male or female;
- Violence against younger children;
- Self-mutilation;
- Bruises and hickeys or both in the face or neck area or around the groin, buttocks, and inner thighs;
- Fear of bathrooms and showers;
- Knowledge of sexual matters and details of adult sexual activity inappropriate to age or developmental level;
- Combination of violence and sexuality in artwork, written schoolwork, language, and play;
- Extreme fear or repulsion when touched by an adult of either sex;
- Refusal to undress for physical education class at school.

In my training of counselors on working with this population, I cover these and other behavioral specifics but also stress that it is important to note that the existence of any one or even a combination of several of these behaviors does not automatically mean that a child has been sexually abused. While this statement may seem obvious, let me give an example. If a five-year-old girl is found to be chronically masturbating in her kindergarten class, it is likely that the teacher will assume some type of inappropriate sexual activity has occurred. And why not? This is not typical behavior for most kindergarten girls. It is certainly a possibility that the child has been exposed to some type of sexual trauma. Another possibility may also exist. Suppose this girl had recently had a rash in her vaginal area (it is possible for a child that young to have a yeast infection). It is only natural that she would scratch where it itches. The child might discover that scratching and rubbing in that area is pleasurable, and the masturbation then becomes a habit. The problem is that public masturbation is definitely not socially acceptable, even if the child's motivation is no different from another child's habit. Obviously some intervention is necessary—but not calling out the cavalry.

I should probably make a point about investigations for child sexual abuse. Although people in the field disagree on this subject, I generally believe that it is not appropriate for a therapist to be a sexual abuse investigator. I am principally a therapist with children, and even after a disclosure has been made once therapy begins, I prefer not to take on an investigative role. The potential for damaging the therapeutic relationship is too great. I will make the required child-abuse report and will cooperate with an investigation, but I will not begin interrogating the child for purposes of investigation or prosecution. It may be beneficial for an investigator to take on a child's case therapeutically in some situations, but I would be quite reticent about going back to investigating once therapy has begun. If it is handled well, the investigation process can be therapeutic, but it can also retraumatize the child. A colleague of mine has developed a sexual-abuse interviewing protocol that incorporates play-therapy techniques within the investigation process.

I assert that a play-based approach to treating child sexual abuse is the most beneficial. The child who has experienced this devastating trauma has internalized a variety of negative messages about self, others and the world. Play provides an opportunity to process and externalize these messages. Children, through the fantasy of the play, manage the clearly unmanageable—the abuse itself.

> The emotional dynamics resulting from abuse must be
> matched by an equally dynamic therapeutic process as is
> found in the play therapy relationship. Children who have

been abused cannot be expected to verbally describe their experience and their reaction because they lack the cognitive-verbal ability to do so. Abused children come from inconsistent environments. The play therapy relationship provides children with an absolutely consistent environment, for without such the child cannot feel safe, and it is this dimension of predictable safety that allows children to express, explore, and resolve through play deep-seated emotional pain. Abuse and neglect cause serious inner conflicts and relationship problems for children, and play therapy provides the modality necessary for children to develop adaptive and coping mechanisms on their own terms and at their own emotional pace.[12]

Play is sexually abused children's way of making sense of the traumatizing experience. In their effort to make sense of what has happened to them, children often "act out" the sexual abuse in the play. The child who has been abused while still in the crib may regress to infancy in the play. The child who has been forced into oral sex may stick all manners of toys into his or her mouth. The child who has been sodomized may shove objects into the buttocks area of dolls and animals. The child who has been penetrated may mount and "hump" the inflated bop bag. I have seen all of these in the playroom. It is my belief that these children would not have been able to process these horrible experiences adequately without the safety of play. The wounds of sexual abuse begin to heal as children build a safe relationship with a counselor who understands and accepts them (and their awful experiences), and they process issues in their natural medium of communication—play.

There are many issues to be considered when counseling children who have been sexually traumatized. Although not a complete list, I would propose the following summary as some fundamental considerations when working with this challenging population:

◆ Sexually abused children, like all children, naturally communicate through play. Effective counseling of these traumatized children should, therefore, take a play-therapy approach.

- Sexual exploitation is extraordinarily intrusive. Therefore, the therapist's interventions should be nonintrusive, allowing the child sufficient freedom to explore, to process and to grow.
- While children must explore and process their pain in the therapeutic process, verbal acknowledgment is *not* always necessary.
- Sexual abuse most often occurs within the framework of the family, thus family therapy and parent training may be crucial elements of the therapeutic milieu.
- Additionally, because of this relational framework, children can benefit from the experience of building a safe, appropriate and affirming *relationship* with a trusted helper.
- Children who have been sexually abused may be vulnerable to secondary trauma related to the abuse because of psychological and physical maturation. Treatment of these children may need to be ordered and cycled over time to respond to these development vulnerabilities.
- Positive and affirming therapeutic messages should be frequent and passionate to be heard and felt by the wounded and hyper-vigilant child. The low self-esteem and lack of self-acceptance that abused children feel must be actively worked against.
- Sexually abused children are often forced, shamed or threatened to keep the abuse secret. The therapist must be intentional regarding the allowance and promotion of *self-expression.*
- Traumatized children often employ elaborate or bizarre defense mechanisms to cope with the trauma. While this should be addressed, these defenses should not be torn away by professionals but must be given a place for full expression.
- The needs of the child may not be entirely met by a therapist working alone, without the support of others involved with the child. A treatment team approach is frequently necessary, including medical, legal, and governmental persons—and, perhaps most importantly, the child's caregivers.
- Treatment must attend to a continuum of issues, including physiological, cognitive, psychological and spiritual concerns.

Sexual exploitation may involve damage to any and all of these areas.

◆ Because of the developmental process of therapy and the developmental change of children in therapy, ongoing assessment is crucial.

◆ Sexual exploitation is an activity that is forced. Counseling should therefore be facilitative instead of forced by therapeutic prescription.

◆ Children who have experienced sexual exploitation frequently evidence damaged or distorted boundaries. These children should benefit from learning skills to employ in both difficult and everyday circumstances. Group psychoeducational work may be helpful here.

◆ Clinical work in the area of sexual trauma often involves direct encounters with horrible and horrifying circumstances. The professional and personal impact of this on the therapist should never be underestimated.

◆ The focus of treatment should never be the sexual trauma or the child's symptomatic response to the trauma. The focus of treatment should always be the child.

CONCLUSION

A few years ago a young girl who had been molested was referred to me. She had been in therapy, and the progress had stagnated. We went into the play-therapy room. She immediately sat down and said, with a flat affect: "I suppose you want to talk about the molestation?" I was flabbergasted. This was my very first contact with this child, not to mention I am a male therapist. I thought, *Is this what this girl assumes counseling is all about?—What a shame.* After my initial surprise, I responded by reminding her *that this was a place and time where she could talk about anything she wanted to, or not talk at all. This was her time.* Now it was her turn to be flabbergasted. After a couple of sessions of awkwardness and discomfort on her part (she had never had an experience like this before), she began to play out her hurt, fear and anger. Her parents reported renewed therapeutic progress.

Wounded children need to work through their pain through play. If sexually abused children did not have the opportunity to

126

experience the healing power of play, the emotional wounds might never close. We as Christian counselors must work against leaving a generation of hurting children to live out lives of fear and anxiety. Their survival may depend on it. Remember, time does not heal wounds. Rather, the power of relationship heals wounds—relationship with God and relationship with God's children. One author writes: "Consider the play of the child, and the nature of the kingdom will be revealed. Christ is that fiddler who plays so sweetly that all who hear him begin to dance."[13] For the sake of the children, let's join in the play.

Notes

A portion of this chapter has been adapted from the chapter author's book *Counseling Children Through the World of Play* (Wheaton, Ill.: Tyndale House Publishers, 1997).

[1] G. Landreth, L. Homeyer, G. Glover, and D. Sweeney, *Play Therapy Interventions with Children's Problems* (Northvale, N.J.: Jason Aronson, 1996).

[2] L. Shengold, *Soul Murder: The Effects of Childhood Abuse and Deprivation* (New Haven: Yale University Press, 1989), p. 2.

[3] L. Terr, "Child Trauma: An Outline and Overview, *America Journal of Psychiatry* 148 (1991): 10–20.

[4] B. James, *Treating Traumatized Children* (Lexington, Mass.: Lexington Books, 1989).

[5] G. Landreth, *Play Therapy: The Art of Relationship* (Bristol, Pa.: Taylor & Francis, 1991), p. 10.

[6] Ibid., p. 14.

[7] *Diagnostic and Statistical Manual of Mental Disorders: DSM-IV,* 4th ed. (Washington, D.C.: American Psychiatric Association, 1994).

[8] Landreth, et al., *Play Therapy Interventions with Children's Problems,* p. 241.

[9] C. Schaefer, "Play Therapy for Psychic Trauma in Children," in K. O'Connor and C. Schaefer, eds., *Handbook of Play Therapy,* vol. 2 (New York: John Wiley & Sons, 1994).

[10] M. Piers and G. Landau, *The Gift of Play* (New York: Walker & Co., 1980).

[11] B. James and M. Nasjleti, *Treating Sexually Abused Children and Their Families,* (Palo Alto, Calif.: Davies-Black Publishing, 1983).

[12] Landreth, et al., *Play Therapy Interventions with Children's Problems*, p. 1.

[13] R. Neale, *In Praise of Play: Toward a Psychology of Religion* (New York: Harper & Row, 1969), p. 174.

Recommended Reading

Sweeney, D. *Counseling Children Through the World of Play*. Wheaton, Ill.: Tyndale House Publishers, 1997.

Landreth, G. *Play Therapy: The Art of the Relationship*. Bristol, Pa.: Taylor & Francis, 1991.

Landreth, G., L. Homeyer, G. Glover, and D. Sweeney, *Play Therapy Interventions with Children's Problems*. Northvale, N.J.: Jason Aronson, 1996.

Gil, E. *The Healing Power of Play*. New York: The Guilford Press, 1991.

10

Creating a Healing Environment for Sexually Exploited Adolescents

Ann Noonan

The atrocities of sexual exploitation either in the context of war or family interactions can bring us face to face with the evil (fallenness) of human nature. To examine exploited youngsters causes us to bear witness to horrific events and become aware of the potential God has allowed us to harm and destroy. May we as helpers use this information to enable us to understand so that we may be more effective in God's plan for redemption and restoration. Can we as helpers for healing believe as Joseph did: "You intended to harm me, but God intended it for good to accomplish what is now being done, the saving of many lives" (Gen. 50:20).

Traumatized youth learn two extremely important and sad lessons:

1. The world is unsafe, no one is trustworthy; and
2. I do not have control over my life.

> In situations of terror, people spontaneously seek their first source of comfort and protection. Wounded soldiers and

raped women cry out for their mothers, or God. When this cry is not answered, the sense of basic trust is shattered. Traumatized people feel utterly abandoned, utterly alone, cast out of the human and divine systems of care and protection that sustain life. Thereafter, a sense of alienation, of disconnection, pervades every relationship, from the most intimate familial bonds to the most abstract affiliations of community and religion. When trust is lost, traumatized people feel that they belong more to the dead than to the living.[1]

This chapter will present a brief description of adolescence, the sexually abused adolescent, problems a helper may encounter, the nature of the helper, the healing process, and suggestions for creating a restorative (healing) environment.

Adolescence is a time marked by change—a bridge between childhood and adulthood. It is often confusing for the individual and can be even more confusing for adults who are unaware of struggles associated with this period of life. With the onset of puberty the youngster may experience growth spurts both physically and emotionally, accompanied by raging hormones. The major question for the adolescent to answer is, Who am I? This pursuit begins in adolescence and can continue throughout life. According to Eric Erikson, having an identity—knowing who you are— gives adolescents a sense of control that allows them to navigate through the rest of their life. Without achieving an integrated identity an adolescent often looks to others to evaluate how they are doing. Youngsters may become whatever they perceive their environment needs them to be in order to receive the needed acceptance, approval and affection. Maurice Wagner says individuals have three basic needs—belongingness, value and competence. If unmet, the individual can go through life trying to satisfy or meet these three basic needs.

One of my regrets from an earlier career as a secondary special-education teacher for mildly handicapped youth was not knowing what to do and not knowing enough to follow my instincts when working with a young woman I will refer to as Jean. She was a bubbly, effervescent 18 year old who was loved by the 1,000+ student body, professional and nonprofessional staff. She endeared herself to me, and although the tests classified her handicapped, I always wondered because of her quick wit and sharp intuition. She managed to complete academic requirements and to pass the required basic competency tests for high school graduation, which qualified her to graduate with a diploma.

One day during one of my many conversations with Jean regarding, "Who are you? What do you want to do with your life?" Jean revealed to me that her alcoholic father had been sexually abusing her and threatening to harm her mother, who was suffering with cancer, if she told. I believed Jean and informed her that I would need to tell her mother and report it to the authorities. Later that day Jean told me it was all a joke and that there was nothing to report. After talking with her for some time, I believed her, did not report, and we turned our attention to helping her graduate.

Jean was so cheerful and effervescent, I forgot about the abuse story until years later after I had become a therapist and Jean called my office for counseling. When she came in she was able to tell me her story of sexual abuse from her seventh birthday to the present. The current abuse was emotional and sexually covert, in the form of threatening phone calls from her father. Her mother had died of cancer, and Jean was living in an apartment with another female. She was struggling with flashbacks and nightmares. She entered the counseling process very afraid, yet willing to face her long history of abuse and work toward recovery.

I share that story to illustrate two main features of working with the adolescent survivor. One is a survivor's ability to present a "false self" that frequently is what he or she perceives as needed by the hearer or one who will protect the survivor from more harm. Figure 1[2] illustrates one author's understanding of the "false self/ true self" phenomenon. Notice that "Mary" presents positive, acceptable traits to those around her, while she buries and carries what she has learned as unacceptable inside.

Youngsters who have been sexually exploited have a highly developed "false self" and may have lost awareness of their "true self." The most important component to getting past the false self is relationship: "Relationships are everything. No work can be done in the absence of mutual affection and regard. The first step in

OUR LOST SOUL

The False Self
Also called the image,
persona or mask

**The Soul,
or True Self**

Hidden emotions, beliefs,
perceptions and desires.
Undeveloped abilities.
Unfilled needs.
Our need for God.

The false self consists of attitudes and
behaviors intended to protect us
from judgment and gain the
attention we desire

MARY

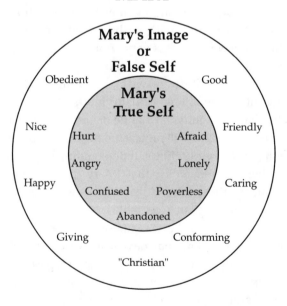

Figure 1

developing a relationship is in helping the girl develop trust—for me, for the therapeutic relationship, and for herself."[3]

The second feature is the need for a helper to listen with what Theodore Reik calls "the third ear"; this is also known as *active listening.* The heart of counseling and supporting is listening. In James 1:19 we read "Be quick to listen, slow to speak." Proverbs 18:13 says:

> If one gives answer before hearing,
> it is folly and shame" (*NRSV*).

All helpers could benefit from studying and applying Proverbs 18:13. We involve ourselves in the helping process because we truly want to help, but we often perceive that to mean giving answers or solutions. Answers, solutions and advice often are for the benefit of the helper and not beneficial for the helpee. Notice that Proverbs 18:13 describes this as the listener's folly (foolishness) and shame (a feeling of somehow being defective). Eugene Peterson's paraphrase of this verse in *The Message* reads, "Answering before listening is both stupid and rude."[4]

The following poem describes how the survivor feels and allows the helper to "crawl inside" that wounded person. I have used this poem with many adolescent and adult survivors, who have consistently testified to the accuracy of its description.

Please Hear What I'm Not Saying
author unknown

> Don't be fooled by me.
> Don't be fooled by the face I wear.
> For I wear a mask. I wear a thousand masks.
> Masks that I'm afraid to take off.
> And none of them is me.
>
> Pretending is an art that's second nature with me;
> But don't be fooled, for God's sake don't be fooled!
> I give you the impression that I'm secure.
> That all is sunny and unruffled in me.
> Within as well as without.

That confidence is my name and coolness is my
    game.
That the water's calm and I'm in command.
And that I need no one.
But don't believe me.

My surface may seem smooth, but my surface is a
    mask.
My ever-varying and ever-concealing mask.
Beneath lies no smugness, no complacence.
Beneath dwells the real me, in confusion, in fear, in
    aloneness.
But I hide this.
I panic at the thought of my weakness and fear being
    exposed.
That's why I frantically create a mask to hide behind.
A nonchalant, sophisticated facade to help me
    pretend.
To shield me from the glance that knows.
But such a glance is precisely my salvation.

That is, if it's followed by acceptance.
If it's followed by love.
It's the only thing that can liberate me from myself.
From my own self-built prison walls.
From the barriers that I so painstakingly erect.
It's the only thing that will assure me of what I can't
    assure myself.
That I'm really worth something . . .
But I don't tell you this, I don't dare . . . I'm afraid to.
I'm afraid your glance will not be followed by
    acceptance and love.
I'm afraid you'll think less of me, that you'll laugh . . .
And your laugh will kill me.

I'm afraid that deep down I'm nothing, that I'm just
    no good.
And that you will see this and reject me.
So, I play my game, my desperate pretending game.
And my life becomes a front.
I dislike the superficial game I'm playing

The superficial, phony game.
I'd really like to be genuine and spontaneous, and
    me,
But you've got to help me.
Even when that's the last thing I seem to want or
    need.
Only you can wipe away from my eyes the blank
    stare of the breathing dead . . .
Only you can call me into aliveness.

Each time you are kind and gentle and encouraging.
Each time you try to understand because you really
    care.
My heart begins to grow wings . . .
Very small wings, very feeble wings, but wings.
With your sensitivity and sympathy, and your power
    of understanding,
You can breath life into me.
I want you to know that.
I want you to know how important you are to me,
How you can be a creator of the person that is me, if
    you choose to . . .

It will not be easy for you.
A long conviction of worthlessness builds strong
    walls.
The nearer you approach me, the blinder I may
    strike back;
It's the irrational, but despite what the books say
    about man,
I'm irrational!!

I fight against the very thing that I cry out for.
But I am told that love is stronger than strong walls,
    and in this lies my hope.
My only hope.
Please try to beat down those walls with firm hands.
But with gentle hands—for a child is very sensitive.
Who am I, you may wonder?
I'm someone you know very well . . .
For I am every man or woman you meet.

SKILLS THAT FACILITATE THE HEALING PROCESS

You bring "who you are" to the helping process and who you are will be a major determinant of your effectiveness. Of course, we do not want to negate the healing power of the Holy Spirit in the process, but your personhood and the level of your relationship with God can be an asset or a hindrance.

Much research has been done on the qualities of an effective counselor, and most of the research supports Carl Rogers's 1967 findings.

> Rogers and his colleagues conducted a 4–year study that seemed to cut to the bone. The findings were unequivocal. People are more likely to improve when their counselors are (1) warm, (2) genuine, and (3) empathic. Without these traits a person's conditions may actually worsen regardless of the technical knowledge of the counselor.[5]

Warmth

Warmth, sometimes referred to as nonpossessive warmth, does not mean the helper approves of everything he or she hears; it does, however, mean "I accept you where you are." Our Lord has offered each of us this same type of unconditional acceptance, which was clearly illustrated in Jesus' attitude toward the woman at the well. He respected her and treated her as a person of value, without condoning her behavior. This warmth is not superficial—presenting a bubbly, cheerleader-type attitude of "Oh, let's just praise the Lord." A person who has nonpossessive warmth knows how to "speak a word fitly." Doing so does not demand that the struggling adolescent present a behavior that isn't his or hers to receive the helper's approval; that is, it does not encourage the development or propagation of a "false self." Rather, it fosters self-acceptance and honesty instead of a performance-based spirituality that lacks grace.

Genuineness

Adolescents more than any other group can spot a "fake" (an insincere person) even at a distance. They not only evaluate words, they read the sincerity in eye contact, posture, tone of voice and questions.

136

Genuineness cannot be faked. Either you sincerely want to help or you are simply playing the sterile role of a "helper"— hiding behind masks, defenses, or facades. In other words, authenticity is something you *are*, not something you *do*. Genuineness has been described as a lure to the heart. Jesus said, "Blessed are the pure in heart." Or, to put it another way, "Consider the counselor in whom there is no guile." When genuineness is present, a hesitant and skeptical adolescent is likely to stay with you and invest energy in the counseling process.[6]

Empathy

A third skill integral to the healing process is empathy—that quality of not only hearing another's words, but also the person's feelings, thoughts and wishes. Responding to a struggling youth who has just had her first sexual experience—in the form of a violent rape—with platitudes, reassurances that everything will be OK, reading Scripture, or even prematurely praying can be damaging and leave the youth feeling isolated and hopeless. We who want to come alongside hurting youth need to be ever praying that God will help us in our insight and our timing.

> A word fitly spoken
>   is like apples of gold in a setting of silver" (Prov.
>   25:11, *NRSV*).

That is to say that expressions of empathy which demonstrate not only hearing but also understanding and feeling are crucial in giving hope.

For example:

> "It's terribly hard to put such strong feelings into words."
> "It makes you sick to your stomach every time you think about what happened."
> "Everything seems so confused now."
> "You are so scared."
> "You felt so alone, defenseless and helpless."
> "You wish you could wake up and find that it was only a bad dream."[7]

In counseling it is the relationship that brings healing to suffering people. And so, along with psychologist Carl Rogers, we ask, How can I create a helping relationship? To help us understand this larger question Rogers asks ten more specific questions:

1. Can I be perceived by the other person as trustworthy, dependable or consistent in some deep sense?
2. Can I be expressive enough a person so that what I am will be communicated unambiguously?
3. Can I let myself experience positive attitudes toward this other person—attitudes of warmth, caring, liking, interest, respect?
4. Can I be strong enough as a person to be separate from the other?
5. Am I secure enough within myself to permit the counselee his or her separateness?
6. Can I let myself enter fully into the world of the counselee's feelings and personal meanings and see these as he or she does?
7. Can I be acceptant of each facet of this person which he or she presents to me?
8. Can I act with sufficient sensitivity in the relationship that my behavior will not be perceived as a threat?
9. Can I free him or her from the threat of external evaluation?
10. Can I meet this other individual as a person who is in the process of becoming, or will I be bound by his or her past and by my past?[8]

It is difficult for those who have not experienced or been exposed to sexual trauma to understand the depths of pain an exploited individual feels. A helper may feel as though she herself is in mourning. Leonard Shengold refers to the "via dolorosa" of psychotherapy with survivors. Therapists working with survivors of the Nazi Holocaust report being "engulfed by anguish" or "sinking into despair." Unless therapists have adequate support to bear this grief, they will not be able to fulfill their promise to witness and will withdraw emotionally from the therapeutic alliance.[9]

We, as those working with sexually exploited youth, must be absolutely sure that we have our lives built on the right foundation—

Jesus Christ. Otherwise, when we get into the work, we will be "engulfed," as Herman describes it, or we will "fall with a great crash," as Jesus describes it in Matthew 7:27.

The following poem, *Because of You*, was written by a young woman whose stepfather had sexually abused her from the time she was four or five years of age until she left home for college.

Because of You
Unnamed

Because of you I hurt inside.
The River of Pain runs deep and wide.
You stole my pride, my dignity
    those times you dumped your filth in me.
You robbed me of my childhood years
    and filled my life with shame and fears.

It's over now, and yet it's not
Because of all the scars I've got
That remind me of so long ago when
    I was young and you were bold.
Of all the times that you were nice,
Knowing later I'd pay the price.

You say you're sorry—
    That may be true,
But I still hate those thoughts of you.
For I know that you will never be
The daddy that was meant for me.
You cannot earn the respect you'd like—
I was born to be your daughter, not your wife!

This bright young woman entered therapy because of her inner turmoil and her inability to cope with herself. She was an excellent student at a Christian college, and yet she was suicidal, depressed and self-destructive. During her recovery she needed hospitalization, followed by a group-home residency. Today she lives independently and is self-supporting. She entered a psychiatric hospital one year after therapy had begun. While in the hospital she found several caring support people who managed not to be "engulfed by her anguish" and could stand firm in their knowledge of a loving God who heals.

THE HEALING PROCESS

It is of utmost importance that the helper view the abused as one with potential for healing and acknowledge the individual's strengths as a survivor. The healing process involves a number of stages or steps. The helper and helpee need to ask God to:

1. Give the courage to be honest and take a look at the damage—as Nehemiah did before he set out to rebuild the walls of Jerusalem, and
2. Help them to give God permission to turn the Holy Spirit's light on their thoughts, feelings and actions, believing "our God will fight for us" (Neh. 4:20b).

Jan Frank, author of *A Door of Hope*, offers a helpful outline of the steps to recovery:

Ten Steps to Recovery
1. Face the Problem—1 Corinthians 11:28
   Symptom identification: examine self-depression, anger, fear, guilt, difficulty establishing relationships, repeated victimization, sexual problems in marriage, poor self image, shut-off emotions.
2. Recount the Incident—Nehemiah 2
   Verbalize in detail with knowledgeable support person.
3. Experience the Feelings—Nehemiah 2
   Experience feelings both past and present. Allow the child within to express previously suppressed emotion.
4. Establish Responsibility—Joshua 7; Hosea 2:14-15
   Establish the perpetrator(s) as 100% accountable, as well as any co-contributors. The victim is innocent.
5. Trace Behavioral Difficulties/Symptoms
   Look at current behavior patterns, trace them back to their origin, begin implementing practical steps to change.
6. Observe Others/Educate Self
   Associate with others who have had similar experiences. Read material which will provide knowledge, support, and encouragement.

7. Confront the Aggressor—Matthew 18:15
   (Note: Do not do prematurely) (The perpetrator can be confronted within the victim if not in person.) Bring face to face. Goal of reconciliation. From position of strength. Format compliment, confess, confront, commit. *[Author's note: This step is highly individual and should never be made mandatory. It should be done only with much preparation and prayer. See Frank's Door of Hope for complete instructions.]*
8. Acknowledge Forgiveness—Colossians 3:13
   This is a process that involves: acknowledging the pain, releasing your rights, desire for reconciliation and re-building relationships.
9. Rebuild Self-image & Relationships—Nehemiah 4:17
   See ourselves as God sees us See God for who he really is. View our circumstances from God's perspective.
10. Express Concern & Empathize with Others—2 Corinthians 1:3-4
    Reach out and comfort.[10]

It is important for one in a helping relationship to be aware that these ten steps are guides, not rules, and their accomplishment may or may not be in sequence. There is potential for great damage in the "confronting the aggressor" step. Within the Christian community we seem to want to move too quickly to forgiveness and not do the emotional work needed to understand the process. This shortcut results in the survivor becoming discouraged and even frustrated to the point of invalidating his or her salvation experience. Therefore, it is of utmost importance that we helpers exercise the skills described earlier and rely on the guidance of the Holy Spirit.

It is best not to rush the process. Be aware that the abuse occurred within the context of some kind of relationship and that healing will most often occur within the context of a different kind of relationship. We are the connection for the injured to a loving and restorative God. It is essential for those of us who are willing to walk into the pain of abuse to know that

The LORD will surely comfort *[survivor's name]* and will look with compassion on all her ruins; he will make her deserts like Eden, her wastelands like the garden of the Lᴏʀᴅ. Joy and gladness will be found in her, thanksgiving and the sound of singing (Isa. 51:3).

and to believe:

> The spirit of the Lord Gᴏᴅ is upon me [Jesus Christ],
>> because the Lᴏʀᴅ has anointed me;
> he has sent me to bring good news to the oppressed,
>> to bind up the brokenhearted,
> to proclaim liberty to the captives,
>> and release to the prisoners;
> to proclaim the year of the Lᴏʀᴅ's favor,
>> and the day of vengeance of our God;
>> to comfort all who mourn;
> to provide for those who mourn in Zion—
>> to give them a garland instead of ashes,
> the oil of gladness instead of mourning,
>> the mantle of praise instead of a faint spirit.
> They will be called oaks of righteousness,
>> the planting of the Lᴏʀᴅ, to display his glory (Isa.
>> 61:1–3, NRSV).

May we as helpers see the abused adolescent as future "oaks of righteousness . . . displaying his glory."

Notes

[1] Judith Lewis Herman, *Trauma and Recovery* (The US: Basic Books, 1992), p. 52.

[2] Kenneth A. Schmidt, *Finding Your Way Home* (Ventura, Calif.: Regal Books, 1990), pp. 45, 46.

[3] Mary, Piper, *Reviving Ophelia: Saving the Selves of the Adolescent Girls* (New York: Ballantine Books, 1994), p. 253.

[4] Eugene H. Peterson, *The Message: New Testament with Psalms and Proverbs* (Colorado Springs: Navpress, 1995).

[5] Les Parrott III, *Helping the Struggling Adolescent* (Grand Rapids, Mich.: Zondervan Publishing House, 1993), p. 25.

[6] Ibid., p. 27. Emphases added.

[7] G. Keith Olson, *Counseling Teenagers* (Loveland, Col.: Group Books, 1984), p. 3.

[8] Ibid., p. 16.

[9] Herman, *Trauma and Recovery*, p. 144.

[10] In her excellent book *A Door of Hope* Jan Frank outlines ten steps to healing from sexual abuse. In my practice I have used Jan's material with adolescent and adult survivors to enable them to acquire necessary information in the healing process. *Ten Steps to Recovery* is taken from a handout Jan wrote and which she distributed at an Abuse and Recovery Conference in Rochester, New York, in 1987. For more thorough information, please read her *A Door of Hope*, rev. and updated (Nashville: Thomas Nelson Publishers, 1995).

Recommended Reading

In addition to the works directly referenced, readers in this field also will benefit from the following works.

Erikson, Erik H. *Childhood and Society*. New York: Norton & Company, 1963.

Langberg, Diane Mandt. *Counseling Survivors of Sexual Abuse*. Wheaton, Ill.: Tyndale Press, 1997.

McDowell, Josh, and Bob Hostetler. *Handbook on Counseling Youth*. Dallas: Word Publishing, 1996.

Rogers, Carl R. *On Becoming a Person* (Boston: Houghton Mifflin, 1961).

Santrock, John W. *Life-Span Development*. Madison, Wis.: Brown and Benchmark, 1997.

Skinner, Alicia, and Daniel S. Dworkin. *Helping the Bereaved: Therapeutic Interventions for Children, Adolescents, and Adults*. New York: Basic Books, 1992.

Wagner, Maurice E. *The Sensation of Being Somebody*. Grand Rapids, Mich.: Zondervan, 1975.

Warshaw, Robin. *I Never Called It Rape*. New York: Harper Perennial, 1994.

Whitfield, Charles L. *A Gift to Myself*. Deerfield Beach, Fla.: Health Communications, 1990.

11

Spiritual Healing

Dan Brewster

Surely it is profoundly significant that rather than telling children to be like adults, Jesus tells adults to be like children (Mark 10:15)! God values children. And most fundamentally, the spiritual healing of sexually abused children begins with this fact. One of the dominant themes throughout the Bible is God's concern and care for victims. That concern and care flows most especially to the victims of the ugliest kind of victimization, sexual abuse.

Jesus often reminded us about the very special place that those who are younger and smaller had in his eyes. It is significant that Christ himself dignified childhood by experiencing it (Heb. 2:14).

The Oxford statement on Children at Risk[1] expresses particularly well the special concern God has for children, and God's anger when they are abused or mistreated:

> Scripture clearly shows that God is outraged about what is happening to children. Our own anger is but a pale reflection of God's own fury and indignation. Our compassion for hurting children and the righteous anger that arises within us reflects nothing less than the jealous love and righteous anger of our Heavenly Father. Our anger is predicated

upon God's anger, and our actions on his actions. Over and over again God's warning throughout the Bible is "Don't touch my precious children!" (Exodus 22:22; Psalm 68:5, Ezekiel 16:4–14, Deuteronomy 24:17) He indicates terrible consequences for anyone harming his children: " . . . it would be better that a millstone be hung around his neck and [he] be drowned in the depths of the sea" (Matthew 18:6).

In the light of such clear biblical affirmation, and in the light of common decency, we are appalled at the depravity inherent in the sexual abuse of children. "Unfortunately," the Oxford statement continues, "we live in a world where an attitude of cynicism towards the dignity of human life has resulted in a tragic loss of respect for humankind. Children are increasingly the undeserving victims of human and demonic forces." Nowhere is this more evident than in the sexual abuse of children.

SPIRITUAL AND PSYCHOLOGICAL HEALING GO HAND IN HAND

This chapter is about the *spiritual* healing of sexually abused children. But spiritual healing will always go hand in hand with emotional, psychological and sometimes physical healing of the child. Complete restoration must be holistic. As with emotional healing, the spiritual healing process can begin as soon as the abuse ends but may extend well into adulthood. Occasionally, a person may receive quick healing. But most require an extended process, during which the Holy Spirit brings to light the layers of experiences that need the Spirit's touch.

Let me be frank. Sexual abuse damages the soul. Every year we are gaining a deeper understanding of the harsh reality of life after abuse. For many, it is a life robbed of the joy and beauty that God intended. For not only has a precious child been sexually abused, that child has been wounded at the deepest level of his or her being.

One of my favorite movie lines is from *Hook*, where young Jack is goofing off in the plane and his father, the now grown-up and thoroughly matured Peter Pan, gets frustrated with him and yells, "Stop acting like a child." His son looks up incredulously and says, "But I am a child!"

How quickly we forget! God made us children first. He values childhood. In fact, God thought it was such a good thing that he spent most of his earthly life being one. God wants children to be children. He wants us to be children before we are adults. He wants us to experience dependency before we try independence. God wants us to have joy in the simple things, to be carefree, to think more about play than about work. Unfortunately, sexual abuse stops a childhood short. It makes a child not think like a child, not feel like a child. For protection, abused children need to think like adults. They cannot be innocent. They cannot be vulnerable. They dare not trust. We cannot turn back the clock and relive a childhood. Some things cannot be redone; some realities will not be changed, and most often these experiences have an impact on a person's relationship with God.

Childhood sexual abuse may result in physical injury. It invariably results in emotional and spiritual injury. Sexual abuse activates a very specific psychological dismantling process that destroys the psychological inner core of a person. The child has been raped psychologically. Eventually so much has been ripped from the child's life that the child doesn't know what to believe, or whom to trust.[2] Healing of such trauma must address both its psychological and spiritual consequences. Clearly, physical injury or trauma must be detected and treated. But it is no less important to deal competently and lovingly with the psychological and spiritual damage.

Some people distinguish between surface-level healing and deep-level healing. Surface-level healing has to do primarily with the physical side of the person. "Deep-level" healing deals with the emotions and psyche of the victim and with restoring the damaged relationships—with God, with others and with self. Deep-level healing is the healing of the mind, the emotions, the painful memories. It is the process whereby we are set free from guilt, resentment, bitterness, depression, self-pity, inferiority, self-condemnation and a sense of worthlessness. It seeks to bring the power of Christ to bear on the roots from which damage springs.[3]

GOD AS AN "ACCOMPLICE"

Not surprisingly, many sexually traumatized children experience questions and conflicts regarding their spirituality. Sexual

146

abuse strikes at the core of the individual. The two deepest forms of intimacy are sexual intimacy and spiritual intimacy. Violation of sexual intimacy has implications for our spirituality. Compound this problem by violating this level at an age and stage of development when basic assumptions about life and self are being formed and disruption of spiritual development is inevitable. Both psychological and spiritual development may be arrested at the time of abuse.

Sexual abuse may create several obstacles that hinder spiritual development. A primary obstacle is mistrust and an inability to develop trusting relationships. Sexually traumatized children often do not feel safe with authority figures, and to the extent that God is viewed as an authority figure, their mistrust can extend to God. Children may transfer their feelings about the perpetrators to God.[4] In some ways they may even view God as an accomplice. Since God is all-knowing, he knew of the abuse. Since God is all-powerful, he could have stopped the abuse.

Another obstacle to spiritual responsiveness may be despair. Sexually traumatized children have a history of being crushed and may have difficulty believing that life can offer anything better. They may lack faith in the future. Their spiritual questions frequently center around meaning and purpose: Why did this happen to me? What's the point of all of this? Or their questions may reflect more of their anger: What kind of God would let this happen?[5]

Satan seeks to destroy the lives of children through sexual abuse. According to some statistics the highest incidence of sexual abuse is in the age group of three to four years—the stage where the child is still classified as "pre-verbal," unable to verbalize what has happened to him or her, and physically defenseless. This is the stage where we as adults should be most protective and nurturing of children and help them develop a healthy self-image and a wholesome, positive concept of God. Sadly, it is at exactly this stage that Satan has brutally intervened. If these children do not receive the correct help in healing this damage, they will rarely be all that God wants them to be. Their concept of God will be twisted and confused.[6] They will struggle against a multitude of problems.

Children and adults who suffer emotional wounds usually respond by suppressing the emotion and quickly "bandaging" the

147

wound, so no one can see. The wound, then, not having been cleansed, festers. Later in life the bandages begin to break down and the "infection" surfaces. The unhealed wounds, though the result of long-past experiences, begin again to influence the person's present life. Most of us have scars somewhere on our bodies from physical injuries incurred in our past. The wound the scar represents once hurt very much. But it hasn't hurt for a long time because it was dealt with at the time it occurred and soon healed. The truth of the fact that we were injured was not changed when the wound was healed. But it doesn't hurt anymore.

Emotional wounds are similar. Healing does not change the history. Those wounds remain a part of the person's life story. There is, however, an enormous difference between wounds that are still open and festering and those that have healed and turned into scars. God is willing and able to turn festering emotional wounds into painless scars.[7]

Let's look at the most common of the emotional wounds that occur as a result of childhood sexual abuse and see how God can work to heal physically, emotionally and spiritually. I am not an expert on counseling those who are spiritually and emotionally injured through sexual abuse. But the truth is that none of us has any special gifting or power in ourselves to solve their problems. Rather, we are coming alongside as partners with them and the Holy Spirit in a team effort.

1. DAMAGED-GOODS SYNDROME

Perhaps the most common and devastating consequence of child sexual abuse is the victim feeling damaged by his or her experiences. The result is low self-esteem and a poor self-image. The feeling of being "damaged goods" will very often surface even when no actual physical injuries occurred. This impression is a combination of reactions. Obviously, there may be actual physical injury or the fear of physical damage. If physical injury or pain did occur, the child has good reason to believe that he or she was damaged. And, even if the pain or discomfort was temporary, the fear of permanent damage may remain if steps are not taken to address it.

The response of family members or the community to the child after the sexual abuse has become public knowledge may also contribute to the damaged goods syndrome. "The fact of the child's premature and inappropriate sexual experience may become a trigger for the conflicts, ambivalence, guilt and fear regarding human sexuality which are harbored by members of his or her family and community."[8] (This damaged goods syndrome may be even more prominent and damaging in non-Western cultures, since the child may be cruelly rejected or considered ineligible for future marriage.)

Healing the child who feels he or she is damaged, with the inevitable consequence of low self-esteem, must start with a competent physical examination to ensure that any physical injuries are properly treated. If there is no physical damage, this should be emphatically communicated to the child and family. Then the child must be gently led to understand that God loves him or her regardless of what has been done, regardless of what has happened, and regardless of what others think.

It is hard to convince some abused children that what happened to them was the result of the badness in someone else rather than in themselves. Such children have difficulty believing that they can be loved just for who they are, rather than for what they can do or how they can please. They have difficulty grasping that they are truly forgiven. Most significantly, survivors of abuse often don't feel lovable. Since they do not love themselves, and often loathe themselves, they cannot conceptualize a God who loves them.

It may be helpful in sensitive and prayerful counseling to review God's attitude toward us as we reach toward a healthy self-image. When we study what God thinks of us, we come up with a lot of ammunition to counter the enemy's lies and our negative feelings about ourselves. We find, for example, that God planned and chose us before the foundation of the world (Eph. 1:4; Jer. 1:5). God created us in his image and likeness (Gen. 1:26). God formed us and cared for us while we were in our mother's womb (Ps. 139:13, 15). Then, after we had sinned and turned our backs on him, God redeemed us while we were still in our sinful condition (Rom. 5:8). Beyond this, God chose us and called us his friends (John 15:15–16). In addition, we are continually referred to in the

New Testament as saints (Rom. 1:7, 1 Cor. 1:2). God even calls us his children (1 John 3:1–2, John 1:12), chosen to inherit the kingdom with Jesus (Rom. 8:14–17). As children of the King, we are princes and princesses—just the opposite of what many abused children feel about themselves!

Children may also need to be reminded of how precious they are in Jesus' sight. Jesus wants us all to go back to the point of being a little child, simply to acknowledge our problems as we do our sins (1 John 1:9), then to give them unashamedly to him (Matt. 11:28, 1 Pet. 5:7). Being God's child means freedom, healing, self-acceptance, self-love and self-forgiveness. It also means the right to come boldly to God without shame (Heb. 4:16) and the ability to receive God's love and forgiveness. God chose us and invited us. We can receive the rights God has given us.

Charles Kraft suggests that it may be helpful to have victims close their eyes and picture the throne room of Isaiah 6:1–4, in which the prophet saw God sitting on his throne, high and exalted with his robe filling the whole temple and a multitude of heavenly creatures worshiping and praising God. Kraft suggests that we should help the child

> feel the awe, the worshipful atmosphere (not just to think about it). Then, once people are really into it, have them imagine a thump on the door to the room and a whole bunch of kids running into the throne room. Have them imagine the kids running right past the angels, the cherubim and seraphim bowing low with their foreheads to the floor, disrupting the whole worshipful scene, running noisily right up to the King and climbing into his lap. Have them notice the King loves it, because they are his kids and always have a right to barge into the throne room. Kids have different rules. And we are God's kids, invited to come any time "boldly" into his presence.
>
> Have [victims] see themselves as children welcomed onto Jesus' lap, with the Lord's arm around each child's shoulder. See Jesus putting a crown on each child's head. Then, as this picture sinks in, have [victims] picture themselves growing up on Jesus' lap.[9]

The popular Bill Gaither children's song of a few years back is a helpful reminder of how important children are, and how precious they are in God's sight:

> I am a promise, I am a possibility;
> I am a promise with a capital "P";
> I am a great big bundle of potentiality.
> And I am learning to hear God's voice,
> And I am trying to make the right choice.
> I'm a promise to be
> anything God wants me to be.[10]

The point is that God is the one who knows their hurt. God knows how many hairs are on their head, and God surely knows and cares about their hurts and fears. It is God who restores dignity, sense of self-worth, self-respect. God can bind their wounds. God loves each child no matter what happens to that child. God will always love us. God also gives each of us the promise that God will not leave us.[11]

> O LORD, our Lord,
> how majestic is your name in all the earth!
> You have set your glory above the heavens.
> From the lips of children and infants you have
>   ordained praise (Ps. 8:1–2a).

> But now thus says the LORD,
> he who created you, O Jacob,
> he who formed you, O Israel:
> Do not fear, for I have redeemed you;
>   I have called you by name; you are mine.
> When you pass through the waters, I will be with
>   you;
>   and through the rivers, they shall not overwhelm
>   you;
> when you walk through fire you shall not be burned,
>   and the flame shall not consume you.
> For I am the LORD your God,
>   the Holy One of Israel, your Savior.

> I give Egypt as your ransom,
>> Ethiopia and Seba in exchange for you.
> Because you are precious in my sight,
>> and honored, and I love you,
> I give people in return for you,
>> nations in exchange for your life (Isa. 43:1–4,
>> NRSV).

2. GUILT, SELF-HATRED AND DEPRESSION

Nearly all child victims will experience bouts of self-hatred and depression either during or after the disclosure of sexual abuse. Because they conclude that their parents hate them or even that God hates them, abused children will often hate themselves. And children who hate themselves very often hate others. They are often self-destructive and may make suicidal gestures or attempts.

Another common injury in sexual abuse is the intense guilt feelings that follow disclosure of sexual abuse. The enemy works hard to get children and adults to feel shame and guilt even from things over which they had no control. They reason: If these things happened to me, I must somehow have deserved or allowed them. Therefore, I am to blame for them happening. This must be because I'm bad.

Frances Porter reports that children who have been sexually victimized usually experience guilt on three levels:

> a. *Responsibility for the sexual behavior.* Many child victims feel as if they are responsible for the sexual activity which took place. By definition, the sexual abuse was initiated by an adult or by someone who occupied a power position over the child. Nevertheless, the children tend to feel guilty about their participation as soon as they perceive the societal response to their sexual activity. . . . Amazingly, the perpetrator's assertion that a seductive child is responsible for the sexual behavior is often given credence by judges, attorneys, police officers, physicians, social workers and the like.
> b. *Responsibility for disclosure.* Almost invariably . . . child sexual abuse is treated as a secret by both the perpetrator and the victim. When the secret is disclosed by the child victim, he or she is obviously responsible for the disclosure.

c. *Responsibility for disruption.* Disclosure of child sexual abuse can be expected to cause profound disruption for the victim, the victim's family and the perpetrator. In intra-family child sexual abuse, the disruption is even greater. If the child was directly responsible for the disclosure, he or she can be expected to feel guilty about the disruption that follows which (in all likelihood) will be greater than anticipated by the youngster.[12]

Counselors must first help the child to identify his or her guilty feelings and to understand that he or she can *never* be held responsible for sexual activity with an adult or an older person. The child must also be repeatedly and consistently assured that he or she cannot be held responsible for "telling" on the perpetrator or for any disturbance following disclosure. The child needs to know he or she had a right to expect protection, not abuse, from the adult, no matter who it was, and that he or she was right in revealing the secret of the inappropriate sexual activity.

It is possible that the child does bear responsibility for some behavior. Occasionally an older child victim may become manipulative or seductive as a result of a favored position with respect to the perpetrator and may behave very inappropriately. While such behavior may be part of the child's unconscious coping strategy, he or she may also experience some appropriate guilt feelings. The sensitive counselor must help them to make such distinctions.[13] We must remember though that it is no more helpful to absolve a youngster of appropriate guilt feelings than it is to ascribe guilty responsibility inappropriately. Even child victims must take responsibility for any of their actions or reactions which may have been sinful.

All sin must, of course, be admitted and confessed to the Lord. And God's promise of forgiveness is sure (1 John 1:9). But hurting people need to be led very gently to deal with any sinfulness of their natural reactions. It is preferable to focus on the freedom Jesus offers to those who want release.

> Something beautiful, something good.
> All my confusion, he understood.
> All I had to offer him was brokenness and strife,
> but he made something beautiful of my life.[14]

3. ANGER AND HOSTILITY

An inevitable byproduct of physical pain and fear is anger. Abused children typically are enraged children. They have learned to suppress or control their rage and often express it only in indirect ways through a variety of behavior symptoms, including expressions of anger at weaker and more helpless beings than themselves, such as younger children and animals.[15]

Although they may appear outwardly passive and compliant, most child sexual abuse victims are inwardly seething with anger and hostility. First, victims are angry at the perpetrators who abused and exploited them. They are also angry with parents or family members who failed to protect them from the sexual abuse or, in some cases, may have set them up to be abused.[16]

During counseling, it is important to affirm the child's right to be angry and even unforgiving. Anger is a very effective motivator. Righteous anger, a feeling that something must be done to right a wrong, can be very healthy. It can lead to wise decisions, such as getting help, identifying the abuser and holding the abuser accountable for what he or she has done. Moreover, sexually abused children have been badly wounded, and affirming the fact that their feelings are appropriate can be very freeing. Many Christians have been led to feel that the anger itself is sinful. This is not the case, as we can learn from Ephesians 4:26: "If you become angry, do not let your anger lead you into sin, and do not stay angry all day. Don't give the Devil a chance" (*Good News Bible*). God even allows us to be angry at him. God knows we don't understand. With our human limitations, we probably would not understand even if God explained things to us. And God doesn't.

God doesn't deny our right to choose even a reaction that God knows will be damaging. The problem is not with the angry reaction. It is with *keeping* the anger. God, knowing that keeping anger will damage us badly, has made it possible for us to give him our right to anger and revenge. God simply invites us, saying in essence, "Give me your burden. Keeping such burdens as anger, bitterness and unforgiveness will enslave and destroy you." When he says, come to me with your heavy burdens so I can give you rest (Matt. 11:28; 1 Pet. 5:7), he has burdens like this in mind.[17]

One other point. We must not confuse anger with hatred. Anger is a sign that we are alive and well. Hatred is a sign that we are sick and need to be healed. Healthy anger drives us to do something to change what makes us angry; anger can energize us to make things better. Hatred does not want to change things for the better; it wants to make things worse.[18]

4. INABILITY TO TRUST

Obviously a child who has been sexually abused by someone he or she knew and trusted will have difficulty in developing new trust relationships. The inability to trust is directly linked to the victim's low self-esteem and past experiences of betrayal.

Part of the mistrust of abuse victims will extend to God. Opening ourselves to God requires vulnerability, acknowledging our dependence on and need for God. Victims of abuse frequently have learned to cope by not needing others. The essence of our relationship with God is that we are to be his children. Children who lose parts of their childhood due to abuse have a very difficult time seeing their heavenly Father as someone they can trust. Counselors may be surprised that abused children with whom they work may not respond immediately and openly to their kindness, love and good intentions. Clay Jorgensen notes that

> where their abuse has been severe and prolonged, such children cannot afford the trust that this responsiveness demands. They have pent-up rage that cripples their ability to respond to love. They are children without self-respect, empathy for others, or the anticipation of reward that would enable them to appreciate others' good intentions. They have come to see people as being dangerous, undependable, and unrewarding—and they react accordingly.[19]

A further cause for mistrust is confusion on the part of the child. The child is confused not so much because he or she is abused but because the abuse is unpredictable. We have to understand the context in which the child experiences abuse. Jorgensen points out that

> the child usually does not have a background of experience with consistent, safe, nurtured life against which to judge

155

the abuse to be unusual, aberrant or undeserved. The child experiences the abuse as painful, frightening and confusing, but cannot see (as we do) that it is something outside of himself, something that is aberrant.[20]

Many abused children have been in a figurative if not literal life-and-death struggle. Trusted caregivers have been capricious and unpredictable. The absence of abuse for a time may merely be an undependable period of relief until they are hurt again. "Children cannot appreciate until they can feel appreciated, they cannot trust until the world is predictable, and they cannot love until they feel both lovable and loved."[21]

> How long, O LORD? Will you forget me forever?
>   How long will you hide your face from me?
> How long must I bear pain in my soul,
>   and have sorrow in my heart all day long? . . .
> But I trusted in your steadfast love;
>   my heart shall rejoice in your salvation.
> I will sing to the LORD,
>   because he has dealt bountifully with me (Ps.
>   13:1–2a, 5–6, NRSV).

FEAR, CONCERNS FOR SAFETY

All child victims of sexual abuse can be expected to be fearful of the consequences of the sexual activity as well as the disclosure. Sexually abused children have had their sense of safety violated at the deepest levels. They may be afraid of further abuse before disclosure, as well as reprisals once the secret is revealed. Victims should be helped to identify their fears and be encouraged to express them and to vent their feelings.

In recovery a sense of safety must be restored. Children need to grow in their ability to experience a shift from unpredictable danger to consistent, reliable safety. Abused children need to learn who "safe" people are and when and where they can experience safety and protection. A safe person is someone who is consistent, respectful, has a good sense of self and has healthy boundaries.[22]

He who dwells in the shelter of the Most High will
    rest in the shadow of the Almighty.
I will say of the LORD, "He is my refuge and my
    fortress, my God, in whom I trust. . . .
He will cover you with his feathers, and under his
    wings you will find refuge;
For he will command his angels concerning you to
    guard you in all your ways; . . .
"Because he loves me," says the LORD, I will
rescue him; I will protect him, for he acknowledges
    my name.
He will call upon me, and I will answer him; I will
    be with him in trouble, I will deliver him and
    honor him (Ps. 91:1–2, 4a, 11, 14–15).

FORGIVENESS—THE ONLY WAY TO CHANGE THE PAST

One mistake made by inexperienced counselors of sexually abused children is to minimize the amount of work involved in effecting spiritual healing. "Just pray about it and forgive," they glibly advise. Unfortunately, sexual abuse wounds are so deep that such counsel sounds trivial and meaningless. Worse, it may be nonproductive or dangerous. On the other hand, counselors also must not make the opposite mistake—that of trivializing prayer and forgiveness. Fundamentally, the long-term spiritual healing of sexual abuse is forgiveness and letting the Savior wrap loving arms around its victims to heal the inner wounds. Sometimes psychological healing may have to take place before spiritual healing can begin. But spiritual healing may also be the trigger for psychological healing.

Sexual abuse is an offense so personal and deep that it requires the serious work of forgiveness. It turns up the heat a bit when the abuse comes at the hands of those whom the child has a right to trust the most—parents or caregivers. Nothing cuts more deeply. Tender personalities can scarcely bear such treachery.

But what is forgiveness? The child needs to know that forgiving is not being weak—it takes incredible strength. Forgiving is not excusing. Excusing is just the opposite of forgiving. Excusing is for people who can't control what they do, even if it hurts someone.

That person needs help, not forgiveness. Forgiving is also not tolerating. We can forgive someone almost anything, but we cannot tolerate everything. The child should understand that though he or she may forgive the perpetrator, he or she will never again tolerate what the perpetrator has done.

Forgiving is also not forgetting. We are only human. If we can forget, there is no need to forgive. Forgiveness is needed precisely because we cannot forget what the perpetrator has done; our memories keep the pain alive long after the actual pain has stopped.

> The pains we dare not remember are the most dangerous pains of all. We fear to face some horrible thing that once hurt us, and we stuff it into the black holes of our unconsciousness where we suppose it cannot hurt us. But it only comes back disguised; it is like a demon wearing an angel's face. It lays low for a while only to slug us later, on the sly. ... Once we have forgiven, however, we get a new freedom to forget. This time forgetting is a sign of health; it is not a trick to avoid spiritual surgery. We can forget because we have been healed.[23]

Forgiving is being realistic. "To be able to forgive we must have the guts to look hard at the wrongness, the horridness, the sheer wickedness of what somebody did to us. We cannot camouflage; we cannot excuse; we cannot ignore. We eye the evil face to face and we call it what it is. Only realists can be forgivers."[24]

Forgiving is like spiritual surgery inside the child's soul. It is cutting away the wrong that was done and letting it go. Just as the child would open his or her hands and let a trapped butterfly go free.[25]

One objection to forgiving abusers of children is that the abuser's wickedness is so profound that they must not—cannot—be forgiven. But the truth is that even "monsters" must be forgiven—not for their sake, but for the child's sake:

> If we say that monsters are beyond forgiving, we give them
> a power they should never have. Monsters who are too evil
> to be forgiven get a stranglehold on their victims; they can

sentence their victims to a lifetime of unhealed pain. If they are unforgivable monsters, they are given power to keep their evil alive in the hearts of those who suffered most. We give them power to condemn their victims to live forever with the hurting memory of their painful pasts. We give the monsters the last word.[26]

Lewis Smedes has said that forgiving is the only way to change the past. Although we cannot change the actual event, we can change how it affects us. Forgiving is also the only way to keep the hurt from polluting the present and poisoning the future. Until the abused child forgives, he or she will be tormented each day with the hurt the child still feels. Forgiving is the only way to set the prisoner—the abused one—free.

Forgiving is love's revolution against life's unfairness. When we forgive we ignore the normal laws that strap us to the natural law of getting even and by the alchemy of love we release ourselves from our own painful past. Every human soul has a right to be free from hate.[27]

The souls of sexually abused children need that freedom.

Notes

[1] "Children at Risk: Statement of an International Consultation at Oxford," January 1997, printed in *Transformation* (April/June 1997).

[2] Marlene Du Plessis, untitled notes of the RP Clinic in Johannesburg, South Africa, presented in the Children's track of GCOWE 97.

[3] Charles Kraft, *Deep Wounds, Deep Healing* (Ann Arbor, Mich.: Servant Publications, 1993). p. 37.

[4] Marily A. Fling-Ganje and Patricia McCarthy, "Impact of Childhood Sexual Abuse on Client Spiritual Development: Counseling Implications," *Journal of Counseling and Development*, vol. 74 (January/February 1996), p. 254.

[5] Ibid., p. 254.

[6] Du Plessis, notes.

[7] Kraft, *Deep Wounds, Deep Healing*, p. 113.

[8] Frances Sarnacki Porter, Linda Canfield Blick, and Suzanne M. Sgroi, "Treatment of the Sexually Abused Child," in Suzanne M. Sgori, *Hand-*

book of Clinical Intervention in Child Sexual Abuse (Lexington, Mass.: Lexington Books. D. C. Heath and Company, 1982). p. 113.

[9] Kraft, *Deep Wounds, Deep Healing*, pp. 176, 177.

[10] "I Am a Promise" words by William J. and Gloria Gaither, copyright 1975, William J. Gaither, Inc. All rights reserved. Used by permission.

[11] Katheryn Goering Reid, with Marie M. Fortune, *Preventing Child Sexual Abuse* (New York: United Church Press, 1989), p. 62.

[12] Porter et al., "Treatment of the Sexually Abused Child," pp. 115, 116.

[13] Ibid., p. 117.

[14] "Something Beautiful" words by Gloria Gaither, music by William J. Gaither. Copyright 1971, William J. Gaither, Inc. All rights reserved. Used by permission.

[15] E. Clay Jorgensen, *Child Abuse: A Practical Guide for Those Who Help Others* (New York: Continuum, 1990), p. 37.

[16] Porter et al., "Treatment of the Sexually Abused Child," p. 120.

[17] Kraft, *Deep Wounds, Deep Healing*, p. 154, 155.

[18] Lewis B. Smedes, *Forgive and Forget* (New York: Pocket Books [Division of Simon and Schuster], 1984), p. 39.

[19] Jorgensen, *Child Abuse*, pp. 29, 30.

[20] Ibid., p. 34.

[21] Ibid., p. 31.

[22] Ann Noonan, "A Healing Environment for the Sexually Abused," in Phyllis Kilbourn, *Healing the Children of War* (Monrovia, Calif.: MARC Publications, 1995), p. 121.

[23] Smedes, *Forgive and Forget*, pp. 60, 61.

[24] Ibid., p. 179.

[25] Ibid., p. 45.

[26] Ibid., p. 107, 108.

[27] Ibid., p. 126.

12

Involving Families and the Church in the Healing Process

Janey L. DeMeo

Jerome's face contorted with hatred. The endless stream of tears falling down his face and sliding into the bitter lines were rivers of hopelessness. His frail body did not resemble that of a 22–year-old man. He was gaunt—not from malnutrition but from weariness. He was worn out by injustice. The deep creases of despair on his face made him look old in contrast to his body language, which reflected the movements of a small and frightened child. Jerome's only dream was to return to childhood and live the carefree life of a normal child. Since this was impossible, Jerome talked of suicide, for the awful childhood memories locked in his heart tormented him daily.

Jerome, along with several other emotionally scarred, abused people, told his distressing story on a French TV talk show. For 10 years, between the ages of 4 and 14, Jerome was raped regularly by a social worker. Today he is plagued by the damaged self-image of a little boy who was seen as unworthy of love, and whose body was considered a useful tool for the self-gratification of a perverted adult.

Tragically, millions of sexually abused children live in this world—many of whom will not even receive sympathy in their adult years or ever be given an opportunity to heal. They desperately need our help to bring them healing and hope, spiritually, physically and emotionally.

COMPONENTS OF HEALING

Holistic healing must address the spiritual needs caused by the child's deep wounding as a result of sexual abuse. Through prayer, love, God's Word, counseling, godly discipline and forgiveness, children can be set free from the assumed guilt, pain and fears of their traumatic experiences of sexual abuse.

Prayer

If families are to expressly help molested or sexually exploited children, they must learn true intercession. This answer might sound simplistic or a "hyper-spiritual" response to a real physical and emotional problem. It is not. Although molestation is carried out by the flesh of sinful persons, it is nonetheless rooted in the demonic kingdom. It is sent to destroy children's lives and their potential faith in God. The destruction of Satan's stronghold begins with us on our knees. As we pray, we not only tear down the fortresses of fear, hatred and guilt imprinted in the soul, but more practically speaking we open ourselves to be used by God as a tool to bring healing.

Prayer, as a vital part of healing, is key to opening the child's heart. No amount of empathetic counseling, love or other attempts to usher in healing have full effect without prayer. When I use the word *prayer*, I am referring specifically to intercessory prayer-pleading on behalf of the suffering child.

Perseverance in love

It may take years before we see the fruit of our labors in ministering to the abused child. But it is worth it.

Kevin lay bruised and terrified, his tiny body curled up in the corner of a prison in Manila. Fortunately, the four-year-old was taken to a children's center for help. At first, no one could go near him. He would jump at the least sign of contact and refused to eat.

162

His inner wounds were too great. He was especially afraid of men because of the abuse he had known. It seemed he would never heal, never be normal.

Today, Kevin runs and plays with the other children. He accepts the loving touch of several women. He smiles to see his teddy. Thanks to Jesus, Kevin is healing.

What is bringing about the miraculous change in Kevin in spite of his traumatic experiences? I believe that because some people were available to be Jesus' arms and voice, Jesus himself reached into the heart of this little child. Some people were willing to be available channels for the One who is the personification of love and who is the great healer, our God. More specifically, one man gave up his whole life to help children like Kevin in the Philippines.

One person, whether parent or concerned worker, can make a great difference in the abused child's life. But our effectiveness increases if we prayerfully involve other mature Christians. As we communicate the burden to them, they can also pray, minister to the hurting children and build us up. Many parents and child-workers would agree that ministering to hurting children can be exhausting. Sometimes we feel overwhelmed, as if our hearts will burst with the burden. The provision during those fragile moments is often seen in the body of Christ as other loving Christians may hug us through their prayers and embrace us back to life through their encouragement.

As Queen Esther's maidens, in the biblical story, upheld her in her mission, the church should also ideally become a divine support group for our ministry to hurting children. Caring, prayer partners are needed!

God's Word

"You have magnified your word above all your name" (Ps. 138:2b, *Amplified Bible*).

God esteems his Word above his name because it has the power to heal and transform. God's name speaks of who God is, of God's nature. God's Word is the means by which we become like God, because it imparts God's nature to us. To be healed the abused child needs to know God's nature. He also needs God's nature at work in him to reestablish the trust that has been so brutally destroyed. Only God's Word transforming and healing the child's broken heart can evoke confidence and rebuild trust. Healthy family and church life provide both the teaching of the Word and fellowship, both vital to the healing process. "He sent out his word and healed them" (Ps. 107:20a, *NRSV*).

The Bible is filled with verses linking healing with the Word of God. The psalms portray the power of the Scriptures to console in the midst of suffering. Psalm 119 depicts God's Word as the source to deliver the soul from dreadful memories. The application of biblical truth, preceded by prayer, can convert the child's heart and ultimately deliver him or her from morbid memories. The family must teach children the Scriptures to see them healed from the inside out. God's Word is key.

The family, whether biological or surrogate, must be careful to keep confidentiality about the children's problems. To be labeled "the molested children" in people's minds will only give them fresh wounds. We must not look at children in this way but rather as new creatures in Christ, teaching them that "everything old has passed away; see, everything has become new!" (2 Cor. 5:17, *NRSV*). A steady diet of scriptural truth will gradually, progressively give children a brand-new self-image and heal their innermost parts.

Counseling

How then does a family counsel wounded children? Often we initially counsel through acts rather than words. We must begin by loving them, listening to them, sitting with them patiently for hours, winning their broken trust and teaching them God's Word. We must not force them to share their bad experiences. It may be helpful, however, to create stories that reveal or shadow the children's own situations. This strategy could help them when they feel ready to talk.

The counselor, however, should talk about the child's trauma, explaining specifically that the violent adult was wrong, that what happened to the child was not right or normal and that the child, in most cases, is unequivocally blameless. Helping to remove the blame and guilt from children is among the most important aspects of counseling. After establishing that the children are not to blame for what happened, children should be the ones to bring up any communication about their experiences as they choose.

As I have pointed out, prayer and God's Word are the primary keys to healing. They lay the foundation for a child's spiritual growth. Intercession opens the heart so that the power of the Word can penetrate and heal. It also opens our hearts to hear from God and to become a source of healing by using the right words. Our words are weighty and vital to healing; they must not be spoken without thought and prayer.

Children especially need our time, affection, silence, tears, tender words and open expressions of love. Affectionate physical contact is also important, provided the child is not repulsed by this demonstration of affection. Tenderly hugging the children, without expecting anything from them, and repeating that they are loved will assist in their healing. Praying with the children, helping them to pray and talk to God and reading Scriptures to them are crucial keys to their healing.

In summary, love is spelled T-I-M-E. This kind of love promotes healing. Healing takes time, prayer, persistence and patience.

Biblical discipline

Contrary to popular thinking, correct, biblical discipline must not be avoided. Loving discipline is just as important—if not more important—for the equilibrium of the abused child as it is for any child. Many people are so afraid of hurting exploited children that they do not correct their misbehavior. The wounded child is already unbalanced and perturbed and quickly becomes totally unstable and often violent or self-destructive if not disciplined. Abused children must learn that, although they have been victimized, they cannot be excused from their own personal sin.

Children also must learn personal accountability through gentle but firm, loving discipline. I would highly recommend finding creative forms of discipline rather than corporal ones. The idea is to show the children where their boundaries lie and to guide them into respect for boundaries. This accountability is never achieved through harsh methods. Loving discipline is proof of love and protection.

Forgiveness

At the beginning of their healing process, the children's pain is too great and their knowledge of Christ too small to entertain the idea of forgiveness. When children have come through a measure of healing, we can talk to them about forgiveness. Forgiveness brings forth great healing, setting children free from hatred. They are released to forgive and are no longer prisoners to negative emotions. Children who are able to forgive reveal spiritual maturity and deep healing.

THE FAMILY AS A HEALING COMMUNITY

When a child is abused, family members and concerned helpers are the first line of defense in helping the child overcome his or her pain. The child has been damaged physically and (especially) emotionally. We must cater to the specific need for healing in both these domains, and perhaps the family has most opportunity for this part of the healing process.

Since maternal love is said to be the strongest of human sentiments, the suffering child must be as important to the mother in the home as her own child would be. The father in the home may have a lot to overcome in the child. A child abused by a father figure picks up the message that he must have somehow deserved such painful treatment. That child also will have great difficulty believing in a loving God as Father.

Families must understand that to the child his or her wounds seem incurable. Every family member will be called on for patience, wisdom and repeated acts of unconditional love. Tears and sweat and dying to selfishness—laying down our lives for each other—is God's chosen method. This principle of God's Word is never more important than in dealing with an abused child.

THE CHURCH AS A HEALING COMMUNITY

The sexual exploitation of children is one of the most cruel evils perpetrated on children. Children who are victims of such abuse are left with deep inner scars and often with damaged bodies also. Their pain is immeasurable. Their delicate emotions are forcefully plunged into deep despair, hopelessness, guilt, hatred, feelings of worthlessness and deep depression. On the human level there is no hope for these children. In Christ, however, there is every hope: Christ is the Great Redeemer, the Healer and the Father of Compassion. And we, the church, must bring this hope to them. We are Christ's body here on earth. We are his hands, his feet, his voice, and we must reach out to these hurting children and show his immense love to them. The church is called to be the functional family for hurting children.

Children are extremely close to God's heart. Jesus welcomed them and always found time for them, although his disciples did not understand this attitude (Mark 10:13–14). In spite of their innate sinful natures, children depict innocence. For this reason Satan hates them and delights in destroying their lives. Jesus tells us that we should imitate the faith of little children, because their trust and ability to believe are so pure (Matt. 18:3–4). It is no wonder the devil delights in destroying a child's capacity to trust and know God. Sexual exploitation is one of his greatest weapons used to this end. We must fight this epidemic with all our strength.

Pastoral Counsel

The man of God's involvement is described for us in 2 Kings 4. Elisha involved himself in the economic affairs of a poor widow, a woman's personal need for a child and consequently that child's healing. I highly encourage families, where at all possible, to involve their pastors in the healing of the sexually exploited child. It is important to have the pastor pray for the child and show loving interest in him or her. This can help eventually to open the child's heart to God, while enabling God to have greater access through more prayer support. I realize that in many cases this is not feasible. Some have no pastor. Others know pastors who misuse authority and lack compassion, like Elisha's servant. In these instances it is still advisable to seek some support from other Christians as we seek to become channels for healing.

"Why is my pain unceasing, my wound incurable, refusing to be healed?" (Jer. 15:18, *NRSV*). We—the families and the counselors—must understand that the child's wound seems incurable. I purposely use the word *seems* as I believe that, in time, God can heal even the deep scars of molestation. Much of that healing will depend on the sensitivity, spiritual maturity and scriptural wisdom of the families and counselors attempting to help the child. It will depend on how much we give God access to that child through prayer, compassion, specific strategy and wise counsel.

The children who have been victimized often feel as though their souls refuse to be healed. They feel much inward resistance to love when they have not been spiritually primed. They suspect people want to hurt them. Worst of all, they suspect God. Yet, according to the prophet Jeremiah, the deliverance of a damaged soul lies in being cleansed from suspicion toward God. The children's scar tissue will heal as they are able to look at Christ with full-fledged trust. Obviously, such a healing does not take place by waving a magic wand. It takes place through divine intervention as concerned people learn to seek God's face for the children, to intercede for them and to intervene on God's behalf through words, actions and clear-cut teachings on God's love.

Ideally, gently nurturing a child in a healthy church atmosphere creates a healing foundation. Christ said, "I will give you the keys of the kingdom of heaven; whatever you bind on earth will be bound in heaven, and whatever you loose on earth will be loosed in heaven" (Matt. 16:19). According to this verse Peter was given the keys to the kingdom to accomplish God's will on earth. God's will is to heal the hurting child. God has given us—the church—many keys to unleash his kingdom power on earth, to loose the power of healing on those who are hurting.

THE URGENCY OF THE CALL

At the time I wrote this chapter, Europe was grieving over a major case of child abduction for sexual exploitation in Belgium. I personally had been praying for eight-year-olds Julie and Melissa for a year. They had been missing for a year and a half when their bodies were found. For eight months they had been kept in an underground dirt hole and exploited by visiting pedophiles throughout the day. They actually died of starvation, because no one remembered to feed them for several weeks. This scandal is a picture of hell on earth. But I do not intend to highlight its horror. Rather, I would like to point out one thing, one tiny glimpse of hope, which may never efface the pain those children and their families went through in human proportions, but which may encourage us to keep fighting.

Since this case became a showcase to the world, Europe is becoming more severe in its treatment of pedophiles. The world is becoming conscious of its need to act to prevent sexual exploitation of children all over the world. This action is the result of prayer. Perhaps Julie's and Melissa's pain ultimately will serve to bring about the deliverance of millions of other children. We can and must hope so. Meanwhile, may God use our lives to prevent such affliction on little children.

Let us boldly take hold of the keys God has given us to be vessels of healing to others. There is a high price to pay, but it is worth it. There is no greater reward this side of heaven than to see a child delivered of pain, healed of inner scars and enjoying life as he or she walks hand in hand with the loving Savior. May we become the King's hands to the hurting children, bringing eternal healing balm.

"Whoever welcomes one such child in my name welcomes me" (Matt. 18:5, *NRSV*).

13

Empowering Sexually Exploited Children to Help Themselves

Robert C. Linthicum

Surang was a 15-year-old girl in a village far from the burgeoning capital of her Asian country. A man came to that village and told Surang that he had been sent by her older sister, who was working in a restaurant south of that city. She was in trouble, he said, and wanted Surang to come to her. In total innocence Surang believed the stranger's story and accepted his offer to escort her to her sister. She ended up imprisoned in a dingy brothel with 50 other girls in that city. Working each night from 7 P.M. to 4 A.M., and sometimes working days, Surang would service as many as 12 men in a row. The thought of escape tantalized her until she saw what happened to girls who tried. Those beaten into unconsciousness were the lucky ones. For three months Surang toiled in her unwilling prostitution. Then a police raid on the house put Surang in jail. From there she was taken by the police to an emergency home for women and girls rescued from prostitution.

Surang had been extricated from a fate seemingly worse than death. Yet, as I visited with her and observed her as she went about her chores at that home, I was struck by her demeanor. On the face of it, I would have expected her to exhibit signs both of relief at her escape from a life of prostitution and a determination to rebuild her shattered life. Instead, what I observed was an acquiescence, resignation and a compliance that was most alarming. Surang seemed to be withdrawing from life rather than engaging her future. Observing her attitude, I could only conclude that if her attitude did not change, she would eventually gravitate back into prostitution or end up living life victimized in some other way. And then it struck me—despite her rescue and opportunity for reclamation, Surang was exhibiting the classic signs of one who was still feeling powerless.

Rescuing sexually exploited children is not enough. Working for their reclamation is an inadequate response. Providing for the psychological adjustment of the children, their parents or family is insufficient. If attention is not given to the empowerment of such children so that they are able to assume responsibility for the rebuilding and redirection of their lives, then, like Surang, they are unlikely to become productive and effective parts of human society.

What is empowerment? And why is it crucial to the response of children to their sexual exploitation? The essence of any exploitation—whether economic, social, political, familial or sexual—is the overwhelming sense of helplessness. The children feel betrayed by those whom they have always believed can be trusted—parents, family, friends of the family or adults in general. They feel powerless to address the situation or to effect any change. They don't know whom they can trust. They can see no future for themselves, no hope, no possibilities. In other words, they feel thoroughly victimized.

Although I was not sexually exploited as a child, I knew what it meant to be thoroughly powerless, betrayed and unable to control my own future. When I was seven years old, I watched my father die of a heart attack. The only one to whom I could turn for safety, protection and comfort was my mother. But within three months of my father's death, that safety net was ripped away from me. My mother was involved in a near fatal trolley accident. It seemed unlikely that she would live. Faced with her own almost certain death, from her hospital bed my mother made me a ward of the

171

State of Pennsylvania—thus surrendering all legal right to me—and had me enrolled in a local orphanage. I was bundled up and with my limited possessions taken to live in that orphanage.

I will never forget my first night in the orphanage. Having delivered me to the orphanage, my older sister kissed me and walked out the door. I thought she had walked out of my life forever. (She hadn't.) I was stripped, given a medical examination, issued orphanage clothes and told to go out and play with the other orphans. Instead, I cowered in a corner of the playground, overwhelmed by the way my life had crumbled around me. A whistle blew, I was herded into a line with the other students, and we were marched off to the dining room for dinner, then to our studies. (I had nothing to study, so I just sat in a corner of the study hall trying to control my tears and fears.) Then we were all marched off to a dormitory shared by 35 orphans.

For the next ten years of my life I remained an unwilling resident in that orphanage. I marched everywhere in lines, obeyed orders, won a place for myself at the school through my academic and leadership skills, yet yearned for just one loving action or word.

Children who have had life tumble in upon them—whether from sexual exploitation, abandonment, natural or manmade disaster (such as warfare), or even choosing to run away from home to become a street child—no longer feel either protected or in control. There is no one they can trust to look after them. They feel inadequate to look out for themselves. They feel *powerless* or excluded from the decisions being made about their lives, and thus victims of the systems or conditions creating their dilemma.

How do they react to their powerlessness? In one of three ways. According to their personality and the external conditions of their lives, they will withdraw into helplessness, intimidation and fright; they will become hostile, angry and alienated; or they will create (or join) a reactionary culture that will be intentionally distinct from the majority culture. I chose the third alternative—I became a Christian at a decisively secular, humanitarian school—and I became a very aggressive, "in-your-face" Christian the school didn't know how to handle. Its dilemma provided me with a great deal of delight.

When the church or the helping agency seeks to address the conditions such a child faces by providing material or psychological support, but does not address the powerlessness issue, its action has two unintentional but highly destructive results for the child. First, it continues the sense of powerlessness rather than solving it, because it reinforces the child's sense of helplessness, lack of control and marginalization. Second, it treats the child as an object, rather than a self-determining subject of his or her own destiny, thus contributing to the child's lack of self-respect and self-assurance.

How can the church or the helping agency address the vulnerable child's sense of powerlessness? How can such groups work for the empowerment of that child? The biblical illustration of Nehemiah is helpful for enabling us to understand the principles of empowerment, even though the powerlessness faced in that situation was the helplessness of a nation and city rather than that of a child.

When Nehemiah determined to address the crisis facing Israel, he did not choose first to identify the primary problem faced by Israel or a course of action he would follow to solve that problem. Instead, he began by *listening* (1:1-3) He talked with people who were living in Jerusalem and were most directly affected by the vulnerability of destroyed walls. Out of that listening Nehemiah allowed his heart to be broken by the plight of the Jewish people, and out of that pain he wept, fasted and prayed (1:4-11). Nehemiah then *built networks* both with the powerful (2:1-10) and the people (2:11-16) so that, at the proper time, the issue of the broken walls of Jerusalem could be addressed.

Further, Nehemiah gathered the victims of Jerusalem together ("the Jews, the priests, the nobles, the officials, and the rest") and *got them to analyze their situation and to determine their own action* (2:16-20). They owned their own vulnerability regarding their collapsed walls and together considered the possibility of rebuilding the walls. Together, they made the corporate decision, "Let us start rebuilding" (2:18). They then *created their plan of action* (3:1-32). Incidentally, note there is no suggestion that Nehemiah formed that action plan; the text implies the exact opposite. Finally, they *implemented their plan,* carrying it out against massive opposition from the political and economic powers of Palestine and against intensive internal opposition (chapters 4-6).

So the wall was completed (6:15). The people gathered to *evaluate* and *celebrate* (chapters 8-10), and out of this corporate evaluation and celebration *took new actions* to rebuild the corporate life of the people (chapters 11-13).

What do we learn from Nehemiah concerning how empowerment of sexually-exploited or troubled children occurs?

The church or helping agency:

◆ listens to the children;
◆ builds relationships of trust with them;
◆ weeps with them over their pain and prays for them;
◆ works with the children in addressing their issues of powerlessness.

The children (with the guidance, help and support of the people of the church or helping agency):

◆ identify and share about their own problems;
◆ determine their own solutions;
◆ develop their own action plans;
◆ carry those plans to completion;
◆ celebrate their victory;
◆ evaluate both the results and what they have learned;
◆ tackle the next major problem.

How then does empowerment—whether of a slum, a church, an agency or sexually exploited children—occur? The process outlined above makes it quite clear. Empowerment occurs when people take charge of their own situation. No one—not even the best-meaning church or helping agency—can empower another person or group. People must assume responsibility for themselves to identify their own issues, determine their own solutions, develop their own action plans, implement the plans they have created, celebrate their victory, evaluate its results and then move on to the next (or related) issue they need to address. It is the process itself which empowers. And by its very nature that process is one that only can be done by the people themselves. The task of the church or helping agency is to help the process and people—to come alongside and shepherd the people by listening, unobtrusively guiding the people through the decision-making and implementing process, and by learning along with the people.

What are some of the strategies by which the church or the helping agency can work with sexually exploited children to empower them to help themselves? I can only write about those strategies that I have experienced. These are the strategies implemented by the Christian humanitarian relief and development organization World Vision over the past eight years in community-organizing efforts in major cities of the Majority World that led to the empowerment of sexually exploited or street or slum children.

ORGANIZING CHILDREN AND YOUTH

In Madras, India, World Vision worked for the empowerment of slum people through its "Organizing People for Progress" (OPP) project. The people in each of five slums were organized in three "associations": associations of women of all ages, youth associations for males ages 13 to 30, and children's clubs. These associations learned to hold the appropriate government offices accountable to maintain water pumps, care for the slum's public toilets, keep the drainage systems cleaned, keep the slum communities clean and dust-bins emptied, eradicate mosquitoes and supply electricity to the slums. The associations also developed their own programs of skills training; literacy; educational activities for children and youth; tuition-raising to enable community children to go to formal school and to get old-age pensions for the aged, bank loans for beginning small businesses and public health care and services. Youth associations particularly concentrated on skills training and sports, and the children's clubs supported youth and women's activities as well as concentrating on slum community cleanliness, moral education, organized sports and games. Each summer these slum communities would operate camps for the children, each normally having between 100 and 150 children in attendance.

Women from the associations began coming to OPP's women organizers to talk about family and marital problems, especially the drunkenness and brutality of their husbands. This led, initially, to an increasing load of personal counseling in which kingdom values were shared with the women in respect to their relationships.

175

But the concern was so great that the matter of community values (and especially male drunkenness) began to be discussed at association meetings. Out of such reflection these associations developed and executed plans of action to deal with the moral and ethical development of their slum communities.

On November 14, 1991, a particularly important event occurred in one of the slums in which the children participated in both planning and implementing roles. It was national Children's Day. On that day the children's club organized to hold a procession through this and a neighboring slum community, shouting slogans, carrying banners and posters, and seeking to raise consciousness about alcoholism, drugs and environmental cleanliness. Sample posters read: "Fathers, don't beat our mothers" and "Fathers, say no to alcohol." Over 200 children participated in this action. The result was such embarrassment for the men that drinking dropped significantly.[1] This action combined the efforts of the children, the women and the youth in substantively addressing a serious problem affecting that slum. The strategy used was one of mobilizing the newly emerging "people power" of the slum associations to work together in addressing a common problem. Children were not involved in the original formulation of the problem, because it was an issue to the wives of the community whose husbands were coming home drunk and acting abusively. But both the youth and the children were included in the planning process and then in the implementation of those plans. The result was one of both perceived and actual empowerment as drunkenness in the slum substantially decreased.

ADVOCACY AND SELF-DETERMINATION

On July 13, 1990, Law 8069-90, the Statute of the Children and Adolescents, was approved by the national legislative body of Brazil and became the law of the land regarding children and youth. It replaced the former "Underage" law and came about because of the pressure exerted over a considerable period of time by children's-rights groups, such as World Vision Brazil. The Statute of the Children and Adolescents is built on the premise that every child in Brazil has the right to preservation of the family, adequate health care, education, social policies that benefit the child, protection of children from harm, medical assistance, psychological and social assistance and legal services. This sweeping legislation is built upon three premises:

1. Children and adolescents have rights and obligations;
2. They are considered a special development group, needing direct attention;
3. They must be a decisive priority for the nation.

To guarantee both compliance and implementation of this law, the statute called for the formation of both formal and informal bodies to police and to participate in its implementation. Councils are the official legislative bodies at national, state and citywide levels; they are composed of equal government and private civic representation. "Fronts" exist to enable the people to act as advocates and as watchdogs to be sure government compliance to the statute is implemented.

On August 1, 1991, the police commander of Belo Horizonte (Brazil's third-largest city) authorized the violent arrest and imprisonment of 502 street children and youth of the city. Late at night the police swept through the city picking up the children, throwing them into detention camps and violently beating any who offered resistance or sought to escape. When World Vision Brazil heard of this flagrant violation of the statute it immediately, through the Belo Horizonte Front, brought nationwide attention to this violation of the law. As a result, the leaders of the Front (including World Vision) were asked to meet with the superintendent of the State Department of Justice.

The World Vision Brazil representative, as the main spokesperson for the Front, reported to the superintendent a vivid picture of the life of Belo Horizonte's street children, based upon his visiting with and interviewing the children and youth over the previous year. The superintendent, in turn, ordered the release of all the children who had been jailed and asked the Front to work with her in developing a preventive work-and-housing proposal for these street children.

Up to this point World Vision had been an advocate for the street children against forces with which the children couldn't cope. With the superintendent's request for the Front to work with her in addressing the issue of street children, however, the scene underwent dramatic change. The World Vision representative, a highly experienced community organizer, went to the street children and youth themselves and asked them to participate in the Front. They agreed to do so and elected specific children and youth as their representatives. These young street people joined community representatives, slum leaders and evangelical and Catholic pastors in the Front.

Eventually the Front became a powerful advocate for children's rights. The children and youth representing the now-organized street children of Belo Horizonte, together with natural community and church leaders, formulated, advocated for and supervised the implementation of citywide programs to provide opportunities for street children to be adequately housed and educated, to be protected from police harassment and to be provided with both jobs and job training.[2]

In this example the change of roles of the interventionist organization—World Vision Brazil—is particularly important to note. When the street children were vulnerable, unorganized and, consequently the victims of police brutality and illegal action, World Vision acted both on its own and in conjunction with the Front to bring national attention to this infraction of human rights. Once the crisis had been dealt with, World Vision accelerated the organizing of the street children (which it had already been doing for a year) to include the children and youth in the response to the justice superintendent's request that it help reformulate the Front to enable it to work with her in bringing about justice for the street children. With this action the street children gained a voice in the decisions being made about them and, through the Front, could become a strategic force in advocating for their own welfare.

ECONOMIC DEVELOPMENT

In 1993 World Vision Zimbabwe began working intentionally with street children in the capital city of Harare. As the community organizers met with children, the most-often mentioned concern was finding work. Zimbabwe faces a serious job shortage, with over 300,000 youth a year entering a job market that can only supply 10,000 new jobs. The government reports that to address unemployment adequately the nation's economy would have to grow at the rate of over 10 percent annually; in reality, the growth rate is closer to 3 percent. So, for poorly educated street children to find work in the formal sector is an impossibility. All that is open to them for generating income upon which to live is to beg, steal or sell themselves into prostitution.

When the children raised the issue of jobs as their most important concern, the community organizer of World Vision Zimbabwe challenged them not to look for jobs but to create them. The youth chose a unique market niche to create such work—Christmas and seasonal decorations in Harare hotels and public buildings. The youth successfully negotiated with a large Harare hotel to decorate the hotel for Christmas. World Vision helped the youth draw up appropriate contracts, set up adequate bookkeeping procedures, and develop their budding effort in a businesslike manner. They got the Anglican Cathedral to provide space for their design and production units, and these street children began making the Christmas decorations.

To the surprise of all but the children, the decorations were extremely creative and artistic. They became an instant hit. Before long this little informal business run by street children had expanded its customer base to include many of the hotels and public buildings of Harare.

Out of the continued success of this venture additional street children have been trained in income-generating activities, and other businesses have been generated by these youth. Sixty street children have been trained in community theater. Ten budding theater production groups have sprung into being, building human development, self-esteem, personal growth, cooperation and a sense of empowerment through the plays the children write, produce and present. Camps throughout the year temporarily remove the children from the streets to hone job skills; to involve the children in environmental studies, Bible study and prayer; and to participate in sports and recreation in a safe retreat setting.[3]

It is intriguing, in the examination of this strategy, to see the role World Vision played in the empowerment of these street children. The children selected the business or activity they would corporately pursue. They were responsible for doing all negotiations and making all arrangements with the businesses and other partners in Harare. And they were responsible for producing, marketing and distributing their products.

World Vision did not "rescue" them. What World Vision did was mentor them, provide training for them in business development and surround them with a community of youth and adults that gave them the safety they needed to develop these businesses successfully. And the result was the empowering of Harare's street children.

In the accounts presented above we have seen how a helping agency has enabled street or slum children and sexually exploited children to empower themselves and thus to experience more fulfilled lives. The specific strategies were determined by context and by issue, and included organizing, advocacy, creating a political voice and economic development. Numerous other strategies not examined here are equally valid. But underlying all these strategies are common assumptions. These include:

1. Reclaiming exploited children will not occur unless they take charge of their own situation. In the final analysis, the people who can best deal with a problem are those who are most affected by that problem. And what is true of the poor, the politically oppressed, the marginalized or the economically exploited is also true of sexually exploited children. Precisely because they feel so powerless as a result of their sexual exploitation, they will never feel truly liberated until they themselves have dealt with both their exploitation and the conditions that lie behind that exploitation. People, churches, helping agencies can come alongside them, encourage them, be their advocates and even negotiate for them. But the children will continue to feel powerless until they have dealt with their exploitation themselves. That is what street children, organized all over the world, have demonstrated decisively both to themselves and to society in general. Children are quite capable of generating considerable power if they know how to mobilize for action and how to use power.

2. Sexually exploited children can take charge only by acting corporately. There have always been two kinds of power throughout history—the power of money and the power of people. One of the realities of life is that the power of money often wins battles but rarely wins wars. Every revolution has been the result of collective

180

people power. The empowerment of people emerges through collective action and reflection.

Action provides the opportunity to act corporately on one's condition, to confront the forces that have caused the people's misery, to address and resolve their issues and to win back their rights and dignity as human beings. Reflection provides opportunity for the people to encourage each other in their mutual condition, to discern the forces that have created their powerlessness and marginalization and to learn from and evaluate the actions they have taken to liberate themselves. But whether action or reflection, it is collective activity that causes people to feel empowered. And this idea is as true of sexually exploited children as it is of any other group that has experienced sustained powerlessness.

3. The task of the helping agency is to encourage and support the children, to provide technical assistance and to be mentor and trainer. The agency can advocate, defend, encourage, provide support and training, partner with the children and, in particular, use its influence to bring worldwide attention to the issue of the sexual exploitation of children. But the helping agency can't do the work that the child needs to do for himself or herself.

When the church or helping agency becomes aware of the sexual exploitation of children, its tendency is to rush in and initiate projects to meet the discernible manifestations of such powerlessness—provide housing, food, education, safety, health care, security. The helping agency often does not recognize, however, that undertaking only those ministries addresses only the manifestations of the problem and not the problem itself. The real problem has been the aggrandizement of the children both by adults more powerful than themselves and by international economic and political systems that have used those adults to benefit from the exploitation of these children.

The children will have a hard time confronting the international economic and political systems. Here the work of advocacy and public exposure by the helping agency is very strategic. But the children themselves must address together the direct realities of their sexual exploitation, the rebuilding of their lives and, when possible, the bringing to justice of those who are directly responsible for their condition. If the children do not do this, they will always be recipients, dependents and victims. And that is because they have been treated as objects for care, not self-determined and competent subjects capable of molding their own destiny. So the primary task of the church or helping agency that ministers to sexually exploited children must be to enable those children to empower themselves.

We began this discussion by examining both the tragic story and the resulting helplessness of Surang, both during her sexual exploitation and during her stay at the home for girls rescued from lives of prostitution. I want to conclude by telling you about another such home dedicated to the same purpose in the city of Natal in Brazil's northeast. All 47 of the girls in this home have been sexually exploited; most have been prostitutes. Three of them had children. They were all between the ages of 7 and 16.

Whereas the atmosphere of the home in which Surang lives is grave and subdued, Casa Renascer in Natal abounds with life and joy. The girls were delighted that my wife and I could visit. They quickly organized themselves to present for us a drama they had written and were rehearsing. Through dance and drama they shared the trauma in their lives of sexual exploitation and their enthusiasm for rebuilding their lives. Casa Renascer has a full spectrum of programs both to equip these girls for life and to enable them to deal with the exploitation they have known. But what most struck me as I talked with the girls about their hopes and their efforts to rebuild their lives was the power of the place. They were not defeated, hopeless girls. These were energetic, effervescent girls with a future. They were taking charge of their lives. And they were not going to be defeated by the exploitation and perversion through which they once had suffered.

As Jeremiah promised to the Israelites living in Babylonian captivity, so God was saying to these girls,

> For surely I know the plans I have for you, says the LORD, plans for your welfare and not for harm, to give you a future with hope (Jer. 29:11, *NRSV*).

With all their determination, will and love, the girls of Casa Renascer were embracing that promise for their lives.

Notes

Some of the concepts expressed in this chapter were first articulated in the book Empowering the Poor *by Robert C. Linthicum (Monrovia, Calif.: MARC Publications, 1991).*

[1] *Evaluation Report: Organizing People for Progress-World Vision India* (Monrovia, Calif.: Evaluation Department, World Vision International, July 1, 1993), pp. 20-21.

[2] *Evaluation Report: Brazil Urban Advance Projects* (Monrovia, Calif.: Office of Urban Advance, World Vision International, December 15, 1994), pp. 29, 81-87.

[3] *Urban Advance Reports, World Vision Zimbabwe* (Harare, Zimbabwe: World Vision International Zimbabwe Office), reports for October 8, 1993; April 15, 1994; October 10, 1994.

14

Intervention Issues and Models: Prevention and Rehabilitation

Phyllis Kilbourn

M eo is a dancer and a prostitute in Pussy Galore bar in Patpong, Bangkok's biggest and most notorious red-light district, known worldwide as a mecca of sexual delights for foreign tourists. Meo despises herself. Meo was just 14 when her mother forced her to have sex with an old man to pay off her mother's gambling debts. This happened several times before Meo drifted to Bangkok and the bars. She now works in a sex show and keeps going by using alcohol and marijuana and sometimes sniffing heroin. Meo claims, "I'm no good for anyone or anything; this is the only life I'm good for."[1]

Sexual exploitation, whether through rape, incest by family members, pornography, cross-border trafficking or sex tourism, causes many physical, psychological and social problems and impairs all aspects of children's development. It is one of the worst violations of their basic human rights. The memory of the trauma may forever cast its shadow over the lives of victimized children. Along with deep psychological wounding, they suffer the deprivation of basic material needs and training or education. The children are often on their own—in an economic, an emotional and a personal sense. Their responsibilities and experiences exceed what could or should be expected of a child.

Compounding their trauma, the majority of the children in commercial sexual exploitation have found that their customers often mistreat them severely. In addition, they practice their job in an environment in which they are the least protected and in places that are characterized by a complete lack of sanitary facilities. One can only speculate on the influence such an environment, along with their experiences, has on the social, physical and emotional development of young children. Some psychologists would claim that children like Meo, who endure so much sexual abuse, can never be restored to emotional health or live normal lives. Furthermore, along with all the destructive consequences, unless the abused child is helped, there is a risk that the victim will turn into a perpetrator, abusing younger siblings or other children.

This chapter highlights some of the basic components of intervention planning for prevention and rehabilitation. These interventions look beyond the immediate needs of food and shelter—the place where too many interventions begin and end. Examples of successful rehabilitation programs are briefly explored to demonstrate how the components can be effectively utilized.

PREVENTION ISSUES

The first consideration in any intervention planning is prevention. We must constantly ask ourselves how we can prevent children like Meo from becoming victimized by sexual abuse. It would have been so much easier for Meo if the abuse had been stopped.

Understanding the problem

Finklehor points out four preconditions to sexual abuse that we must understand when working to prevent sexual abuse.

1. The first precondition assumes that perpetrators have a need for perverted sexual stimulation. However, it must be noted that while their sexual preference may not be by choice, they can, like all other adults, learn to control their desires and impulses.

2. The need for perverted sexual stimulation is not enough for sexual abuse to occur. Even perpetrators imbibe certain moral

185

values through parents, teachers, societies and churches. These help shape behaviors and inhibit desires and give the knowledge that hurting others is contrary to moral values. Therefore the second precondition to abuse is overcoming internal inhibitors.

Alcohol is effective in neutralizing internal inhibitors; so is pornography. Stress stemming from poverty, unemployment or other situations beyond one's control also removes internal inhibitors. A more dangerous form of overcoming internal inhibitors is rationalizing that such actions are not wrong but are also ways of experiencing "love" or of giving some form of "sex education."

Research has shown there are three components for developing internal inhibitors: the ability to empathize, the ability to manage anger and the ability to control impulses. Pedophiles usually lack these components but psychologists believe these skills can be taught. Thus teaching these skills is necessary when working to prevent violence. In addition to helping children heal from their trauma, they also must be helped to not assume the role of abuser.

The ability to empathize, manage anger and control impulses can be developed in the child by the family, the school and the church. The most important internal inhibitors are developed through socialization within the family. A strong family, therefore, is vital.

3. Overcoming internal inhibitors is still not enough to prevent child abuse. External inhibitors must also be overcome to sexually abuse a child. External inhibitors include the stigma attached should the victimization be discovered, perhaps losing a job or a certain position or even confronting punishment for the crime. Both the law and the church can act as external inhibitors, but advocacy that includes active involvement is vital because these external inhibitors can be overcome. The need to strengthen these inhibitors through advocacy is extremely important.

Given the usual conspiracy of silence, external inhibitors to an adult with the need for perverted sexual stimulation are extremely weak. If these are not strong, the offender will overcome them by threatening his or her victims. More often offenders develop relationships with children, making victims feel part of the abuse and thus discouraging them from disclosing it.

4. Keeping in mind the need to develop these relationships, the fourth precondition to sexually abuse a child is overcoming the

186

inhibitors placed by the child. This precondition is the rationale for providing preventive education among children. The family, school or church can provide this teaching. Developing these skills in children is important not only because of the weakened external inhibitors but also the high number of potential abusers, given the cycle of abuse, stress factors within society today, the disintegration of family structures and often the mixed signals from the church, society and family.[2]

Giving children the ability to prevent sexual molestation requires arming them with accurate information and developing their assertiveness skills.

PREVENTIVE EDUCATION

It is imperative that parents and all child workers warn children of the possibilities of abuse and teach them to avoid it. The following ideas help us to do this training.

1. Warn children that "bad people" exist and that they should never talk or approach anyone they do not know. It is wise to avoid letting children wear clothing with their names printed on it. A pervert may take this open door to call children by their names, making them believe they are known.

Children also must be warned that people they know or who are close to them also can hurt them. Be sure to instill in them, however, that there are loving adults who can offer positive and nurturing relationships. Care must be taken to ensure that trust is not totally destroyed.

2. Set clear standards of behaviors and role boundaries, establishing values of what is right and what is wrong. Definitions of actions are necessary. Children armed with a strong understanding of right and wrong will have the courage to act to protect themselves from abuse.

3. Set family safety rules, including how to answer the door when alone at home, not to leave the house after dark, not to go home with strangers for any reason and not to accept gifts from strangers when alone.

4. Teach children that certain parts of the body are private, that no one should ever touch them or ask to see them. Teach modesty. Likewise, if someone displays his body or touches himself in front

of a child, the child should run and find an adult. These are clear danger signs for a child to recognize. Teach them to be assertive in saying no.

5. Build support systems or external inhibitors around each child, such as trusted adults and peers.

6. Teach children how to report. Have them practice various modes, including through the telephone, directly or in writing.

7. Know where your children are; make them accountable to certain boundaries you feel are safe.

8. Never leave your children with strangers or people you scarcely know—no matter how "nice" they may seem. Children have even been abused by church members baby-sitting them.

9. Do not allow your children to wear immodest, provocative clothing.

10. Pray over your children and with your children daily for wisdom and protection.

PHAYAO GIRL CHILD PROJECT
Prevention Project

The Phayao Girl Child project is located in Phayao Province, Thailand, and run by World Vision.[3] Its purpose is to teach income-generating skills to vulnerable girls from poor families before they are lured into prostitution. Middlemen and entrepreneurs convince families to sell their daughters or entice the girls themselves to the city. Many of these girls have been encouraged by their parents to assist the family financially by going to the city, where they are forced into the flesh trade or some form of child labor.

The program's primary objectives are:

◆ To encourage parents not to sell their children. The program has a public awareness campaign to change the attitudes of parents and children. These campaigns stress the importance of keeping children in school and away from the dangers of the sex trade. Children are motivated to become self-reliant and to continue their education. The media also are used to stress the importance of keeping families intact and of not exploiting their children for profit. The campaigns are coordinated at the provincial level, organizing seminars and workshops to emphasize the importance of these issues.

◆ To provide the children with higher education opportunities, stressing education's importance in improving the quality of life for children and their families.

One part of the program provides girls with the chance to become self-sufficient. They learn to raise chickens and market both the chickens and the eggs. They receive formal education in agricultural development at a vocational training center. Through instruction and example they learn to create a future away from the dead-end path of prostitution that so many of their peers have chosen or been sold into.

The program has been successful in its short-term objectives. Since the girls have become involved in income-generating projects, or have received educational funding, workers have seen a drop in the number who normally would have left their homes and schools to go to the cities. Involving parents in the program, especially mothers, is seen as crucial to the program's success.

Long-term program developers hope that as the girls grow up and raise their own families, they will pass their ideals on to their children, hopefully making *Tok Kiew* a thing of the past. *Tok Kiew* is an agricultural term commonly used in Thailand in reference to a deposit for crop loans. Today, the same term is used in transacting "loans" for purchase of children. When a middleman shows interest in a girl of 9 or 10 years, the remainder of the agreed-upon loan is paid to the parents. Their daughter then must leave with the middleman to work off the payment. When this practice is abolished, childhoods will no longer have to be sacrificed.

COMPONENTS OF LONG-TERM INTERVENTION PLANNING

The problems in rehabilitating a sexually exploited child are so complex that there is no single right approach. The following components are vital to the holistic care of sexually abused children. A major goal of intervention planning is to place children in a supportive environment that allows them to escape their exploitative situations and restores a belief in themselves and their future—and in their abilities and worth as those created in the image of God.

Befriending

Before specific interventions can be successfully initiated, we must befriend the children. We must try to win their trust and get to know them as people—people with hopes, fears, pain, anxieties and a complexity of needs. This means being where they are and beginning with their perceived needs. Instead of sharing the gospel in a "preachy" manner, we need to incarnate the gospel for them. In the midst of developing friendships and trying to stay in tune with their struggles, we're presenting the truth that God really loves them.

Reintegration

Reintegration focuses on restoring the reality of childhood for children who have lost theirs through sexual abuse. This process of giving back, restoring, or reconstructing their lost childhood is crucial for children to regain a normal life. The first priority is to give children a physical and community environment that is conducive to the healing process. When the home situation is favorable, this process should include reunification with their families or, if needed, with a surrogate family.

Most caregivers of sexually exploited children view institutionalizing them as a flawed form of reintegration because it creates another form of dependency and a handout mentality that can further psychologically disable them. Institutionalizing children isolates them from the community support group that gives the affirmation and human support normally experienced by healthy children in a secure family. In a family setting children are encouraged to nurture their own abilities, talents and self-reliance; in an institution an abused child relies on the resources of the institution for sustenance.

In sexual exploitation the power or authority of someone stronger over someone weaker leaves children defenseless. Children no longer have a voice in what is happening to them, nor do they have power to stop the abuse. Therefore, a non-authoritarian model of rehabilitation restores and preserves the children's freedom of choice. This model is beneficial in healing the deep psychological scars afflicted by strong authority figures over them.

Supportive talking and listening

For most children a high degree of trauma results from coercive sexual exploitation. The stigmatization and loss of trust in adults often result in difficulty when developing relationships. The pain and anger resulting from the abuse, along with the loss of parental support and bonding, cause children to become withdrawn and noncommunicative. Instead of verbal communication, they often demonstrate their hostility and violence through actions and behaviors. Helping the children talk about their experiences can bring out genuine feelings of anger and even hatred that lie beneath the surface of consciousness. When their suppressed feelings erupt into conscious feeling and are expressed or verbalized, they can be analyzed and the root cause identified. Caregivers must give special support to children during these emotional outbursts, allowing the children to release their feelings of anger and pain in safe and natural ways.

Medical support

Sexually exploited children experience a variety of physical problems stemming from physical maltreatment, many sex partners, unavailable or inadequate medical attention, substance abuse and malnutrition. They are generally ignorant of general health care and safe sex practices, resulting in their vulnerability to sexually transmitted disease including HIV and AIDS. Pregnancy, being an occupational hazard, results in many botched abortions, even when into their fifth or sixth month of pregnancy, resulting in injuries and hemorrhaging. In bars and brothels the children are further exposed to poor lighting, loud music, cold air conditioning and the fumes of tobacco and alcohol. These factors contribute to constant colds, headaches and fever as well as suspected hearing, ear and skin infections.

Psychological healing

The psychological damages inflicted on children are the most difficult to detect and to heal. Enforced prostitution generally conflicts with the social values and behaviors of children. This conflict results in feelings of low self-esteem, lack of self-respect, loss of dignity and self-blame. It also leads to feelings of guilt and loss of trust in adults. Children often perceive themselves as "sinful, dirty and worthless" and become depressed and even suicidal. Society's neglect and nonrecognition of the plight of sexually abused children have further made the children think of themselves as worthless—now they can only be liked, accepted or loved if they allow their bodies to be used and abused. Sexually abused children may feel accepted or loved only by submitting to more sexual abuse. An approach that emphasizes affirmation, support and constant sensitivity to the psychological effects of childhood sexual abuse is essential. Children need to be affirmed as being of value and deserving respect as persons in their own right, even those who have lost their virginity.

Traumatized by constant rape and beatings, starved or tortured if they fail to comply with customers' demands, some girls are broken to the point where they may be unlikely ever to regain self-respect and dignity. Workers with these children need to develop a friendly and caring rapport, helping them rebuild their sense of personal dignity and self-esteem. Their feelings of isolation and rejection need to be replaced with feelings of self-worth, acceptance, understanding and self-confidence. As healing occurs, the children become more open, extroverted and natural in expressing their feelings and relating their experiences. The seeds of self-confidence and self-acceptance grow and enable such children to develop a strong personality and to take control of their lives.

Reconciliation and justice

A betrayal of trust is a major part of the long-term trauma suffered by the children. They often blame themselves for what has happened and are sometimes bitter against their own families even while wanting to be reconciled. With their history of injustice, sexually exploited children are naturally supersensitive to all expressions of hostility, rejection or unfairness. Quarrels and fighting among themselves are spontaneous in the early months of reintegration. It is important to see that children are given justice. In conflict, all sides must be heard and all aspects of conflict discussed with the children. They need to be encouraged to give their opinions and verbalize feelings. Reconciliation based on justice can only be reached in an atmosphere of understanding and the desire to make peace.

Alternative and sustainable income-generating activities

A serious attempt must be made to provide alternative and viable employment options for older children. Without such options a child, like 13–year-old Juliet living in a slum in Manila, has no way out of her life of prostitution, which provides needed support for herself and her younger siblings. Acquiring work skills that increase self-esteem and have potential to gain the respect of others and allow for eventual economic independence is essential. These skills can be acquired through non-formal education and vocational training. Protected work options, where children are able to study and still maintain some earning capacity, are also important. The children should be encouraged and supported in income-generating schemes on a cooperative or an individual basis. Working capital could be provided through a revolving loan fund. Loans need to be large enough to insure the economic viability and sustainability of the projects they will launch. To be successful, income-generating schemes must create products or capture niches that have a demand for the products or services.

As a prevention strategy, alternative incomes also may be needed for families that rely on their children's earning for survival.

Spiritual nurture and moral development

Children who have lost their sense of self-worth and have experienced so much rejection need to hear the good news of Jesus' unconditional love and acceptance, his willingness to forgive and restore and his longing to have them become a part of his family. In a Cambodian study of sexually exploited children,[4] faith in God was found to be important. Naree, one girl interviewed, stated she believes "in God as a person to relieve me of sorrows." Others mentioned taking their problems to God, and their experiences of church being of help in putting their past behind them. In contrast, where a center of faith and the strong support of other people were missing, recovery was slow.

Researchers in the study emphasize that children should be encouraged to seek sources of spiritual strength. The assurance of a God who will not condemn, or a system of values that affirms their worth, has been seen to be a lifeline for many children who have suffered this kind of exploitation. When children need to make decisions about their own lives, they should be encouraged to look to such sources as a basis for their decision-making and be affirmed in the process. A framework of strong moral values also gives hope for the future and diminishes the possibility of these young persons, in later life, abusing others in their care.

Legal issues

Children have a strong sense of justice, and the prosecution of the perpetrator can satisfy this basic need; it also grants the basic right of protection guaranteed a child. When children have initially worked through their trauma to the point where they feel confident and secure enough to pursue the legal prosecution of their offenders, they can find such action strengthening and therapeutic. The children and their families will need help in working through the legal issues involved. Along with sexual exploitation, there may be many other legal issues that need to be addressed, such as international regulations concerning cross-border trafficking of children or kidnapping.

Sometimes legal advocacy will be required. For example, public policy toward street children or others involved in prostitution for a livelihood often is expressed in terms of laws rather than development programs. Often these children are regarded as delinquents who must be arrested and sent to approved schools and other related custodial institutions such as juvenile remand homes. The official success in dealing with the problems is measured by the extent to which the police keep the children out of the streets and enclose them in approved schools and other related institutions.

Many children imprisoned for "crimes" or placed in corrective institutions may not only have to live in a very poor quality environment but also be exposed to further abuse by caretakers. This is particularly true for girls. The children are also deprived of the child-adult relationships and stimulations that are so important for child development.

LONG-TERM INTERVENTION MODELS

The following models were designed to meet specific needs to care for at-risk and traumatized children. The Ja Ela Model Care Home and the Ja Ela Retirement Home for Active Elders exemplify a creative way of combining two pressing needs in Sri Lankan society—sexually abused children and the elderly. The exciting aspect of this project is how these two populations benefit mutually. The New Beginnings program provides a residential rehabilitation program focusing on strengthening the family unit so children can be returned to healthy, nurturing homes. The Hagar Project creates self-sustaining, community-style living for at-risk children and their mothers. All of these projects have been successful because they have been tailored to children's needs in a specific situation. They are presented to stimulate your thinking about how to best meet the needs of those with whom you are working.

The Ja Ela Model Care Home
and the Ja Ela Retirement Home for Active Elders

Social workers in Sri Lanka are confronted with two major social concerns involving citizens on both ends of the age spectrum: young children who are sexually abused and the increasing elderly population. Through the Ja Ela Model Care Home, the Lanka Evangelical Alliance Development Service (LEADS) creatively formulated a strategy for these two vulnerable populations that provides mutual support and care. The Ja Ela Model Care Home is a creative way to provide one of the most basic and urgent needs of any child living in crisis situations—family. This project, using the natural link between the children and the elders of society in the process of reconstruction and healing, demonstrates how children can be helped by becoming receivers and givers in a family situation. The model also stimulates creative thinking in planning other strategies to meet the needs of sexually exploited children.

Elderly population

Sri Lankan society is now known as an aging society. Well-developed medical services have resulted in an increase in life expectancy. Yet there exist very few avenues of development for this group, or even of social support. Sri Lanka is on its way to acquiring an elderly population in a society not equipped to accommodate them. Without meaningful intervention, Sri Lanka's elderly population will live unproductive, less meaningful lives. Between the years 1991 and 1995 suicide rates for the elderly, according to a Central Statistics Report by the Sri Lanka police, registered a staggering 50 percent increase.

Sexual abuse of children

The second concern is for the sexual abuse of Sri Lankan children, especially because this beautiful island is a haven for homosexual pedophiles. Caregivers with LEADS recognized that many children needed more intensive and comprehensive rehabilitation, over an extended period of time, than their drop-in center would provide. Often the children do not have homes that provide even the basic security and structure from which therapeutic work with the child at a drop-in center can take place. The children also need help in reintegration into society. These needs can best be met in a therapeutic care home that offers long-term intensive therapy and support.

Caregivers further understood that the elderly were witnessing a change in family structure, from extended to nuclear families. This change created a need for a social system that would be "elder friendly," one that would enhance the quality of their lives and make provision to tap their resources. They also realized that the sexually exploited children they were attempting to help would benefit greatly from the support of "family members."

The solution

The idea was birthed to plan a holistic program that would fulfill the needs of both vulnerable groups of citizens. The resulting project embraces both the Ja Ela Retirement Home for Active Elders and the Ja Ela Model Care Home, called *Kedella* (meaning "nest") for sexually exploited children. What potential exists with this exciting blend of citizens!

The concept envisions young children receiving help and counsel from mature senior citizens, who become surrogate grandparents, extended family, to the children. Then, as the grandparents age, the children become the givers, assuring the elderly they are still loved and cared for.

Both facilities are located on the same premises to foster interdependency between elders and children, thus adding richness to an extended family atmosphere. The unique feature of the elders' home is the active participation of the elders in the functioning of the children's care center, especially in the teaching program, which is run in the education and vocational center. Elders themselves use this center to study and develop their own skills. They are encouraged to spend quality time giving and receiving from the young people around them.

To provide the best mentoring relationships between the youth and the elderly, the selection process of elders places a particular emphasis on elders who have spent their lives in community service. This focus is vital, because elders are expected to live and work in close proximity to the children, making it necessary for elders to be willing to participate in a community effort and to be available to the children.

A farm also benefits both groups of citizens by providing some of their food, giving children opportunities to learn "nurturance" through animal husbandry and providing small-scale funds. Informal learning and counseling also can occur during routine tasks performed together.

Comparing the goals for each home shows the richness of blending these segments of population. First, for the Ja Ela Model Care Home, Kedella:

1. To restore victims of sexual abuse, to enable them to live healthy lives.
2. To reorient and empower such children to get back into society as productive citizens.
3. To enrich their lives and give them holistic care that will enhance the quality of their future lives.

Second, for the Ja Ela Retirement Home for Active Elders:

1. To provide a care home that can serve as a model, one that offers opportunities for rich, active, meaningful lives.
2. To provide facilities for elders to have access to information and to keep abreast of the changing world, maintaining intellectual sharpness and mental agility.
3. To enrich and enhance lives of all in this community by fostering healthy interdependency—giving and receiving between the young people and the elders—to make it a place where the wisdom of the past meets the energy of the future and together form a powerful community of the present.
4. To provide a secure place for elders to spend their lives with the comfort of knowing that they will be taken care of, even when they can no longer make a contribution to this community. The children will continue to visit them and maintain relationships as the elders move from giving to receiving.

Kedella's program is directed toward the holistic development of the child. The following outline illustrates how the program is uniquely designed to meet the children's total needs.

- *Physical needs:* The children are nurtured in chalet-type homes by skilled and sensitive caregivers.
- *Psychological needs:* The therapy center, with therapist and support team, works according to an individual care plan in an environment conducive to recovery.
- *Educational needs:* In-house education center, library, tutoring programs, technical and vocational training are provided. (Senior citizens help in all the educational programs.)
- *Social needs:* Indoor games and outdoor sports, provision for creative expression (music, art, dance), excursions and family-oriented activities are provided.
- *Spiritual needs:* There are daily devotional and reflection times and weekly youth club meetings.
- *Medical needs:* There is an in-house medical facility.

Structure and functioning

The care home is structured so that each resident child belongs to a family unit, living with his or her family in a separate cottage. Each family unit consists of no more than five children and, ideally, a couple to act as parents. In the absence of a couple for each family, a single staff member is in charge and "foster parents" are trained and assigned to each "family." They are required to visit at regular intervals, take the "family" out, and spend time with the children so they will see how functional family members could relate to each other.

New Beginnings

New Beginnings seeks to promote the care, protection, rehabilitation and development of children to the fullest and to ensure that they have loving, Christian families. New Beginnings provides a residential and rehabilitation center for sexually abused girls age 15 and younger. The program attempts to begin the lifelong healing process that the trauma entails by providing the girls with as many positive reinforcements as possible. The center houses 20 girls, on average, for up to two years.

Rehabilitation programs are based on psychological test results. These programs are designed to suit the children's individual needs and preferences. The girls attend formal classes and receive individual and group counseling. They learn about their rights as children and are encouraged to seek redress in court. Therapeutic activities are used to contribute to their growth and recovery. Art therapy is a much-used tool to help the children express their feelings and develop marketable items. The author attended one of their art shows, which featured outstanding works of art. The event was attended by many dignitaries and received television coverage. The joy of accomplishment and recognition was evidenced in the children's happy faces.

Many cases of child sexual abuse in the Philippines are the result of incest. Therefore, a strong objective of New Beginnings is to strengthen families, to prevent—where possible—the long-term separation of children. An intensive counseling program for the parents is provided with follow-up before and after reintegration. Until such time as the children can be placed back in their home or an alternate living situation, foster care provides an alternative for the girls who need individual family care. A child resides with a foster family temporarily for about three months to a year. The child is treated like a regular family member and receives the affection and attention he or she needs. The foster parents act as surrogate parents to the children until they are placed in a permanent living situation where they can receive healthy nurturing.

Hagar Village: A Community Development Project

Children living in especially difficult circumstances—such as street children, refugees, children in armed conflict and disabled children—are particularly vulnerable to sexual exploitation. Living in unprotected situations, suffering from hunger and poverty, they are at the mercy of perpetrators and pimps. Special care must be given to empower this vulnerable group of children to survive without having to resort to prostitution.

One such project is the long-term rehabilitation program on Khor Kor Island in Cambodia. This program cares for the sexually abused child and also focuses on prevention of sexual abuse for at-risk children and their mothers who live on the streets of Phnom Penh.

Background to the problem

Even before the 1997 uprising in this tiny country, Cambodia had experienced more than 20 years of civil unrest, war and social upheaval. Economic development is slowly beginning, but primarily for those living in Phnom Penh. Eighty percent of the people in the country live in rural areas, where families struggle to make a living. Urban migration occurs with poor villagers leaving their homes for Phnom Penh in search of jobs, income or the basics to survive.

Consequently, most of those living on the streets in Phnom Penh are mothers and their children and unaccompanied children. Begging, prostitution and scavenging have become their professions. Forced migration to Phnom Penh has placed these children and mothers in difficult and vulnerable circumstances. Estimates show that 600 families and 3,000 children are living on the streets of Phnom Penh. In 1996 the National Public Radio reported that approximately 40 percent of all the prostitutes in Cambodia are children. Even items on the Internet advertise that in Cambodia "a 6–year-old is available for US$3."[5]

Non-government organizations (NGOs) and UN agencies report that abduction, trafficking in women and children, rape and child prostitution are also growing at a worrying rate. Local media report the abduction of young women, who are then allegedly sold into prostitution, on an almost daily basis.

Resettlement Plan on Khor Kor Island

In March 1994 YWAM began the Hagar Shelter Project in Phnom Penh to help strengthen and support families by providing assistance to mothers and children living on the streets. A key component of the program is skills training and reintegration assistance to help the family become self-sufficient in its community of origin.

YWAM also recognized the need for a resettlement plan that would meet the ongoing needs of children and mothers who would never be able to leave the Hagar Shelter and return to their community of origin. The government offered them thirteen acres of land on an island forty minutes from Phnom Penh. This leased land was for community development and to provide income-generation projects for homeless mothers and children. The eligible mothers were those who had successfully completed Phase 1 at the Hagar Shelter, including a vocational training course, and were unable to return to their home villages.

The island provides a community for these mothers to establish a home for their children and themselves. To prepare these families for a community-based village life, training in public health, assistance with basic human rights and other psychological preparation were provided. Plans are in place for ongoing evaluation and monitoring.

Objectives of the Khor Kor Community Development Project

♦ to ensure a smooth transition from shelter-based care to a rural community-based livelihood.
♦ to provide a basic community infrastructure for families, including housing, water and sanitation, irrigation, transportation (river crossing), and security.
♦ to facilitate social, economic and cultural development.

201

- to develop a self-sufficient and mutually supportive community.
- to develop long-term sustainability through agriculture, aquaculture, animal husbandry, and sewing and weaving.
- to help preserve and promote the natural resources of the environment.
- to provide ongoing counseling support.
- to facilitate educational opportunities for the children.
- to provide day-care facilities for children of working mothers.
- to provide ongoing health and hygiene education.
- to assist in establishing a community-based savings and loan scheme.

In this supportive and empowering community, sexually exploited children and mothers are finding healing and hope. Trusting, loving relationships are developed and are being sustained through community living.

CONCLUSION

These examples of successful interventions—both prevention and rehabilitation—demonstrate that creative holistic programs, along with liberal doses of love and patience, can be designed to help restore children who have been deeply scared by humiliating and emotionally wounding sexual abuse.

The prophet Jeremiah, observing the pain and suffering of his people, cried out in dismay:

> Is there no balm in Gilead?
> Is there no physician there?
> Why then has the health of my poor people
> not been restored? (Jer. 8:22, NRSV).

Jeremiah, unlike some caregivers who feel these children are hopelessly scarred for life, knew that healing for broken people, including children, is possible. He knew that God's name, *Jehovah Rapha*, means "the God who heals." He knew there is no wound or hurt so great, so horrible, so devastating or destructive that our sovereign God cannot heal it.

But we who care for the children have the responsibility to apply the "balm of Gilead" to children deeply scarred by the horrors and humiliation of sexual abuse. We must introduce these children to the Great Physician. Nothing is too difficult for him.

Notes

[1] Patricia J. Green, "The Women of Patpong," *News on Health Care in Developing Countries*, vol. 10 (February 1996), p. 11.

[2] Finklehor is quoted in R. Kim Oates, M.D., *The Spectrum of Child Abuse: Assessment, Treatment and Prevention* (New York; Brunner/Mazel Publishers, 1996), pp. 40-42.

[3] Mikel Flamm, "Silencing Bells in Thailand," *Together* (October-December 1996), pp. 21–22.

[4] Laurence Gray, Steve Gourley and Delia Paul, "Cambodia's Street Children Prostitutes: A Case Study," *Together* (October-December 1996), p. 12.

[5] Kyle and Ruth Luman, "Slavery of the 1990s: Child Prostitution in Cambodia," *East Asia's Millions* (September-November 1997), p. 6.

PART FOUR:

Areas of Special Concern

15

Essentials of Bonding and Lack of Attachment

Foster W. Cline

L ack of attachment, as a diagnosis, is based on bonding theory. It is based on both observations and clinical assumptions that evolve from clinical experience. The two basic empirical observations appear to be unarguable at this point. They are observations that everyone can validate with his or her own inspection and commitment. These observations were first remarked upon by Bowlby and his followers nearly half a century ago; they have not been seriously contested since that time. Now they are incorporated officially as part of the DSM-IV Reactive Attachment Disorder. The observations are:

1. The normal bonding process between child and mother takes place in infancy, mainly around feeding and physical contact, in a flow that occurs as the mother and child interact around the child's distress.

2. Most severely disturbed individuals have had developmental problems occurring during the time of the bonding cycle with problems occurring early in life, generally around early

parenting techniques or early life developmental disorders. Generally, alone or in combination, such individuals:

◆ have had physical or mental developmental disorders such that the normal cycle of pain followed by gratification and relief could not be achieved.

◆ have suffered early abuse and/or neglect.

◆ have, before birth, been bathed in alcohol or drugs to the extent that the normal early neurologic functioning is impaired.

◆ have been moved from caregiver to caregiver early in life.

◆ have had the physical trauma of either surgery, pain or undiagnosed infantile illnesses such that the normal bond cannot form—such infants generally have problems recognizing or obtaining relief from their distress.

BONDING THEORY

Bonding theory is based on the following two arguable clinical assumptions. These assumptions, at the foundation of attachment therapy, are open to disagreement but believed to be true by the vast majority of practicing therapists:

1. All true bonding has elements of trauma, pain, difficulty or uncertainty followed by gratification and/or relief.

All true bonding involves an ordeal followed by success in the undertaking and/or the expression of love or rescue by another. "Male bonding" in which men are thrown together in tough situations with positive outcome or when groups of men give each other a hard time but show affection as well are but two examples of bonding involving the successful completion of an "ordeal." Bonding, then, is a process that is different from the growth of love, esteem and respect.

Bonding experiences take place in normal infancy; in the armed services; in the use of challenge courses; among survivors following a catastrophe; among cult members (who may follow their leader, to whom they are bonded, in suicide); in interrogation and indoctrination routines; in brainwashing situations; and in reparenting and certain "attachment therapy" routines. Bonding routines can be seen throughout the Bible. Bonding takes place in many other situations, from the shores of Normandy in 1943 to college campuses today, where Greeks involve plebs in "hell week."

208

Trauma bonding is a widely known phenomenon where a person who is in a weaker, helpless and difficult position identifies with a stronger (sometimes threatening) person. The concept of trauma bonding helps one understand why children who were abused, either physically or sexually, want to live with the perpetrator. It helps one understand why abused spouses want to stay with their abusive partners.

In the story *Ninety Minutes at Entebbe* the hostages at Entebbe airport identified and felt a bond with their captors, who simply offered them cigarettes. During World War II trauma bonding of Jews in concentration camps was written about under the term "identification with the aggressor." It is a fact that commonly children of a conflicted marriage identify with the parent of perceived power. This leads a parent to ask with perplexity, "Why doesn't James act like me? I love him, I treat him lovingly, and he acts abusively to me, just like his father."

It could be said that all bonding has elements of trauma. Mothers automatically bond to their infants following the agony of childbirth. Infants bond to their mothers after experiencing the trauma of hunger pangs that could lead to death if food were not provided.

In unhealthy bonding routines the outcome is almost always negative. In loving bonding routines, the outcome, as in normal childbirth and the development of infantile affection, is almost always positive.

Thus it may be seen that bonding routines can be used for good or for evil purposes. In mother-child interactions bonding depends on who is in control, the motives and the outcome.

In childhood bonding relief takes place as we are given milk, touch, movement and eye contact, all of which we later tightly connect with love. For example, when we wish to develop a relationship we ask others to come to our home for a meal or go to a restaurant to eat with us, and Americans use food terms when speaking to loved ones—"sugar," "honey." Prolonged eye contact means physical merger, just as it did in the original nursing position.

Bonding that takes place around infantile trials and tribulations and the rescue that takes place with the mother's feeding and love has far-reaching implications. Few Americans, even therapists, understand that a culture falls or builds on the early years of infant and toddler care.

2. *The lack of completion of the normal bonding cycle results in predictable symptoms.* These include but are not limited to:

♦ The inability to show gratification, basic trust, love, attachment and normal affection to parental figures.

♦ The internalization of rage and anger that leads to childhood cruelty to animals and other children, lack of self-respect and severe control problems.

♦ As there is no development of an internalized "other" or mother, children are unable to put themselves in the shoes of another. Thus the foundation for conscience is lacking.

♦ Other first-year-of-life developmental problems, such as hoarding and gorging on food, an inability to show remorse and a general lack of conscience, are evident.

♦ Often, in cases of neglect or abuse, the care is inconsistent. Consistency must be present for the developing brain to learn causal relationships. These are necessary for the development of the ability to tolerate delayed gratification, which is the foundation for planful thinking.

Elephants on the rampage

The *Chicago Tribune* published an interesting article. Someone, something, was systematically killing the beautiful white rhinos in the African Planesberg Game Reserve. The South African officials found the rhinos had gaping wounds shaped like elephant tusks in their backs. Surprising evidence showed young bull elephants were responsible for this unusual behavior. The only recorded incidence of elephants killing rhinos had earlier occurred at water holes when mothers and young calves felt threatened. But these young bull elephants were going on a rampage for no reason.

The officials came up with a possible reason for this aberrant behavior. In the late 1970s Planesberg became a pioneer in the restocking of animals. Baby elephants that would have been marked for slaughter in other parks (as part of the animal cull to keep animal populations manageable) instead were moved to Planesberg along with only two adult females to care for the seventy or more junior elephants. Clive Walker, chairman of the Rhino and Elephant Foundation of Africa, believes the problem goes back to the childhood trauma suffered by these elephants and the lack of parental authority throughout their formative years. As babies, these elephants watched their parents being slaughtered and then were trucked off to new and unfamiliar surroundings.

The Unabomber saga

Newsweek learned that Ted Kaczynski, the alleged Unabomber suspected in a series of mail bombs in the Western United States, wrote his mother, Wanda, as many as a dozen letters blaming her for turning him into a recluse. He castigated her for his inability to form relationships, particularly with women. Kaczynski told his brother, David, that he wanted nothing to do with their parents, then dismissed their mother as a "dog."

Blaming one's mother is the oldest and least original excuse in history. In Greek mythology Oedipus railed against his mother, along with the Fates, after he inadvertently slept with her and killed his father. Teenagers will blame their mothers for almost anything. It may not be fair to hold Wanda Kaczynski, who is described by her neighbors as a sweet old lady, accountable for turning her son into a convicted serial killer. Yet something must have caused Ted Kaczynski to go on an 18–year bombing spree that killed three people and wounded 23 others.

Why did he do it? Why did the shy, brilliant son of respectable parents become an alleged serial killer? Why did his brother—with the same blood and the same roots—become a gentle social worker? When both dropped out of society, why did only one return? Perhaps it was biological. Or evil.

The first clue is something that happened when Kaczynski was only six months old. According to federal investigators, little "Teddy John," as his parents called him, was hospitalized for a severe allergic reaction to a medicine he was taking. He had to be isolated; his parents were unable to see him or to hold him for several weeks. After this separation, family said the baby's personality, once bubbly and vivacious, seemed to go "flat." Skeptics may scoff, but psychologists see lasting consequences from such

211

episodes. "There is a lot of evidence that painful loss or separation or injury during infancy can be particularly grave," says Dr. Jerrold Post, director of the political-psychology program at George Washington University. "The first two years of life are the time when a sense of security and self-esteem is laid down."

Ann Rule's strange dream

Ann Rule, an ex-policewoman, wrote for *True Detective* magazine and was on the staff of a Seattle crisis center with Ted Bundy. She told me he was a wonderful, charming man. "And imagine, I was locked in a building with him!" Ann went on to write her famous biography of Ted, *The Stranger Beside Me*. In the book she tells of being torn between the facts as told to her by her police friends and her gut emotion telling her that "Ted couldn't be a killer."

Then she had a most amazing dream. A dream that not only indicated Ted's guilt but gave the genesis of the problem. Ted's problem started early in his life:

> It was that night—April 1, 1976—when I had the dream. It was very frightening, jarring me awake in a strange room in a strange city.
>
> I found myself in a large parking lot, with cars backing out and racing away. One of the cars ran over an infant, injuring it terribly, and I grabbed it up, knowing it was up to me to save it. [How many adopting parents feel this way!?] I had to get to a hospital, but no one would help. I carried the baby, wrapped almost completely in a gray blanket, into a car rental agency. They had plenty of cars, but they looked at the baby in my arms and refused to rent me one. I tried to get an ambulance, but the attendants turned away. Finally, in desperation, I found a wagon—a child's wagon—and I put the injured infant in it, pulling it behind me for miles until I found an emergency room.
>
> I carried the baby, running, up to the desk. The admitting nurse glanced at the bundle in my arms. "No, we will not treat it."
>
> "But it's still alive! It's going to die if you don't do something."
>
> "It's better. Let it die. It will do no one any good to treat it."

The nurse, the doctors, everyone, turned and moved away from me and the bleeding baby.

And then I looked down at it. It was not an innocent baby; it was a demon. Even as I held it, it sunk [sic] its teeth into my hand and bit me.

I did not have to be a Freudian scholar to understand my dream; it was all too clear. Had I been trying to save a monster, trying to protect something or someone who was too dangerous and evil to survive?[1]

REACHING UNATTACHED CHILDREN

Many years ago Bruno Bettelheim wrote a book entitled *Love Is Not Enough*. This particularly applies to most seriously disturbed individuals and certainly to all unattached individuals.

If love is not enough, what else is needed?

If the normal bonding cycle has not been completed at a developmentally appropriate time, during infancy, then it must be repaired in a "corrective emotional experience."

This task is difficult to do on an individual level, and nigh impossible to do on a population level. John Bowlby finally, after a lifetime of study, said the only hope was in prevention.

In selected cases the corrective emotional experience, when used in therapy, is the purposeful use of a bonding cycle with the therapist, parents or other significant others. The bonding routines will generally involve, in one way or another, an ordeal or challenge followed by feelings of relief, achievement or gratification.

There are many therapies based specifically on bonding techniques:

◆ challenge courses
◆ ropes courses
◆ wilderness experiences
◆ "boot camp" for delinquents
◆ highly structured and demanding foster and adoptive homes
◆ reality attack therapy
◆ some loving confrontive techniques

The list is nearly endless.

All adoptive parents of unattached or marginally unattached children (and these are being adopted in increasing numbers) tell stories of either the disruption of the adoption or, alternatively, an experience that they and the child went through together that encouraged bonding. The following is a typical story, told by a Denver Colorado social services worker:

> When I adopted Jennifer, at four, I suddenly found that I was in way over my head. Things that worked with the birth children were no longer viable. My love seemed to make no difference. Consequences had little effect. She was impervious to pain, cried without tears. She would walk off with strangers. She hoarded and gorged on food and had all the signs of severe symptomatology. Then an amazing sequence of events took place.
>
> Jennifer fell out of a tree! She injured her spinal column and had to be in a body cast for several months. During that time she was immobilized and completely dependent on me for every need. Since that experience, she has been a wonderful, loving and very bonded daughter. Until I understood bonding theory, I could never figure out exactly why it happened, although I certainly knew what had happened.

CULTURAL IMPLICATIONS

For the past 40 years, as the social situation in much of the Third World has deteriorated, the industrialized world, in spite of this trend (or because of it?), has increasingly become involved in the survival of young children and teens. The industrialized world is continuously concerned with the nourishment of third-world infants, children and teens regardless of their history of early abuse and neglect. This interest is the understandable, loving intercontinental response—a humane response.

However, that policy has far-reaching consequences. As these uncared-for children are nourished physically, they do not grow emotionally or mentally. Then we have scenes of teens running through the streets and shooting all who move. They have sex without affection, producing greater numbers of children with little regard for their ability to care for them. The population increases. The numbers of uncared-for children skyrocket as children raise children who, in turn, are discarded and uncared for. The number of the mentally crippled also increases geometrically. Thus is added an increasing amount of individual and cultural psychopathol-

214

ogy, instability of the population and inability of the culture to plan ahead. There also is a decrease in the population's general morality, in ability to engage in planful thinking and a decrease in collective conscience.

Note

[1] Ann Rule, *The Stranger Beside Me* (New York: New American Library, 1980), p. 199.

Selected Bibliography

Ainsworth, Salter, M.D. "The Development of Infant-Mother Attachment," in *Review of Child Development Research*, ed. B. M. Caldwell and H. N. Ricciuti. New York: Russell Sage Foundation, 1969.

Banham, K. M. "The Development of Affectionate Behavior in Infancy," in J. Genet, *Psychology* (1950), pp. 76, 283–89. Reprinted in *Human Development: Selected Readings*, ed. M. L. and N. R. Haimowitz. New York: Crowell, 1960.

Bettelheim, Bruno. *Love Is Not Enough.* New York: Free Press Division of Macmillan, 1950.

Bowlby, John. *Child Care and the Growth of Love.* Baltimore: Penguin Books, 1953.

Cline, Foster. *Hope for High Risk and Rage Filled Children.* Self-published.

Fahlberg, Vera. *Attachment and Separation.* Deerfield Beach, Fla.: Health Comm., 1979.

Fanshel, David. *Far from the Reservation: The Transracial Adoption of American Indian Children.* Matuchen, N.J.: Scarecrow, 1972.

Feigelman, W., and A. R. Silverman. *Chosen Children: New Patterns of Adoptive Relationships.* New York: Praeger, 1983.

Kadushin, A., and F. W. Seidl. "Adoption Failure: A Social Work Postmortem" *Social Work* (1971), pp. 16, 32–28.

Karen, Robert. "Becoming Attached," *The Atlantic Monthly* (February 1990), pp. 35–70.

16

HIV and AIDS: Orphans and Sexual Vulnerability

Geoff Foster

Where would you be were it not for your parents? Would you be a different person if you had grown up without your father or mother? In the West it is rare for children to be orphaned. But in many developing countries orphans (defined as children whose father or mother has died) are many. And the number of orphans, especially double orphans (children who have lost both father and mother), is increasing dramatically due to HIV/AIDS. Try putting yourself in an orphan's shoes.

You are young. Your father becomes ill. At first his illnesses are not serious; but as time passes by, he gradually becomes weaker. He learns he has AIDS. It is necessary for him to take time off from work; he loses his job. Next he begins to lose weight drastically, becoming dependent, bed-bound and requiring round-the-clock care from your mother. After he dies your life changes dramatically as your family becomes poor. A few years later the same fate befalls your mother. This time you are the one called upon to provide care during her frequent illnesses. At the same time you must look after your younger brothers and sisters. After your mother

216

dies, you drop out of school and try to find work to bring some income into your family. Fearful, vulnerable and open to exploitation, you and your little family try as best you can to cope with your plight.

Most of us have little notion of what it is like for children who have the responsibilities of parenthood thrust upon them. But as a result of the AIDS epidemic, thousands of children are heading families of younger brothers and sisters. Millions more orphaned children are cared for by grandparents. Children are growing up in a world very different from the one in which their parents were raised; they are children living in a world with AIDS. Children bear the brunt of many disasters. The AIDS disaster is no exception.

Let me tell you the story about a girl I'll call Maria. After her mother died from AIDS, Maria (then 16 years old) was left looking after three young brothers and sisters. Her father worked as a gardener in town and visited the family on weekends. But soon he remarried and the visits dropped away. Maria stopped going to school so that she could care for her little family. They were very poor and lived in a mud-and-thatch hut, which was falling apart. At night the boys slept under one blanket while the girls shared the other blanket. In turn, each of the children dropped out of school because they could not find two dollars a year for school fees.

Crises often occurred in the family—hunger, illness, difficulties with the house or problems with the crops in the fields. One day there was an emergency. Tendai, age 8, was sick with malaria. Maria took him to the local clinic where the nurse gave him chloroquine. But Tendai got worse. That evening the children were desperate. Tendai was delirious and looked as if he might die. Maria realized that she must somehow get Tendai to the hospital. She went to a neighbor, the local storekeeper, and begged him to take them in his truck. He said the fare would be five dollars in advance, but he made it clear that if she could not find the money, they could come to some "special" arrangement instead. Maria went home to nurse Tendai, but he was now unconscious.

So Maria made a difficult decision, one that many young girls around the world feel increasingly compelled to make. She decided to trade her body. She went back to her neighbor and agreed to his proposition. He transported Tendai to the hospital. On the way back, he had sex with Maria in the back of the truck. Fortunately Tendai arrived at the hospital in the nick of time. His cerebral malaria improved, and he was discharged a few days later.

THE IMPACT OF AIDS ON CHILDREN

"It pays to take proper care of your children. When you are old, they will take care of you," goes one Zimbabwean proverb. But in countries with severe HIV epidemics, most young adults living now will not enter old age.

According to estimates published by the U.S. Bureau of the Census the HIV epidemic is unfolding in its severest form in countries in east and southern Africa.[1] By 1996, life expectancy had fallen in Zambia from 57 to 36 years, in Zimbabwe from 64 to 42 years, in Uganda from 53 to 40 years and in Kenya from 65 to 56 years. Further falls are anticipated to as low as 29 in Malawi, 30 in Zambia and 33 in Zimbabwe and Botswana as a result of AIDS. One consequence of the fact that most people will die before reaching middle age is a large increase in the number of orphaned children.

Projections of the orphan epidemic for Zimbabwe suggest that by 2005, fewer than 20 percent of Zimbabwean women may be expected to live throughout their childbearing years; only one-third of girls aged 15 are estimated to survive to their thirty-fifth birthday; and one-third of children under 15 may have been maternally orphaned.[2]

Orphanhood has profound implications for child survivors. The traditional method of coping with orphans was the extended family, especially aunts and uncles. But as a result of rapid increases in the number of orphans because of AIDS, the elderly and the young are being recruited for childcare. We interviewed 300 orphan households in Zimbabwe in 1995 and found that nearly one-half of the caregivers were grandmothers.[3] Many of the grandparents were elderly (average age 62), and some were sick and infirm. Some orphan households were headed by older sisters or brothers who took over childcare following the death of an elderly grandmother. As the number of orphans increases and the number of young adults in the population falls, we can expect to see more and more grandparent- and child-headed households.

In 1997 we interviewed 43 child-headed households; in almost all the households, the mother or both parents had died; the youngest head of household was an 11 year-old girl.[4] Older brothers were also heading households and providing childcare. In many cases relatives provided support by regular visits and small amounts of material assistance. Once child-headed households start to occur in countries with severe AIDS epidemics, their numbers will increase and younger children will be recruited into childcare. This is likely to be particularly pronounced in southern Africa, where the epidemic is having its greatest impact and where traditional extended family coping mechanisms are weakened.

Children living in orphan households are at risk in many ways. Most of the problems facing children affected by AIDS can be summarized under the headings of poverty and parenting.

Poverty

AIDS has been described as a poverty-seeking missile. HIV infection not only thrives in impoverished environments—the disease is itself also a potent cause of poverty. Households in which family members have been affected have higher expenditures due to costs of seeking medical care and reduced incomes associated with loss of affected breadwinners' earnings; when the breadwinner dies, the family's resources are further depleted as a result of funeral expenses and property removal by relatives of the deceased. Consequently, the AIDS epidemic is leading to increasing poverty among survivors indirectly affected by HIV infection.

We measured the level of poverty of child-headed orphan households in Zimbabwe by comparing them with their neighbors. Orphan households were likely to be poorer, with fewer possessions, blankets, cows, goats and chickens; the number of rooms per household resident was smaller and the monthly income was less for orphan households compared to their neighbors. As might be expected, orphan households had experienced more deaths in the preceding five years, more moves in the preceding two years and more previous caregivers than children in control households.[5]

	Child-headed	Non-orphan neighbor
	(n=37)	(n=42)
Rooms	2.4	3.4
Cows	0.7	1.8
Goats	1	2
Chickens	2.7	6.9
Household items	0.9	2
Blankets	3.5	5.5
Meals /day	2.4	2.6
Average income (US$)/month	$8	$21
Children in household	3.5	3.7
Adolescents in household	0.6	1.5
Adults in household	0.3	2
Moves in last 2 years	12/37	0/42
Previous caregivers	15/37	1/32
Deaths in last 5 years	1.9	0.7

Figure 1: Comparisons between rural child- or adolescent-headed and control households.

We spoke to groups of orphaned children about their experiences. Here are some of their comments:[6]

"When father was alive, we used to go to school without any problem of school fees; my uncle helped with school fees and now my brother helps." (Girl, 13)

"My father used to buy school uniforms; nowadays it is difficult." (Boy, 13)

"Now that I stay with grandparents, I no longer have new clothes." (Boy, 9)

"We are segregated because we don't have shoes." (Girl, 12)

PARENTING

Orphaned children face many problems because their parents have died. Some children spoke about difficulties they had experienced:

a. Extended family support to orphan households:

> "We moved from our original home and built on another spot after my aunts and grandmother refused to take care of us." (Brother-caregiver)

> "My uncle used to come when he wanted mother to be his wife but when mother refused, he stopped coming." (Girl, 15)

> "Auntie only came when she wanted to take the property." (Girl, 14)

> "Mother is in a sewing cooperative so I am left at home looking after the young children." (Girl, 14)

b. Differences from other children:

> "We steal and sell to earn a living, which is different from them [non-orphans]." (Girl, 15)

> "We want to go to school but I must help uncle in the fields. He said, 'You are not my child so I cannot send you to school.'" (Girl, 16)

> "When my ballpoint finishes, I sometimes absent myself from school and sell manure to get money to buy a pen. I am not pleased being absent from school." (Boy, 13)

> "Father remarried another woman who mistreats me." (Boy, 11)

> "A certain girl assaulted me, saying she did not want to play with those who don't have fathers." (Girl, 13, who then started crying)

> "My friends changed after the death of my mother." (Two 10-year-old boys)

c. Psychological problems:

Children suffer anxiety and fear during the years of parental illness, then grief and trauma following the death of a parent. Stigmatization, dropping out of school, changed friends, increased work load, discrimination and social isolation all increase stress for orphans; this makes coping with their situation more difficult and painful. Difficult relationships with new caretakers also contribute to stress; two children said they were "being given a hard time" by a grandparent and a stepmother.

As a result, children may become depressed, reducing their ability to cope with growing pressures. During one focus group discussion the facilitator asked about changes experienced following parental death. One boy stated his stepmother mistreated him, whereon a 12-year-old boy started crying and continued sobbing throughout the rest of the discussion. Psychological problems are often less obvious than material ones and may remain unnoticed by the children themselves. However, they were a major concern to relatives, neighbors and community workers.

> "My mother is suffering, unlike when father was alive; she cannot carry the burden alone." (Girl, 12)

> "[Because of the situation,] I almost thought of committing suicide." (Brother-caretaker)

AIDS, ORPHANS AND SEXUAL EXPLOITATION

Sexual exploitation during childhood and adolescence is not a new phenomenon. Children who are sexually abused are at high risk of being HIV-infected as a result. But the AIDS epidemic increases the vulnerability of children to sexual exploitation in many different ways:

Children who are orphaned are more vulnerable to HIV infection

By 1996 some nine million children were estimated to have lost their mother due to AIDS.[7] In Zambia the number of children orphaned by AIDS is expected to increase from 80,000 in 1991 to 600,000 in 2000; currently, more than 70,000 children are living on the streets, and 37 percent of families are caring for at least one child orphaned by AIDS.[8] Wherever they are living, orphaned children, especially girl children and those whose mothers have died, are vulnerable to sexual exploitation. Children living with relatives are at risk of continuous sexual molestation or incest. They may even be put to work in prostitution in return for room and board.

"This lady likes mistreating me because my mother is dead,"
said one Ugandan girl. "She wants me to sleep with men
because I stay at their house. She brings these men into her
house and introduces them to me. She often tells me to be
good to them and this is the only way I can continue to live
in her house."[9]

Children living alone are at risk of rape and sexual exploitation. Children living in orphanages, institutions, remand homes
and foster homes are at risk from staff, caregivers and other residents and inmates. These homes, which are supposed to be places
of safety for children, are often places of abuse—both heterosexual
and homosexual abuse. And increasing numbers of orphaned children, escaping poverty and abuse in their homes, are now living
on the streets, where early sexual activity is the norm. Whether
forced or as a form of income generation, sex can be relied on to
bolster children's emotional insecurity.

Men seek childhood sex partners to reduce their risk

The average age at which people are becoming infected with
HIV is falling in countries with severe epidemics; most females
are infected before they reach the age of 21. Girls believed to be
HIV-negative are being singled out by older men for sexual favors
in many countries with severe HIV epidemics. In Zambia the trend
is increasing the severity of the HIV-infection rate among Zambian girls aged 15 to 19.[10] The "sugar daddy syndrome," as it is
referred to, is blamed for the rise in infection rate among these
girls, reportedly six times higher than that of boys the same age.
Zambian schools generally do not inform children about sexual
issues and approximately 50,000 children in Zambia are HIV-positive, with perinatal transmission accounting for 75 percent of the
cases.

AIDS leads to poverty and prostitution

Poverty is associated with increased vulnerability to HIV infection. In countries like Zimbabwe, a large proportion of the next
generation of young adults—this generation's children—will be
at increased risk of HIV infection as a result of orphanhood and

poverty. Orphaned children who are poor are especially vulnerable to sexual exploitation. In some orphan families prostitution is the main source of income. Orphaned girls may become involved in commercial sex to provide basic requirements for themselves or children in their care. And unlike this generation, they will have no mothers available to care for them when they are dying of AIDS. There will be no grandmothers around who can act as caregivers to their orphaned children. Instead of seeing reductions in HIV transmission, the AIDS epidemic may be perpetuated by a vicious cycle of orphanhood, poverty and increased vulnerability.

WHAT CAN CHRISTIANS DO TO HELP?

This chapter has drawn attention to the rapidly increasing numbers of children orphaned as a result of AIDS, children who are at risk of sexual abuse and contracting HIV themselves. What are Christians and local churches doing to protect these children? This final section provides a biblical basis for helping and draws on practical examples of Christian community care in Zimbabwe.

Orphans and the Bible

It is evident from the Bible that the Lord has a special regard for widows and orphans. Over 40 verses in the Bible talk about the ways in which believers are to help widows and orphans:

> [A complaint arose] because their widows were being overlooked in the daily distribution of food (Acts 6:1).

> Honor widows who are really widows. . . . Let a widow be put on the list if she is not less than sixty years old. . . . If any believing woman has relatives who are really widows, let her assist them; let the church not be burdened, so that it can assist those who are real widows (1 Tim. 5:3, 9, 16, *NRSV*).

> Religion that is pure and undefiled before God, the Father, is this: to care for orphans and widows in their distress (James 1:27, *NRSV*).

These verses and other passages elsewhere tell us a great deal about the early church's ministry to support widows and orphans.

224

The early church established an organization within its body to oversee the work among widows and orphans

When the church in Jerusalem was small, it was easy to make sure that widows and orphans were not overlooked. As the number of disciples grew, some of the poor in the church drew attention to the fact that they were being neglected. The matter was resolved when the church leaders appointed seven men to become responsible for the daily distribution of food and other support to needy families. This allowed the leaders of the church to give time to their own area of gifting of prayer and Bible teaching.

It should be noted that this social ministry of the church was not inferior to the spiritual ministry. Visiting widows and orphans was to become one of the church's main areas of ministry. According to Acts 6 this ministry was not something left to a small group of well-meaning "do-gooders." The main requirement for the leaders of this program was being full of the Holy Spirit and wisdom. Among the seven people chosen were Stephen, the first Christian martyr, and Philip the Evangelist.

These leaders had the responsibility of "serving tables," literally overseeing the daily distribution of food to widows in the church. The requirements for these deacons (literally "servers") are listed in 1 Timothy 3:8-13.

Like elders, deacons were required to be men worthy of respect who did not abuse alcohol. But there were other attributes that were required of prospective deacons. They had to be good managers, not only of their own families but also of domestic affairs. Administrative abilities were necessary for deacons to provide efficient service. They had to have no predisposition toward dishonesty—this would counteract any temptation to skim off the church's material aid for their own ends. And their wife had to be able to keep confidences—gossiping about the goings-on in the lives of beneficiaries could destroy the effectiveness of the program.

Deacons were chosen by the voice of the people (Acts 6:3). Only after the men had been proved by a searching inquiry to see whether they were blameless would they be appointed to the ministry of serving as deacons. Success in a deacon's ministry would lead to their strengthening their faith and increasing their spiritual effectiveness.

By the time Paul wrote his letter to Timothy, another group of people had become active in the ministry of supporting widows in the church. These were older widows who were responsible for carrying out ministry to orphans and other widows. In 1 Timothy 5:9 we read about a list of widows. Widows on this list had to be older women who had been faithful to their husband and had a past record of good works. A woman who had a record of hospitality, helping people in trouble and bringing up children would be well-qualified to provide support to other widows in need.

Younger widows were not to be put on the list of widow-deaconesses. Entering this ministry meant permanent acceptance of the state of widowhood; such a promise should not be recommended to young widows, who should be encouraged to remarry.

Therefore, the church's orphan program was to be carried out by an organization made up of older widows. Tertullian, Hermas and Chrysostom wrote about church life in the first three centuries after Christ. They all mention an order of older widows ministering with a sympathizing counsel to other widows and orphans.

The church was selective in whom it helped

Not every widow or orphan in the church was to receive financial help in the church's support program. It is likely that Paul wrote to Timothy because there had been some abuse of the church's orphans-and-widows program. The church was not to assume the role of supporting orphans and widows when there was another family member capable of bearing this burden. Only those who were in need and without other means of support were to receive assistance. Families with members capable of supporting their relatives who were widows and orphans were not to be allowed to escape their responsibilities. In this way the church could concentrate its limited resources upon those who were really in need.

Visiting widows and orphans and distributing food to them were daily activities of the early church

Visiting people in their homes is the only way to assess whether families are really in need. Home visiting for the early church was

226

to be a regular event. During a home visit, material aid could be distributed.

But meeting physical need was not the only purpose of the home-visitation program. Loneliness is a real problem for many widows, and visits to homes can provide friendship. And no doubt such home visits gave opportunities for spiritual ministry and support to widows and orphans.

Orphans, orphanages and the church

For many people the mention of orphans immediately brings to mind the solution of orphanages. Most orphanages have been the result of Christian initiatives. Many people have selflessly dedicated themselves to providing for unaccompanied children by raising resources to construct and run some kind of institution. Some of these orphanages have gone a long way in trying to re-create family caring structures and avoiding problems associated with bringing up children in institutions. But according to experts, orphanages should be considered as a last resort in providing care to those orphaned by AIDS.

Children growing up in orphanages often have difficulty knowing where they belong in society. To which family or tribe do they belong? Who will receive or pay the bride price? In fact, only a tiny proportion of children who have lost one or both parent are being brought up in orphanages. When we conducted a survey in Mancaland in 1991, we found 170 orphans in 19 institutions. However, we estimated that the province held a total of 47,000 orphaned children. Almost all the children were being cared for in a family setting. The number of orphans is rising rapidly as a result of AIDS and will more than double during the next decade.[11]

What should the church do?

We asked community members living in a rural area in Zimbabwe what they thought should be done to cope with the growing number of orphans. No one suggested that sending orphaned children to an institution was an appropriate response. Many said that though they were poor and could not afford to give much material help, they were trying to help orphans cope with their desperate situation.

"We sometimes think about the problem but come up with no solution—at times, we don't even sleep. We want to help the orphans very much but sometimes our endeavors are limited because of lack of resources." (Caregiver)

"People should come together like this, talk about it [the situation of orphans], form societies, build love and help." (Art cooperative worker)

"I wish there were more people in the area willing to help orphans [besides ourselves]." (Community worker)

"We take care of the children voluntarily; some come to us on their own and others we come across during home visits." (Caregiver-visitor)

"Sometimes we visitors noticed that the children were seriously ill and saved their lives by getting them to the hospital." (Caregiver-visitor)

"The late husband's family takes everything but sometimes the community elders intervene." (Homecare volunteer)

Practical example

Let me give a practical example of what some churches are doing about orphans. In late 1992 a volunteer working with Family AIDS Caring Trust (FACT) in Mutare visited a church in eastern Zimbabwe. The women's group of the church was aware of several needy orphan families in their area and on a number of occasions had provided material support. The volunteer spoke about the important role that Christians and local churches had to play in providing social, emotional, material and spiritual support to orphans and widows.

As a result the women organized themselves into a committee and started visiting orphan households. They identified 55 needy families. A gift of US$1,000 enabled the program to function for a year. Six women, mostly widows, started regularly visiting orphan households and distributing modest amounts of food. In return they received a small gift of maize meal to help them provide for their own orphans.

Since that inauspicious beginning the program has grown. Families, Orphans and Children Under Stress (FOCUS), is a program administered by FACT, supports community-based orphan initiatives in six sites in Zimbabwe. At each site volunteers from different churches are identified. In most cases these are women, many of whom are widows themselves. They are provided with basic training so they can identify and register orphans in the community. The most needy are then visited regularly. Here are some comments by community members in these areas:

> "The FOCUS coordinator gave us corn to pop; we sold the popcorn and made almost $500 (US$50); we used the money to buy books and pens for the orphans." (Caregiver-visitor)

> "On Saturdays the orphans spend the whole day playing at the center. We teach them knitting, sewing, carving, moulding and gardening. They take part in football, netball and traditional dances." (Caregiver-visitor)

> "The church sometimes helps us by donating clothes. FOCUS also helps with food, school fees, and blankets." (Caregiver)

> "The church also helps the orphans; sometimes everyone contributes one dollar to help the poor." (Community worker)

> "People are becoming more sympathetic to each other and offer love and comfort to the bereaved." (Community worker)

In the last six months of 1996 the program involved 3,192 orphans from 798 families at four rural sites. The 88 volunteers made a total of 9,634 visits. Families receive an average of 1.5 visits per month; particularly needy families, such as child-headed households, receive weekly or twice-weekly visits. Volunteers made an average of 18.2 visits per month; this is possible since volunteers live in villages and visit only families living nearby.

Some material assistance is provided in the form of food, clothing, blankets and primary school fees. Income-generating projects have been established to encourage self-reliance. The cost of supporting orphans in the community is much less than the cost of supporting them in an institution. The total cost of the FOCUS program in 1996 was US$26,000. Of this amount, most was spent within the communities affected, in the form of material assistance

(31%), volunteer meetings (11%) and incentives (9%). Indirect costs were staff salaries (27%), transport (13%) and office administration (9%). The cost per month per family was US$2.70 and per orphan child US$0.68. The cost per visit was US$1.55.[12] The community-based model of providing support to orphaned children in their families is not only biblical and culturally sensitive, it is cost-effective as well.

HOW TO START ORPHAN PROGRAMS

Christians have an important role to play in providing support to orphaned children. When the church gets involved in such activities, we act as "salt of the earth" (Matt. 5:13). Instances of sexual abuse and exploitation fall as people realize that children are being watched over, cared for and protected.

It is not difficult for churches to establish support programs. After forming a committee, the next step is to visit families in the neighborhood. During visits the needs of the family should be assessed; sometimes it is possible to persuade relatives to assume their family responsibilities rather than the church taking over a role of material support.

A register of orphan households should be established. This needs to be updated because situations change over time. We have heard of child-headed households that later start being supported by family members. An increasing concern with the AIDS epidemic is for orphans to be taken into a new home only for the new caregiver to become sick and die from AIDS. So it is necessary for committees to update their orphan register regularly.

Material support is the most obvious need in many orphan homes: food, clothing and school fees. But when we asked groups of caregivers what they really wanted, many of them said, "Teach us some skills so we can provide for the children ourselves." Similarly, many of the older orphans are also looking for help to earn a living.

In time we hope it may be possible to help orphans and widows be taught a skill by others in their community. In this way our programs may help move people away from handouts and into looking after themselves.

Finally, we need to remember the spiritual needs of orphan children. I was recently with a group of widows. As they described their efforts to bring up their children singlehandedly, it became obvious that they often felt weary. It was difficult to find time to pray or read the Bible to their families. In administering our material support programs, let's not forget the spiritual needs of orphans and widows.

According to Proverbs 14:31b, "Whoever is kind to the needy honors God." What an amazing statement. Helping a poor person is like helping out the One who created all things! God is concerned about the poor. So it is no surprise that God wants his people to have the same concern. If we are kind to the poor, we are in actual fact giving our lives to our God upon whose heart is the plight of countless numbers of widows and orphans.

Notes

[1] U.S. Bureau of the Census, *The Demographic Impacts of HIV/AIDS— Perspectives from the World Population Profile: 1996* (Washington D.C.: International Programs Center, Population Division, U.S. Bureau of the Census, 1997).

[2] S. Gregson, et al., "Determinants of the Demographic Impact of HIV-1 in Sub-Saharan Africa: The Effect of a Shorter Mean Adult Incubation Period on Trends in Orphanhood," *Health Transition Review* 4, supplement, pp. 65-92.

[3] G. Foster, et al., "Supporting Children in Need Through a Community-based Orphan Visiting Programme, *AIDS Care* 8: 389-403. The research reported in this chapter is based on published scientific studies from Family AIDS Caring Trust (FACT), a Christian AIDS service organization founded by Dr. Foster.

[4] G. Foster, et al., "Factors Leading to the Establishment of Child-headed Households—The Case of Zimbabwe, *Health Transitions Review* 7, supplement 2, pp. 157-70.

[5] Ibid.

[6] G. Foster, et al., "Perceptions of Children and Community Members Concerning the Circumstances of Orphans in Rural Zimbabwe, *AIDS Care* 9 (1997): 393-407.

[7] Fact sheet titled *UNAIDS and UNICEF Launch the "Children in a World with AIDS Initiative,"* August 28, 1996, Stockholm.

[8] Africa News Online, "'Sugar Daddy Syndrome' Blamed for AIDS Infection," July 15, 1997, CDC National Center for HIV, STD, and TB Prevention.

[9] PANOS Media Briefing, "AIDS and Children: A Lifetime of Risk," 20-page mimeograph (London: Panos Institute), p. 5

[10] G. Foster, *Orphans in Zimbabwe—A Descriptive and Enumerative Study,* abstract POD 5158, VIIIth International Conference on AIDS, Amsterdam, 1992.

[11] PANOS Media Briefing, "AIDS and Children: A Lifetime of Risk," n.p.

[12] G. Foster, *Low Cost Replicable Orphan Support Programme in Zimbabwe,* abstract submitted to XIIth International Conference on AIDS, Geneva, July 1998.

17

Sexual Abuse and Pregnancy

Janith Williams

At 18 Lee convinced her mother and younger sisters that the abuse in their home was never going to stop. To save their lives they fled from the father and husband whose violent attacks were becoming more explosive and frequent. Lee had attended a Billy Graham crusade a few months before where she asked Christ to be Lord of her life. As she boarded the bus with her family, Lee looked forward to a new life—an easier life where fear and physical pain were not a part of her daily routine.

Eager to begin anew, Lee quickly found a job and a small apartment for herself, her mother and sisters. One evening Lee decided to attend an after-work get-together with some co-workers. She was the first to arrive. In a few minutes, after being violently attacked by a company representative, her life was shattered and changed forever. While just beginning to deal with the aftermath of the attack, she realized she was pregnant. Her mother told her she would have to leave their tiny home. Lee was alone, broken, angry and hurt. She wondered where this God was in whom she had just begun to believe. She found a temporary place to live. The following Sunday Lee hesitantly walked into a nearby church, wondering whether she would receive comfort and acceptance or judgment and ridicule.[1]

Maybe you are seeking guidance in how to reach out to someone like Lee. Or perhaps you are working in a country where children are coerced into a life of prostitution through sex tourism or war. In such cases children often are forced to have an abortion when they become pregnant.

SEXUAL ABUSE: A WEAPON OF WAR

During times of civil or international war, pregnancy often results from forced rape. The resulting trauma can be wrenchingly painful and intervention complex. The war in the former Yugoslavia resulted in many forced rapes and resulting pregnancies. Torture, murder, imprisonment and relocation are used to terrorize and demoralize the citizenry. Rape and "bordello camps" were part of the "ethnic-cleansing" campaign by Bosnian Serb soldiers. Girls and women who became pregnant had more often than not been raped multiple times, often in the presence of other family members. They were suffering from multiple physical attacks and multiple traumas, including the loss of homes, family members and their uncertain status as refugees.

Pregnant adolescents and women were allowed to go to clinics for care; early in their pregnancies they could apply for legal abortions. Others who were kept from obtaining medical help until later in their pregnancies had no option but to give birth. Both groups appeared depressed, anxious and would depersonalize their experience when speaking about it. Survival is the most pressing need, and even when psychotherapy is available, it is often refused.

One group of therapists attempting to offer care to women in Zagreb noted:

> All of the women who gave birth to children conceived by rape abandoned them in the hospital. It was clear that each woman considered the fetus to be a foreign entity in her body, and all displayed a sense of elation after delivery that was in sharp contrast to the symptoms of depression and anxiety they presented prepartum. All of the women refused any further psychiatric help, particularly after they had given birth.[2]

It is easy to feel inadequate in dealing with such tragic situations and to question why God would allow such overwhelming suffering. This chapter focuses on the needs of sexually abused young people who are pregnant or parenting. Such complex issues cannot be comprehensively covered in one chapter, but an introductory discussion of issues and interventions that experts and Christian workers have found to be effective will be helpful.

The Bible is not silent about the issues of rape, physical and sexual abuse, incest and pregnancy. Yet current Christian literature, or the church, rarely discusses these agonizing problems. Surprisingly, an extensive review of professional literature reveals that although articles and books on this subject do exist, sexual abuse and pregnancy are not comprehensively studied and documented. It is not surprising, therefore, that many lay and professional Christian workers do not feel well qualified to help children and teens deal with abuse and pregnancy.

THE RELATIONSHIP BETWEEN SEXUAL ABUSE AND PREGNANCY

Without question, sexually abused females are at high risk for pregnancy. One study of minority adolescent mothers in Texas showed that 54 percent reported some form of sexual abuse. The mothers who had been abused were younger (age 15–16) than first time mothers not reporting abuse. Ninety-seven percent of the perpetrators were male: 22 percent were fathers and stepfathers, 30 percent were male relatives, 28 percent were male family friends, 19 percent were male strangers; 4 percent of the perpetrators were females. Half of the mothers reported two previous abusers; 24 percent reported at least three abusers.[3]

Families in which sexual abuse takes place teach their children that self-worth and self-esteem are based on sexuality. Children who learn that the only way they can expect love is through sexual activity often voluntarily become sexually active at a very young age. These young teens have more partners than their peers and often do not consistently use contraception. Child sexual abuse frequently leaves a child with such poor self-esteem and depression that she may seek pregnancy as a way to feel better about

235

herself and to have someone to love. In cases where the sexual abuse continues into adolescence, young women often become pregnant from the abuse itself or become pregnant intentionally as a way to escape their abusive situations.

Girls who have been abused are more likely to see themselves as damaged goods. They may seek pregnancy as a way to validate themselves. Girls who have been sexually abused are more likely to have older boyfriends who encourage them to conceive. In an effort to please their partners, they may consent.

EMOTIONAL IMPACT AND PHYSICAL EFFECTS

Young survivors of sexual abuse are often dealing with emotional problems that make it difficult for them to manage a pregnancy and become effective parents. The severity of the emotional impact of sexual abuse depends on a number of variables and circumstances. The emotional problems faced by young sexual abuse survivors continue into adulthood.

When working with adolescent parents it is critical to identify those who have been sexually abused to prevent the cycle of abuse from continuing. Children who have been physically or sexually abused are much more likely to abuse their kids. Intervention, mentoring and treatment are pivotally important to break the vicious cycle of violence. The following issues result from the emotional impact and physical effects of sexual abuse of abused children.

Risk of Suicide

Abused adolescent parents are more depressed, more stressed and often have less family support than adolescent parents who have not suffered abuse. Pregnant survivors of sexual abuse are more likely to report a history of a previous suicide attempt and to think about committing suicide while they are pregnant. Young pregnant abuse survivors have conflicting feelings about sexuality and the physical changes that accompany pregnancy. The internal conflict may cause the young woman to feel that suicide is the best and only solution.

The pregnancy can trigger memories of abuse. The young woman may have intense difficulty dealing with feelings of grief, anger, abandonment and neglect, which she has previously been able to repress or deny. She may fear that she will not be able to protect her own baby, and that she will herself become an abuser. Long-held feelings of rage and grief against herself may result in her seeing suicide as the best solution for her and the baby.

The feelings of helplessness, victimization and vulnerability may cause profound fear about the possibility of the infant suffering through the same kind of abuse. The mother may feel she will be unable to protect her baby from a similar fate. This may cause her to consider suicide as the best way to protect herself and the baby from further abuse.

Pregnant adolescents and young mothers with a history of abuse are seven times more likely to attempt suicide than young mothers with no history of abuse. A history of a previous suicide attempt is a major risk factor for actually committing suicide. Depression, a known risk factor for suicide, in conjunction with the effect of the increased emotional, physical and financial responsibilities associated with new motherhood, may place these youth who are already at risk for suicide attempts at even greater risk.[4]

Substance abuse

Research consistently demonstrates that sexually abused adolescents are more likely to become substance abusers, no matter which country or population is being studied. One Swedish study confirms the results of U.S. studies and others which report that sexual abuse in childhood is the strongest predictor of alcohol dependence and abuse.[5]

Substance abuse makes it impossible for a teen to take care of herself properly during a pregnancy. Young women who use drugs and alcohol place their unborn baby at risk for malnutrition, physical deformities, mental problems such as retardation and attention deficit disorder and being born addicted to drugs. Teens who use drugs also cannot provide their infant or their young children with the physical and emotional nurturing needed to grow and thrive.

Inadequate nutrition

Survivors of abuse are more likely to have eating disorders, placing the mother and her infant at risk of malnutrition during the pregnancy. One study in Australia found that half of the patients hospitalized with eating disorders had a history of sexual abuse, compared with one-fourth who reported physical abuse.[6]

Young abuse survivors trying to survive outside their parents' home frequently have limited financial resources and inadequate housing. Young parents in these situations usually have nutritional deficiencies because they cannot afford to purchase food for a balanced diet.

Risk of injury

Sexual and physical abuse may increase during pregnancy when the young teen is more vulnerable and less able to defend herself. Battering during the pregnancy places the mother and her infant at risk for physical injury, pre-term labor, infection of the amniotic fluid that surrounds the baby and injuries severe enough to cause death.

Early childhood sexual abuse or neglect significantly increase the risk of children becoming prostitutes. Young prostitutes are at extreme risk for physical and sexual battering during their pregnancy.

Homelessness

Sexual abuse and incest can force kids into becoming homeless. Once they are on the street they are further victimized, often sexually. Homeless youth have poorer health status and less access to health care than non-homeless youth—especially since they are usually uninsured. Street youth, however, are more likely to report previous exposure to violence and having been victims of forced sex.

Inadequate housing also makes it more difficult for youth to keep themselves and their infants and children clean. They may not have the use of a safe water supply or a place to store and prepare food safely.

Sexually transmitted diseases

"Sarah" (not her real name) is a 14–year-old whom this author first met when she came to a clinic for an exam six weeks after she had delivered her first child. Sarah told about her life in a quiet voice that spoke of her hopelessness and resignation. At 12 years of age she had no sexual experience and was still playing with her stuffed animals when her brothers and sisters weren't home. While Sarah was beginning seventh grade, her mother invited her 42–year-old boyfriend to move in with the family and be their "stepfather." Sarah's "stepfather" began molesting her when she was 12 years old and by age 13 she was pregnant as a result of his abuse. Sarah and her baby lived with her mother, who blamed Sarah for seducing her stepfather. The stepfather had been arrested and was forced to move out of the home while awaiting trial.

Sarah had been successfully treated for gonorrhea during her pregnancy. This spared the baby from being exposed to gonorrhea during delivery. After her delivery she also needed extensive treatment for genital warts. The treatments were painful, but Sarah submitted to them stoically, telling us she felt she somehow deserved them. Genital warts are caused by a virus that is not curable and may increase Sarah's risk of cervical cancer. It is very important that she get a yearly PAP smear. Sarah dreads gynecological examinations because they remind her of the abuse she suffered. During this time of trauma Sarah lived in a city with one of the highest rates of church attendance in the U.S. Her troubled home was minutes away from a large, nationally known church with a major radio ministry. Yet she was facing her situation by herself.

Although Sarah felt she had somehow been singled out, she is not alone. Sexually transmitted diseases are epidemic in sexually active adolescents, especially those with a history of multiple partners. Sexually abused boys and girls are at even greater risk for sexually transmitted diseases. Sexually abused girls are more likely to have become pregnant, to have initiated sexual intercourse at a younger age, to use illegal drugs, to be depressed, to feel suicidal and to have been physically abused.

Miscarriage

Miscarriage, also called a spontaneous abortion, is very common in all pregnancies. Young women feel conflicting emotions when they become pregnant, even if the pregnancy was planned and desired. Abuse survivors may have even more difficulty dealing with their conflicting emotions when dealing with a miscarriage.

Induced abortion

Induced abortion (when the fetus or embryo is intentionally removed from the uterus or womb) is probably the most controversial subject of our time. It is certain that the readers of this book will have differing opinions about this issue. Whatever your beliefs about abortion, it is very likely that you will work with young women who have chosen abortion in the past because abortion is very common in most countries. And it is very likely that you will work with pregnant teens who are considering abortion. A young woman may ask you for counsel as she tries to decide what is best in her situation. For this reason we will briefly look at current data about the physical effects of abortion. We will then examine the emotional and spiritual effects of abortion. It is impossible to present a comprehensive discussion of the ethical issues surrounding this highly controversial topic. But no discussion of ministering to pregnant young women would be complete without delving into this difficult subject.

Physical effects of induced abortion

When abortion is legal and performed in a safe, licensed medical clinic, physical complications are less common than for a full-term pregnancy. The rate of death after childbirth in developed countries is 9 per 100,000. During pregnancy 22 percent of pregnant women are hospitalized while pregnant due to complications of the pregnancy.[7] In countries where abortion is legal, death caused by abortion is very rare. Women who choose abortion in countries where it is illegal, however, are much more at risk. The rate of complications and death after abortion is as many as 100,000 deaths annually (about two in ten maternal deaths), mainly in poor countries where abortion typically remains illegal.[8]

Emotional effects of induced abortion

As you work with sexually abused teens, you are certain to deal with young women who are either facing a decision about abortion or dealing with their feelings about an abortion in their past. The teen sexual abuse survivor, pregnant as a result of consensual sexual relations, may be experiencing intensely conflicting feelings. A young woman suffering through the emotional impact of

240

sexual abuse resulting in a pregnancy will usually feel very confused about her feelings and choices regarding her pregnancy. Or she may tell you she wants to end the pregnancy as soon as possible to rid her of the reminder of the abuser. If her pregnancy occurred as a result of sexual abuse, especially incest, the young woman may experience pressure from her family and health-care providers to have an abortion.

Young women who are physically or emotionally coerced into having abortions usually have significant feelings of guilt, grief, powerlessness and depression after the procedure.

Adolescents who have chosen abortion show a wide range of emotional reactions in the months and years after the procedure. Many express conflicting feelings about their decision. They may say they are relieved that they are no longer pregnant, but they regret what they did to their babies. Others may say they have no feelings of guilt or regret. Very young teens often do not fully grasp the meaning of their decision. Some may feel very positive about their decision immediately after the procedure, only to have intense feelings of grief and guilt later in life. Adolescents who regret their decision to have an abortion frequently become pregnant again within a few months after the procedure to fill the "empty place" left by the "baby" they aborted.

As you work with teens facing a decision about an unplanned pregnancy, you will probably encounter health-care professionals who tell you that abortion has no negative impact on the young woman. You may also hear from volunteers working in crisis pregnancy centers who state that all teens who choose abortion will have physical and emotional problems for years afterward.

While the physical effects of abortion done in a certified medical clinic in countries where abortion is legal are minimal, unbiased research does support that, emotionally, many adolescents and women do have significant conflicts and problems after the procedure is over. Evaluating the studies regarding the emotional impact of abortion must be done very carefully. The conclusions reached in research studies have the potential to be greatly influenced by the biases of the people doing the studies. This is especially true when looking at the emotional impact of induced abortion.

241

DEVELOPMENTAL TASKS OF PREGNANCY

Abused teens may have difficulty progressing through the normal developmental stages of pregnancy. They may deny or completely repress their feelings about the pregnancy and the babies they are carrying. The normal developmental stages of pregnancy include:

1. Decision to have children;
2. Acceptance of pregnancy;
3. Pregnancy;
4. Birth experiences;
5. Immediate postnatal period;
6. Parenthood.

Young mothers need to progress through the four major tasks of pregnancy, namely:

1. Safe passage through pregnancy for mother and the newborn;
2. Acceptance of pregnancy by significant others and society;
3. Letting go of former identities and giving of oneself;
4. Bonding with the child.

Bonding with the child is often the most difficult task for the survivor of pregnancy-related sexual abuse. The young mother may be using all of her emotional resources simply to live with the memory of the abuse. She may be in denial of the pregnancy or of her traumatic memories, which could prevent her from properly bonding with her baby.

TRAUMATIC LABOR AND DELIVERY EXPERIENCES

The labor-and-delivery experience may be traumatic for survivors of abuse. If you are acting as the friend, outreach worker, or maybe the labor coach to young women who have survived sexual abuse you will want to understand how the abuse experience may affect them during labor and delivery. You may also need to help doctors and nurses understand their reactions and explain to these health care providers how to make the delivery experience more positive and less threatening to them.

During labor, sexual abuse survivors, especially those with a long history of sexual abuse, may display the following behaviors:[9]

♦ strong reluctance, or even refusal, to have an internal examination;

♦ ambivalence or some denial of the pregnancy, such as not taking recommended precautions and advice;

♦ expression of fears that the unborn child may be abused.

The birth experience itself may trigger memories. The physical discomfort and pain may be similar to what the young woman felt during the abuse. She may feel mutilated or violated, as she did from the abuse. She may experience flashbacks. Abuse survivors often have a strong desire to maintain control, especially over their bodies. For such a woman the birth experience can be very disturbing. She may even withdraw, making it difficult to stay in control of the birth. She may feel out of control and unable to make decisions and choices during the birth. Strangers touching her body in intimate ways may magnify these memories. It is important not to be put off if the young woman pulls back slightly or recoils when touched. Survivors of sexual abuse may never have been touched in a kind way. Creating an emotionally safe environment is critical.

Young women may avoid telling their health-care providers about their abuse, fearing they will be judged, yet at the same time they may be desperate to share their stories. Before they can talk about what happened they need to be sure that the person in whom they are confiding is concerned and nonjudgmental.

The gynecological exam can mimic the original abuse. Abuse survivors may delay or avoid gynecological and obstetrical care because these exams remind them of the abuse. Patients need to be given a sense of control and a feeling of comfort and safety. All procedures should be carefully explained, and patients need to be comforted, supported and informed during procedures and exams. This may be the first time the survivor has the opportunity to be asked and to give permission.

Survivors may have complaints of chronic pain where no pathology can be found. Chronic pelvic pain or painful intercourse may be an ongoing problem. Some women who have been forced to have oral sex may have jaw, neck and throat pain.

For many survivors abuse took place at night. Instead of the bedroom being a cozy and restful place, it became a dangerous place where they were forced to participate in unspeakable acts. For many survivors sleep disorders are common. Fatigue can be an ongoing problem. The ordinary fatigue and sleeplessness that can accompany pregnancy are magnified for many survivors.

The childbirth experience can be especially threatening for women who are used to maintaining control. Women who feel they are losing control during labor may become aggressive and difficult. They may withdraw and become submissive and passive. They may try to control every moment of their labor. Or they may create a crisis that forces those around them to drop what they are doing to meet their needs.

During those moments when the labor-and-birth experience triggers reminders of the abuse some young women may emotionally remove themselves from what is happening. They may appear withdrawn or stoic. When this happens young women need to be reminded that they are safe and to be helped to involve themselves in what is happening. Getting the young women up walking and moving may be helpful if that is appropriate for the stage of labor. Touching in non-threatening ways may help to keep them in the present.

If a laboring teen suddenly has a look of panic, has a far-away look in her eyes, becomes rigid or changes how she is breathing, she may be experiencing a flashback to the abuse experience. Ask her what she is remembering and give her the opportunity to express what she is feeling. Remind her over and over that she is safe.

If you are acting as a birth coach or health-care provider, be careful to use non-threatening words when describing what is happening during the process itself and during procedures. If you hear someone using an inappropriate expression like "just spread your legs now for the exam," don't be afraid to take the person aside and explain the impact of that statement for someone who has experienced sexual abuse.

After a successful birth the survivor may feel a strong sense of accomplishment. The birth can help her have positive feelings about her sexuality. She may be able to feel more attached to her physical self instead of feeling estranged from her body, as she has in the past. The childbirth experience may help a young woman feel creative and capable. The people helping her through the birth

244

can encourage her to achieve these changes in how she feels about herself.

BIRTH EXPERIENCE: A CASE STUDY

"Marina" (not her real name) arrived at the labor-and-delivery suite gripping the ear of her brown teddy bear, tears falling from her wide-open eyes and clutching her large abdomen as a contraction began. Her mother held her hand as she walked through the big double hospital doors. Marina was from a protective, loving family that had watched over her all of her 16 years. Then her family's life was abruptly, radically changed one night when she was raped by a man whose face she never saw. Her father retreated from her, unable to deal with his rage and feelings of inadequacy about not being able to protect his only daughter.

Months later Marina finally summoned the courage to tell her mother that she was pregnant. The two struggled through the pregnancy together.

The only room left when she arrived in labor and delivery was shared by another laboring patient and her doting husband. Marina's roommate, Anna, was surrounded by flowers, balloons and stuffed animals. Anna's husband coached her through each contraction, handing her chips of ice afterward. Anna's parents and in-laws made frequent excited inquiries about her progress. She progressed quickly and was whisked to the delivery room. Marina and her mother heard Anna's family shout and clap with joy when they first glimpsed their long-awaited baby.

Marina and her mother quietly endured her long labor. When she finally delivered her baby, a perfect little girl, Marina and her mother looked at each other in a combination of wonder and anguish. The next day the papers were signed, and Marina's baby went home with another couple who promised, through the social worker, to love and care for her. Marina left the hospital sore and tired, holding a piece of paper showing her baby's footprints and looking so much older than she had two days before.

Marina was struggling to deal with the normal problems of adolescence when she was forced to adjust to the aftermath of a violent attack. She was confused, hurt, withdrawn and angry. Suddenly she had to deal with alienation from her father, adjusting to a pregnancy she never chose or wanted and her grief when she decided to allow another couple to adopt her baby. Marina would need further counseling after her delivery to deal with the aftermath of the rape, her father's reaction to her pregnancy and her very normal feelings of grief about relinquishing her baby.

Relinquishment

Marina wanted her baby to have a safe, secure home where she would be loved and nurtured by a mother and a father. She and her mother agonized about which choice was best. After much prayer she decided that the most loving choice she could make would be to relinquish the baby to be adopted by a loving couple. She did not "give her baby away." She did what she felt was the most loving thing she could do to provide her baby with the best home possible.

Adoption is one of the most difficult decisions a young woman will ever make. When ministering to an adolescent who is considering adoption, encourage her to work through a well-known, reputable (preferably Christian) adoption agency if one is available in the country in which you are working. Help her find an agency that advocates for both the birth parent(s) and the adoptive parent(s). Aid her in obtaining comprehensive counseling during the pregnancy and afterward, if these services are available in your area. Trained counselors can assist her to ensure that she is making the best decision for her and her baby and that she will be at peace with her decision after the adoption takes place. Close family members should be involved in the counseling.

Family members also may need help to work through their own feelings about the pregnancy. They also may need help in knowing how to support the young woman in making the best decision for her and her baby, even if this decision does not match the needs and wishes of family members.

The issues surrounding relinquishment will be determined by the culture in which you are working. Cultural awareness and sensitivity is critical to being effective in dealing with abuse survivors who are pregnant. If you are new to the country where you are working, or if you are working with pregnant abuse survivors from cultures with which you are not familiar, seek out people who will teach you about the culture. Read relevant books or articles if they are available. Open conversations with statements like, "Please help me understand what sexual abuse means here" or "How is pregnancy resulting from abuse dealt with?" Ask whether people talk openly about sexual issues and how adoption is viewed. Knowledge and understanding will make you much more sensitive and effective when you attempt to reach out to youth facing decisions regarding adoption.

HOW CAN WE HELP?

Churches, independent ministry organizations and individuals can play key roles in helping survivors of sexual abuse achieve emotional and physical healing and wholeness. When survivors are also dealing with a pregnancy, the need for the help of caring Christians is even more urgent.

Post-abortion intervention

As you work with parents of babies lost to abortion or miscarriage, they may tell you about unresolved feelings of guilt, sadness, loss, regret and emptiness. They may try to repress these feelings using emotional denial or even resorting to drugs or alcohol to numb the pain their feelings cause. These parents may never have had the opportunity to grieve for their babies. The feelings may be even more intense and confusing for adolescents who have survived sexual abuse and have endured the losses that accompany abuse.

Allow the adolescent to talk about her feelings. The teen may need you to help her obtain care from someone trained in post-abortion counseling. The teen and her family may wish to have a formal ceremony for their lost baby. Many lay workers and professionals who work with parents of babies lost to abortion (either induced or spontaneous, that is, miscarriage) have seen freedom and healing after parents are allowed to have a formal ceremony. Many parents find that a formal ceremony like a Eucharist can be even more effective and freeing than months of psychotherapy.

Others may prefer a less formal ceremony than a Eucharist. The ceremony can be solitary, or it can include a counselor or pastor; it may also include other loved ones. It can be conducted at the request of the mother, father, sibling or grandparent, who-ever is dealing with unresolved grief. Regardless, a ceremony to mourn a baby lost to abortion can assist the healing process. When appropriate during the ceremony sin is confessed and forgive-ness requested. The baby is prayed for and recognized as being in heaven with our loving Father. A simple ceremony can bring healing, release and freedom.

You, the reader, may find that reading this chapter brings to mind a personal experience that you have never dealt with. Know that just as certainly as you can touch the pages of this book, Jesus is waiting to heal your pain, and the pain of the adolescents you are working with who have experienced sexual abuse and abortion.

ACHIEVING HEALING AND WHOLENESS

> Jesus went throughout Galilee, teaching in their synagogues and proclaiming the good news of the kingdom and curing every disease and every sickness among the people (Matt. 4:23, *NRSV*).

The local church can play a pivotal role in reaching out to chil-dren and adolescents, becoming an agent of healing in their lives. Church leaders need to educate themselves and sensitively inform their congregations about the sad reality of sexual abuse. Pastors can play a key role in preparing and training interested church members to reach out to children and youth recovering from the impact of sexual abuse.

Embrace

Lee, the 18 year old mentioned at the beginning of this chapter, found a church where she was accepted and loved. No one ques-tioned her about the fact that she was single and pregnant. The congregation simply reached out to her with love and acceptance at the time in her life she most desperately needed their kindness. Lee relinquished her baby for adoption and went on to become a successful Christian speaker and author, wife and mother. She was reunited with her daughter 21 years later. Lee tells her poignant story in the book *The Missing Piece*.

A church responding in this way to a pregnant sexual abuse survivor can be instrumental in demonstrating Christ's love and giving her hope for a blessed future.

Mentoring

The young person you are working with may never have known the love of a parent. She may not know how to love and bond with her child. Wanting to be a good parent, she may find herself lashing out uncontrollably at her child.

Pregnant teens recovering from sexual abuse need adults who will support them through their pregnancy and teach them how to be nurturing parents. An adult mentor may act as a labor coach or may teach housekeeping, budgeting and parenting skills.

Get others involved. Perhaps there are mature people in your church who are willing to share their wisdom with some of the teens in your ministry. Or a Sunday School class may be willing to share the task of teaching a young person the skills she needs. If there is a Mothers of Preschoolers or similar groups in your area, they may be able to reach out to one of the young mothers you are mentoring.

Basic needs

As discussed earlier in this chapter, pregnant or parenting teens who are survivors of abuse are more likely to be homeless or living in minimally adequate housing. These teens and their children need safe, adequate housing and nutritious food. Many churches, ministries and individuals worldwide play a key role in meeting this need. Find out about local job-training programs that are willing to help youth obtain job skills. You may also want to learn about local government-subsidized programs or private programs that help homeless and poor youth.

Meeting these basic needs is crucial when intervening with youth who have been forced or have chosen to survive financially through prostitution. Rarely will these youth leave this lifestyle without an alternative way to survive financially, or without training and mentoring to help them learn other ways of making a living for themselves and their children.

Counseling

Pregnant or parenting teens often deal with depression, anger and thoughts of suicide. Your friendship and caring are healing tools God will use in the lives of those to whom you are ministering. However, some of the youth you are dealing with will need the help of professional counselors. The resources available will vary depending on where you live and the country in which you are working. If available locally, establish a network of experienced counselors willing to accept referrals. Perhaps your church or ministry can support a part-time or full-time professional mental-health counselor who can provide care for the young people to whom you minister.

Substance abuse treatment

If the children or teens you are working with have drug, alcohol or other substance-abuse problems, one of the most important things you can do is to encourage them to get into a treatment program. Substance-addiction intervention is a complicated process. Ultimately it is up to the abuser to decide to pursue treatment. But those working with teens need to be aware of any local treatment programs they can refer adolescents to for counseling and treatment when they do express an interest in pursuing treatment.

Although not as dangerous as street drugs, cigarettes are a threat to the health of pregnant and parenting youth. Encourage them to quit smoking when they are ready to deal with that aspect of their lifestyle.

Medical care

Children or teens who have been sexually abused need compassionate medical care to rule out or treat any injuries caused by the abuse. It is also important that they receive screening and treatment for sexually transmitted diseases.

A history of abuse makes it more likely that a young woman will delay obtaining medical care when she is pregnant. Pregnant youth and their infants are at high risk for complications during the pregnancy and immediately after birth. Encouraging pregnant teens to obtain medical care is important. The teen may want you to accompany her on medical visits.

Obtain a few good reference books or pamphlets regarding pregnancy and delivery, baby care and childrearing to share with the youth you are working with. These books can help you teach basic information about topics such as warning signs that indicate the need for immediate medical attention during pregnancy. They will also help you teach about first aid, medical care and parenting skills for infants and children. If you are working in a city or small town that has a local bookstore, browse through its shelves for some good resources. In cities or more rural areas the local community or public-health clinic health educator can probably assist you in finding simple references and booklets written in the language spoken by yourself and the youth with whom you are working.

Talk with local health-care providers and clinic personnel. These health-care providers may be dealing with young people who desperately need your help. Let them know about your ministry and your ministry's current capacity to care for sexually abused youth.

A CHALLENGE

Measure success by involvement—not by always having the perfect outcome. Sexual abuse is one of the most wrenching experiences a child or adolescent can face. It may take years for the survivor to work through the healing process. When the abuse experience includes a pregnancy, the healing process is even more complicated. As a caring mentor or outreach worker you may not see the immediate change you would wish for. Your caring and involvement, however, does make a difference—even though that may not be apparent to you now. Youth are "works in progress," and your kindness will have an impact during one of the most difficult times a person can ever face.

Your willingness to come alongside children and youth dealing with sexual abuse also will be one of the tools God uses to make a difference in these young lives. The fruit of your labor may not be apparent now or for years to come, but never doubt that your friendship, love, time and caring make a difference, especially when those youth are themselves pregnant or parenting.

This author has witnessed and experienced firsthand the ability of abuse survivors to be warm, loving, compassionate individuals and parents. Paul, such a survivor, is one of the people I

251

love most in this world. Paul's steadfast faith and love are tools God has used to teach me about himself.

The professional literature regarding the long-term outcomes for sexually abused children and youth can be sobering and discouraging. But as a Christian working in this field I know that our God is a God of miraculous emotional healing. God can help any one of us who reaches out to him to be whole. The scars will remain, but survivors of abuse can be fulfilled adults capable of being nurturing caring parents and spouses.

Notes

[1] Lee's story told in L. Ezell, *The Missing Piece: Finding God's Peace for Your Past* (Eugene, Ore.: Harvest House Publishers, 1986).

[2] D. K. Kozaric, et al., "Rape, Torture, and Traumatization of Bosnian and Croatian Women: Psychological Sequelae," *American Journal of Orthopsychiatria* 65:3 (July 1995).

[3] D. Esparza and C. Esperat, "The Effects of Childhood Sexual Abuse on Minority Adolescent Mothers," *Journal of Obstetrics, Gynecological and Neonatal Nursing* 24:4 (May 1996). The total exceeds 100 percent because some victims had more than one abuser.

[4] D. G. Koniak and J. Lesser, "The Impact of Childhood Maltreatment on Young Mothers' Violent Behavior Toward Themselves and Others," *Journal of Pediatric Nursing* 11:5 (October 1996).

[5] L. Spak, et al., "Factors in Childhood and Youth Predicting Alcohol Dependence and Abuse in Swedish Women: Findings from a General Population Study," *Alcohol* 32:3 (May-June 1997):267–74.

[6] L. Brown, et al., "Experiences of Physical and Sexual Abuse in Australian General Practice Attenders and an Eating Disordered Population," *Australia New Zealand Journal of Psychiatry* 31:3 (June 1997):398–404.

[7] D. A. Grimes, "The Morbidity and Mortality of Pregnancy: Still Risky Business," *American Journal of Obstetrics and Gynecology* 170:5, pt. 2 (May 1994): 1489–94.

[8] A. Kulczycki, et al., "Abortion and Fertility Regulation," *Lancet* 347:9016 (July 15, 1996): 1663–68.

[9] A. Cassin, "Sexual Abuse and Motherhood," *Nursing Times* 92:15 (April 10, 1996).

18

Outcast Children Belong in Families

Jennie Woods

Every child is a gift from God, loved into being, infinitely precious to God, created for greater things: to love and be loved.
—*Mother Teresa*

Childhood, designed by our heavenly Father to be a time of nurture, love and hope, has tragically become a crisis of despair and pain for millions of children. Boys and girls who should be surrounded with laughter, encouragement and careful training are instead held captive in exceptionally difficult circumstances that most of us reading this chapter cannot imagine. When there is suffering, why do the children always suffer most? Why are satanic forces concentrated against the young? Perhaps it is because the powers of darkness know that when a tender, fragile life is damaged, the poison will continue to pollute throughout a lifetime.

Through the power of the gospel it is possible to bring hope and healing to adults who have suffered abuse as children. A better strategy is to seek and reach little ones in danger before they become adults and are enveloped by evil. The greatest challenge for God's people is to reach these children at risk, at the youngest age possible, with the good news of the gospel of Jesus Christ and lovingly celebrate their lives and childhoods.

When we discuss evangelism with children, we must realize that it is simply not enough to preach the gospel. Rescuing a child is a process, not an event. In this chapter we shall look at three principles that must be understood as we labor to bring children out of darkness and into righteous, fruitful living.

1. It is possible for a child intentionally and decisively to close the door on the old way of life only if he or she is given a vision and a provision for a new life.
2. A broad range of ministry options must be available, but emphasis should be given to the biblical model of placing children within families.
3. All must work together. Resources must be multiplied by developing partnerships, using all available and potential resources, both lay and professional, especially those within local church congregations.

Ministering to outcast children begins with the message that God loves them exactly as they are and that God hates what is happening to them. They need to know that Jesus' love can free them from the bondage and guilt of their personal sin, and that he is ready to forgive anything they have done, been forced to do, or have had done to them. No matter what condition they may be in right now, Jesus can give them a pure, fruitful, abundant life. New birth is the beginning of that wonderful life. Yet every "out of" must have an "into." A child who is released from the ownership of evil people must have an alternative way of life.

It is possible for a child to close the door on the old way of life only if he or she is given a vision and a provision for a new life. Children must not be brought into new birth and then left with no provision to live that new life. Is it realistic to expect that a young person rescued from sexual bondage will be able to fend for his or her own physical and emotional needs? If we are to disciple traumatized young people successfully, we must be able to introduce a community of security and of belonging that is equal to or better than the one they are being asked to leave behind.

Children need to belong

Fifteen-year-old Ruby had lived in many different homes and been used by many different men before she came to study at a Christian boarding school. The first few weeks Ruby was overflowing with happiness at being in a clean, safe room and having people around her who would pray for and encourage her. But soon she began to get depressed. When her counselor tried to talk to her about her deep sadness, Ruby said through her tears, "I'm lonely. I like it here, but I'm just so lonely." After only three months at the school, Ruby ran away, back to her old way of life.

The deepest need of a child rescued from sexual exploitation may not be economical, physical or even social. Contrary to common perceptions, the burning question probably is not, How will I support myself? but rather Who will love me? Inconceivably, the old life may have held something the child perceives as love. He or she was wanted, and life held value even if only for profit. Life was exciting and risky. The world was narrow, but it was a world where one belonged and, to a certain extent, where one was appreciated by others.

When trying to imagine moving out from beyond the known sphere, an exploited child may be filled with fear. The child may not be able to see a place for "me" in that other world. Not only are basic living skills lacking, but his or her worldview is radically askew. The child may hear, "Jesus loves you." But love has always meant lust. Mention of a heavenly Father may bring remembrance of a father who sold his child for less than the price of a chicken. Friends are viewed with suspicion. Survival has come by manipulating through deception, winning favor with artful lies, coveting money and power, sleeping till noon and stealing. The pain, alienation and hopelessness of these children is an inseparable part of who they are, and how they perceive themselves and others.

Sarie was only three months old when her mother abandoned her the first time. Over the years Sarie's mom reclaimed her daughter repeatedly, only to leave her again. At age 14 Sarie stood out on the balcony of the home of her foster parents and enticed a young stranger into her bedroom. It was the beginning of a life of prostitution during which Sarie would often say, "I'm O.K. I know what I am doing, and I like it." Sarie had found a way to make herself wanted.

Unlike so many others, Sarie's story has a happy ending. Jesus Christ came into her life shortly after her first child was born. Knowing she needed help with the baby, Sarie agreed to move in with a Christian family. After many months of prayer and unconditional love, she was finally able to forgive and conquer the pain of abandonment and realize her special place in the eternal family of her heavenly Father.

No two children are identical

Our God is a creator of infinite variety. No rainbow is the same as another, no fingerprint is identical to another and no child is exactly like any other. Different interventions must be available for different children. A broad continuum of care extending from prevention to intervention to rehabilitation must be developed. A child who needs basic parenting will prosper in an adoptive or foster home, while one who cannot control violent anger will need the safe structure of a group home. For the older, mature child, the ideal place to grow may be a vocational training center. Because children respond to the same circumstances in dramatically different ways, ministering to their individual needs is possible only if we have choices as we make plans for them.

A broad range of options must be available, with emphasis on the biblical model of placing children within families. The revelation of family is essential in grasping the full measure of the meaning of the gospel. God established his family on the earth, redeeming the family of man from sin through the death of his only begotten Son. The love of a perfect father can only be understood when we grasp the anguish of God as he chose to sacrifice his only Son to redeem us, and provide the way for every man, woman and child to be adopted into God's eternal family.

Anyone who has grown up in an abusive family or been removed from a family and brought into an abusive situation lacks a reference point to grasp or understand the loving promises of Father God. God's Word deals with us through family models all the way from Cain's slaying of Abel to the father's joy when the prodigal son returns from his frivolity. Jesus was born into a family.

256

Even from the cross Jesus took care to provide for his mother by designating John to assume the responsibility of a son.

Understanding God's love means understanding family love. When 14–year-old Juanita moved into a home for expectant mothers, she did not reveal that the baby she was carrying belonged to her father. Throughout the six months Juanita was in residence at the home, the women who ran the home prayed for her and loved her. Juanita caused no trouble. She obeyed the rules and quietly did her studies and her chores. But all the ministry efforts simply did not affect Juanita. She became friends with the other young women in the home, but whenever the talk turned to our heavenly Father, Juanita simply became quiet and said nothing. After placing her newborn baby up for adoption, she left the home. Can we imagine what images the word father brought up in Juanita's mind?

Family, the keystone for spiritual understanding and development, is usually also pivotal for the sexually exploited child. Attempting to minister to the outcast child without addressing the need to belong to a family is likely ignoring the strongest felt need that is burning within the wounded child. Is it possible to restore the nurture of lost hugs, soft words, selfless instruction and dependable structure? Yes, it is! The godly meaning of family can be ignited within children who are from incomplete or dysfunctional families or who are without families altogether. The love and truth of the gospel, demonstrated through God's people, can draw these outcast children into holy living and into healthy, loving, homes and families.

Although Rebecca was only 4 years old, she had lived with repeated sexual abuse. Her father and his friends were the men responsible for the regular exploitation. Glad for an opportunity to rid herself of the child, Rebecca's mother signed relinquishment papers enabling us (the House of Samuel, the mission I directed) to place her into an adoptive home. After placement in her new family the adoptive parents were shocked by the self-destructive behavior of this little girl. She banged her head against the wall. She bit her hands and arms until they bled. She drew pictures on the walls of her bedroom with her feces. But Rebecca's parents had determined, "We will never, never give up!" Over and over they assured her by their words and by their actions that she was "our very own little girl forever and forever." Today, these parents are proud grandparents! Rebecca is a good mother, with a loving husband and delightful children of her own. The cycle of rejection was broken only by selfless family love.

In a family, everyone wins

Clearly, family is the best intervention. It is also the only intervention that has the potential to reach such an enormous number of the world's needy children. As an example, let's look at Zambia, Africa. Zambia has an extraordinarily high birth rate coupled with an HIV/AIDS pandemic conservatively estimated to reach 25 percent of the population. Already an estimated 70,000 children live on the streets of this sub-Saharan country. Most of the street boys, and likely all of the girls, are sexually exploited. The number of Zambian orphans is expected to soar to more than 700,000 by the year 2000. Orphanages are overcrowded, and staffs overworked and often overwhelmed. One prominent international leader suggests that Zambia must begin building megaorphanages that can house and feed 10,000 children in each facility. Even if this could be done, Zambia would need 60 such institutions by the year 2000.[1] But God has commissioned the church to bring these boys and girls into our homes and communities (James 1:27).

According to *Operation World*, Zambia has 6,586 Protestant churches with 808,400 church members. If each one of these churches would be responsible for just 11 children, there would be more than enough homes and families for every child who is now living on Zambia's streets! The church at large must be mobilized, trained and equipped to bring outcast children into Christian homes, families and the fellowship of the Christian community. There is simply no other way to reach such an enormous number of children. Everyone can do something for children. And unless we willingly turn our backs, everyone must do something for children. If we employ this biblical manner of ministry, children will have families, the church will have a rich resource in these young members, and the community will have the light of compassionate witness.

BIBLICAL MODELS FOR INCORPORATING CHILDREN INTO FAMILIES

The following models provide some alternatives for placing children in homes and families.

Adoption

Whenever a rescued child is young enough, or receptive enough, the most ideal intervention is adoption. Adoption is far more than a permanent and safe family environment. In its pure meaning adoption is the grafting in of a new branch. Think of those large genealogical charts or family trees, where all the lines connect back into the beginning line. A family is indeed like a large tree, with deep roots to the past and high boughs reaching to the future. It is an organism that began and continues to grow on foundations that have been laid for generations. The new branch, a child or even a young adult, who has been cast off from the family tree of birth is carefully prepared. Through the acceptance of the adoptive family (often proven in much pain and trauma) the grafted branch gradually begins to allow the life sap of the tree to flow and so becomes an integral part of the family tree. In time it will be impossible to tell which branches were grafted in and which branches originated with the tree.

When considering an adoptive placement for a child the following four questions should be addressed:

1. Is the child able and willing to accept a relationship with another? Children who have closed the door to honest relationships will find it difficult to respond to the emotional demands of a family.
2. Does the child have realistic expectations of adoption, and does he or she want the adoption enough to invest in its success? The evidence of an affirmative answer is made apparent by yet another question. Will the child agree to abide by simple household rules and accept responsibility and correction when necessary?
3. With encouragement and support from its local church, is an appropriate family prepared to accept the child?

259

4. Is the child legally free for adoption? If not, can the child be placed in a substitute or foster family?

Although international adoption can be a wonderful alternative for a few children, adoptive parents within the Christian population in the child's own community and country should always be the first priority. International adoptions should be pursued only when it has been determined that adoption is the best placement for an individual child and no family is available within the child's country.

Although most adopting couples want healthy infants, many people in every nation on earth would adopt an older child or a child with special needs if they knew they could get training and support and if they could afford the initial fees.

Substitute families/foster families

Substitute or foster family outreach is probably the best yet most neglected option. Substitute or foster families are capable of providing excellent personal care in a cost-and-labor effective manner. Often all the pieces are not in place for an adoption, especially when a child first comes into care. The child is not legally free. The parents may have disappeared, they may not have valid identity papers, or the child may not have a birth certificate. Sometimes adoptions are not possible because the local court system will not approve adoptions. A foster-family or substitute-family placement offers the benefits of family living without the paperwork hassles of adoption. The drawback is that it does not provide the established permanency of a legal adoption.

An efficient foster-placement ministry is an innovative way to involve the entire local church body in personal ministry. It demands screening, training, supervising and systems of accountability. But it yields the high benefits of family care with a minimum of legal paperwork. Given the proper tools and preliminary consultation, the pastoral and administrative offices of the church are perfectly suited to manage foster-care placements. The potential number of children who could have a family of their own through a foster-care program is exciting. Could each small congregation provide two families? Could a larger church produce ten? The possibilities are enormous.

Group homes and institutional families

A group home or larger facility is usually managed by paid staff. These settings do not offer the individual attention or the interactive family modeling available in other family settings. However, placement into a group family can be ideal in certain circumstances, when the home functions in these ways:

1. A receiving home for new children where evaluations and testing can be done.
2. A safe environment where the pressure to relate to others on an intimate basis does not have to be present.
3. A professionally staffed facility where problems can be evaluated and assessed.
4. A transit home for older children who may soon be living on their own.

The obvious drawback of residential programs is the lack of fundamental family bonding, which includes permanency, identity and inheritance. Yet, even in a group setting, basic family values can be taught and modeled. Sometimes the group home may have permanent parents who, with the help of support staff, can transform the group into a family. Adults from local churches can affirm the value of individual young people by becoming special friends and mentors.

Vocational training and livelihood programs, especially if they are offered in a caring, residential setting such as a boarding school, are a proven answer for older children who can eventually live on their own or in groups. Again, the maturity and growth of children will depend largely on the response and commitment of the neighborhood church. Children can learn the meaning of family as they become an integral part of a church family.

All must work together. We must use all available and potential resources, both lay and professional, especially those within local church congregations.

A worldwide focus on children living in exceptionally difficult circumstances is likely to produce partnerships. We know we can't handle it all by ourselves. The fact is, it's not just too big for me, its too big for us—we need God, and we need each other. So the question becomes, What can we do better *together* than we can do on our own?

The world of business is making good use of partnerships. When the Boeing 777 airplane was being designed and built in Everett, Washington, Boeing itself manufactured very few of the needed parts. Instead Boeing researched where the best of each small part—every connection, every seat, every control—could be obtained. Boeing enlisted the services of 35,000 subcontractors from over 20 countries to build its 777.

The parts were made and shipped to Everett, the pieces assembled and the airplane took off—a stunning success. Every one of the 35,000 partners shared the credit!

How many of us in ministry to children are still trying to provide for all the needs of all our children by adding new programs to our individual ministries? The scenario is familiar. In the 1970s I directed a crisis-care ministry that focused on temporary and long-term care to Native American children. When the ministry outgrew the house, we expanded our operations by starting a program to train Christian foster families. We also purchased land to build several group homes. A few years later we felt it was time that the special educational needs of the children be met, so we opened an ACE[2] school. An adoption program, crisis pregnancy counseling, a group home for expectant mothers, parent-training courses, bonding therapy and a program of international adoptions were also eventually added. Along with these diversified programs we had to add new offices, a fifteen-station phone system, a small fleet of vehicles, elaborate flow charts, a whole bookcase of manuals and policies, daily staff meetings, court hearings, expensive insurance policies and mountains of paperwork.

After quite a few more years of experience I am now convinced that a more effective procedure would be to find the very best school (or parent training, or bonding therapy), contribute everything we could to make that particular school the very best it could be and allow the programs of others to prosper, while they make it possible for us to concentrate on conducting our own area of ministry with excellence.

Differences make partnerships powerful

An effective partnership must allow all its members to maintain distinct, separate identities, procedures and dogmas. Partnership involves two or more individuals or organizations who collaborate to achieve a common purpose. Meaningful partnership presupposes that the partners have different resources and assets. That's what makes partnerships so effective! The form of each partnership is as unique as its members and can vary greatly according to such factors as the number of partners involved, the complexity of the purpose being pursued and the time frame.

Just how many professional disciplines are needed to minister adequately to one child? Evangelism, social work, counseling, placement and follow-up, medical and dental services, basic and Christian education, intercession, vocational training and fundraising are all required. Workers in rural areas who rescue children before they can be sold to pimps cannot recruit and train church members to open their homes. A vocational training school cannot house infants. The mission that is operating in the red-light district of a city cannot become involved in the labyrinth of documents and red tape of adoption. Resources simply are not sufficient for any one person or any one ministry to do the job independently.

Several years ago a missionary family in the Amazon jungle felt a burden for abandoned infants. For an unwanted baby to be discarded in the dump or dropped into the river was not unusual. One day a mother brought her newborn baby to the missionaries and begged them to adopt him. The missionaries could not adopt the baby themselves, but since they had friends in the U.S. who had been wanting to adopt, they decided to take the tiny baby and give him to their friends. Their intentions were good, but their knowledge of adoption procedures were not. After many months of frustration, expense and a miracle or two, the complicated adoption was completed. The missionary's first reaction was to say, "Never again!" Later he contacted a reputable international adoption agency that interacted with local churches whose members wanted to adopt and formed a consensus-based partnership to ensure that in the future babies would have families—and he would never have to appear in another adoption court!

The local church is the place to begin

It's time for us to utilize all presently available and potentially available resources. Children need professional interventions, but they also need meaningful relationships with ordinary people. They especially need the Christian community that is found within local church congregations. Every church is composed of people with a diversity of talents, resources, and spiritual giftings. Everyone can contribute something to children. Everyone has a place within the partnership.

Incorporating the local church within a partnership will bring the ministry from an institutional level to a people level. It becomes approachable, both to the adult wanting to help and to the child in need of help. Some can pray, others can give, others can donate their services in their own area of professional expertise, others can adopt or foster, yet others can share the vision with friends and neighbors. When child welfare partnerships are formed, operated and evaluated within the local church context, everyone can have a part. It is exactly this kind of involvement that must happen if we are to succeed in reaching the suffering children of the world.

On a recent visit to Zambia, Africa, I was blessed to meet the elders of a Baptist church in the capital city of Lusaka. Their church had been left with eight children when both their parents died. A distant relative was willing to care for the children but, because of extreme poverty and many children of her own, was not able to do so. The challenge was met by the church family. The children were all placed in this relative's family because partners from the local church family made it possible by providing for their needs. The four small cell groups within the church each took the responsibility of providing for the children, one month at a time. By rotating months, each cell group is financially responsible for only three months each year. Lusaka Baptist Church is a shining example of a local church congregation partnering together for children.

A partnership is not a marriage

Consensus-based partnership is formed on an informal agreement to work toward achieving a common purpose without the need for a contract or constitution. In the context of Christian partnerships it includes praying, planning and working together. A strategic, consensus-based partnership for the welfare of children is a vertically integrated group of agencies, missions, churches and individuals. Each retains its autonomy and identity but is committed to pray, plan and work together for the planting of a culturally relevant, multifaceted, self-sustaining, Christian child-welfare outreach within a specific area. The partnership is strategic because it is an overall plan to reach destitute and outcast children within a specific area. It includes as many of the necessary interventions as possible, linking such ministries as evangelism, social work, medicine, education, counseling, fundraising and livelihood. The partnership is consensus-based because the different parts of the body of Christ agree to pray, plan and work together, each contributing resources and what it does best to contribute to the overall whole.

A Christian child welfare partnership incorporates biblical interventions on behalf of children in crisis situations. As a basis for consensus is reached, there can be commitment to joint action, responsibilities and timetables. Each partner can focus energy and attention on aspects of child welfare where it is the expert. The goal of each strategic consensus-based partnership for the welfare of children is to engage all available resources in an effort to transform outcast children into effective, reproducing disciples of God.

The children are worth the effort!

The potential for such consensus-based partnering is great. We must not be discouraged, however, if progress is slow. A small project attempted and successfully completed will go a long way in paving the road for larger partnerships in the future.

Jesus prayed that we would be one, so that the world would see and believe. As we work together to bring abandoned, abused and exploited children into the kingdom, let's reach across organizational, racial, cultural and doctrinal lines toward unity in the family of God.

> If you've gotten anything at all out of following Christ, if his love has made any difference in your life, if being in a community of the Spirit means anything to you, if you have a heart, if you care—then do me a favor: Agree with each other, love each other, be deep-spirited friends. Don't push your way to the front; don't sweet-talk your way to the top. Put

yourself aside, and help others get ahead. Don't be obsessed with getting your own advantage. Forget yourselves long enough to lend a helping hand (Phil. 2:1–4, *The Message*).

Notes

[1] *Zambia Daily Mail*, February 14, 1997, from an interview with G. Miyanda, former minister of Sport, Youth and Child Development.

[2] The Alliance for Children Everywhere facilitates the placement of outcast children into families by developing consensus-based partnerships, especially in developing nations, in cooperation with existing mission agencies through local church networks.

19

Mobilizing to Protect Children from Sexual Abuse

Pam Kerr

Eight-year-old Shima is a small-built girl who never smiles. She is regularly beaten by her present mistress, so much that the entire neighborhood knows about it. She is beaten and burned with a hot iron spatula, a shoe, or whatever is at hand. Her back is full of scars from burns and blows. On occasions, Shima is locked in the bathroom and has to go without food. Shima never goes out, not even to take out the garbage. When her employers leave, she is locked in. Her mistress said that she is a little devil and if she is not locked in she will steal things and run away.[1]

Barely a day passes without a new report from somewhere in the world about the abuse of children. Children enslaved like Shima, as domestic servants; children conscripted into armies; children bonded into hazardous labor; children trafficked across country borders; children sold by their own parents into modern-day slavery in brothels and subjected to sexual exploitation at the hands of adults.

Adults like the six Westerners reported by the *Asian Age* newspaper in October 1996 to be facing child sex charges in the western Indian resort state of Goa. A member of this pedophile ring had advised that operations be shifted to southern India so they could "continue in peace"! Peace for whom? Certainly not the innocent children whose lives may be physically, emotionally and spiritually scarred by this abuse.

Who *is* trying to stop these things, and what is our role as Christians? What is our response when we are confronted by these horrors, sometimes in our own backyard? It is normal and easy to despair when we review the numbers of children being exploited in the world today. Surely God has something to say to us about this situation.

OUR STARTING POINT: GOD LOVES AND CARES FOR CHILDREN

We know how God views children. Scripture is clear: a child is a unique individual who is valuable in God's eyes. Before we were born, God knew us (Ps. 139:13–16). God does not want children to be harmed in any way. Jesus said, "Let the little children come to me, and do not stop them; for it is to such as these that the kingdom of heaven belongs" (Matt. 19:14, *NRSV*). Unfortunately, too many children are hindered from coming to Jesus. The adults in their lives are often abusive, manipulative, domineering, cruel and neglectful. How can such children begin to comprehend a loving God when their experience of love is so lacking? Jesus made it very clear how he felt about those who would harm children: "If any of you put a stumbling block before one of these little ones who believe in me, it would be better for you if a great millstone were fastened around your neck and you were drowned in the depth of the sea" (Matthew 18:6, *NRSV*).

Given the importance of children in God's eyes, we ought to be advocating that every child has a right to experience a time in which he or she is nurtured and protected, free from neglect and abuse, to develop into a physically, mentally and spiritually whole adult:

> The children of the world are innocent, vulnerable, and dependent. They are also curious, active, and full of hope. Their

time should be one of joy and peace, of playing, learning, and growing. Their future should be shaped in harmony and cooperation. Their lives should mature, as they broaden their perspectives and gain new experiences.[2]

BACKGROUND: PROTECTION OF CHILDREN

The last two decades have seen a dramatic increase in the level of awareness about the exploitation and abuse of children around the world. In *Children First: The Story of UNICEF, Past and Present*, author Maggie Black describes the gradual emergence of international concern about problems relating to children:

> During the International Year of the Child in 1979, many problems relating to children—exploitation, abuse, child prostitution, children on the streets—that had previously been denied or ignored by city authorities projecting a travel-poster image were given an international airing. One of those imperceptible changes in the moral climate began to appear.[3]

The subcategorization of children experiencing obstacles in addition to poverty itself, "Children in Especially Difficult Circumstances" (CEDC), was coined by UNICEF in the mid-1980s. Such recognition was due in great part to efforts of child rights activists. Quoting from *Mayors as Defenders of Children* (UNICEF) Maggie Black, an author with many years' experience researching and writing about children's issues, pointed out that

> the CEDC designation indicated a heightened perception of children and childhood being subject to special problems of deprivation beyond those of the natural physiological vulnerabilities of the very young. It also pointed in a different direction as far as responses were concerned. Relieving "difficult circumstances" required not only rehabilitative care for the victims; it required preventive actions to stop exploitation occurring, confirmed by legislative action to bring perpetrators to book.[4]

While UNICEF continued developing public policy perspectives, key international non-governmental organizations (NGOs) focused on advocacy and legislative concerns. These joint efforts were behind the development of the United Nations Convention on the Rights of the Child, which was adopted on November 20, 1989.

PROTECTING CHILDREN FROM SEXUAL EXPLOITATION: AN IMPORTANT FOCUS

Article 34 of the Convention says that State Parties undertake to protect the child from all forms of sexual abuse:

> For these purposes, State Parties shall in particular take all appropriate national, bilateral, and multi-lateral measures to prevent:
> (a) The inducement or coercion of a child to engage in any unlawful sexual activity;
> (b) The exploitative use of children in prostitution or other unlawful sexual practices;
> (c) The exploitative use of children in pornographic performance and materials.[5]

In August 1996 a landmark event took place in Stockholm, Sweden. The World Congress against Commercial Sexual Exploitation of Children brought together for the first time in an international meeting, on an equal footing, governments, international and United Nations agencies, NGOs and others working on a global mobilization against the commercial sexual exploitation of children. The congress came on the heels of international outrage at the uncovering of a murderous pedophile ring in Belgium and the discovery of the bodies of four abducted young girls. The response to these disclosures was dramatic, particularly in Belgium, where tens of thousands of persons marched in protest against such evil.

Children in prostitution, trafficked for sexual purposes or used in the production of pornography are clearly sexually exploited; but, as the congress highlighted, children often experience sexual abuse in addition to their already-difficult situations. According to the 1997 *State of the World's Children,*

> Children in domestic servitude may well be the most vulnerable and exploited children of all, as well as the most difficult to protect. They are often extremely poorly paid or not

paid at all; their terms and conditions are very often entirely at the whim of the employers and take no account of their legal rights; they are deprived of schooling, play, and social activity, and of social support from family and friends. They are the most vulnerable to physical and sexual abuse.[6]

Children caught up in war are often similarly affected, but protection from sexual abuse for children swept up in war is not even guaranteed with the arrival of peacekeeping troops. In her United Nations–commissioned report, *Impact of Armed Conflict on Children*, Graça Machel points out, "In 6 out of 12 country studies on sexual exploitation of children in situations of armed conflict, prepared for the present report, the arrival of peacekeeping forces has been associated with a rapid rise in prostitution."[7]

Developing standards for ministry

What is being done to children is an abomination. But it is important to be mindful of the words of Jesus, "For with the judgment you make you will be judged, and the measure you give will be the measure you get" (Matt. 7:2, *NRSV*). Jesus did not tell persons that they could not judge; rather, he made it clear that the same standards used to judge others should be applied to themselves. Are the standards we expect to see applied for the welfare of the world's children the standards we apply to children within our spheres of influence and involvement? For example, consider the following questions in light of your own ministry:

- Are children viewed as active participants and treated with respect and dignity?
- Are there organizational policies and procedures to protect them from harm?
- Do surveys and assessments include an assessment of child exploitation, including children in exploitative situations involving labor, sexual exploitation and/or trafficking of children, and children with disabilities?
- Are efforts mainly focused on "rescue," with limited focus on healing and rehabilitation?
- Is there a concerted effort to keep current on the state of the world's children?

- ◆ Are advocacy efforts viewed as important?
- ◆ Is there partnership and networking with others involved in similar work and also with organizations advocating the end of child exploitation?
- ◆ Is there prayer? Lamentations 2:19b implores

  > Lift your hands to him
  >> for the lives of your children,
  > who faint for hunger
  >> at the head of every street (*NRSV*).

- ◆ Are workers supported, trained, valued and provided with the resources they need to do the job?

Of all these concerns one that is most often overlooked is that of protecting children from sexual abuse. The Stockholm Congress strongly emphasized, first and foremost, the need for prevention and protection.

Protection starts at home

Over the past 15 years many churches and other ministries have had to face the issue of sexual abuse of children in their care by staff or volunteers and, in some cases, donors. Confronting sexual abuse is particularly uncomfortable for many persons. All too often within the church and Christian ministries such confrontation of the potential for sexual abuse results in denial.

Christian ministries are not immune to the machinations of those who may have ulterior motives in mind in their selection of a place of ministry. As noted in End Child Prostitution, Pornography and Trafficking's (ECPAT) resource kit, "It is a comforting thought to classify people who sexually exploit children as criminally insane and/or extreme deviants. The belief that these people are out of the ordinary creates a safe distance from ourselves. It also creates a safe but mistaken belief that no 'normal' person would harm a child."[8]

Does that translate into "no Christian would harm a child?" Why not? All Christians know from their own struggle in striving to let God work out God's purposes in them that all are sinners. According to a book by the Church Law and Tax Report organization, *Reducing the Risk of Child Sexual Abuse in Your Church:*

Sexual molestation in the church is not something new. Only within the past decade has it become a topic for discussion. To a large extent, this new openness has been forced upon the church through litigation and media attention. Often, an attitude of denial or minimization has existed among church leaders concerning this tragic problem. Many local leaders still cannot believe that sexual molestation would ever occur in their churches.[9]

The same attitude of denial still exists today in many Christian organizations. Teo van der Weele has spent many years counseling and working with the victims of sexual abuse. In his book *From Shame to Peace* he describes very clearly a reason for this denial: "The effect of humanism on Christianity seems to show up in an evolutionary idea of people becoming better and better as time goes on. The reality of sin and the possibility of sexual deviance which is hurtful to children needs to be more openly discussed."[10]

We do not propose here to enter a debate about whether or not a person intent on child abuse is likely or not to be a Christian, or whether or not the abuse is more likely to take place within a church than a parachurch organization, but to acknowledge that abuse of children within Christian ministries does happen and to discuss ways in which the risk may be reduced.

Ministries at risk

In addition to denying the issue and finding it difficult to believe people would deliberately target a Christian ministry to have access to children, there are several other reasons why a Christian ministry may be at risk:

1. Persons and organizations of trust are not by nature or experience suspicious of people's motives for working in ministry with children.
2. There is a belief that "nice" Christian people don't abuse children. 1 Timothy 5:24 says, "The sins of some people are conspicuous and precede them to judgment, while the sins of others follow them there" *(NRSV)*. We cannot always determine a person's character by his or her outward appearance.

3. There is a lack of safeguards, or if they are available, they are not always implemented.

4. Evidence of misconduct may be ignored. It is so much easier to accept an apology or an employee's explanation of inappropriate behavior in a spirit of forgiveness than to raise questions about character or motives.

Is this really necessary?

Measures to protect children should be considered in the same light as any other internal process intended to ensure accountability and integrity. Strengthening current procedures reduces the risk of children being sexually abused within a system for the following reasons:

1. Designing and implementing safeguards assumes a greater urgency when the reason—children and their welfare—is considered. Children need to be accorded the respect and dignity due them as unique individuals, valued in every way. There is *never* an excuse for sexual abuse of a child.

2. Children who are sexually abused may be traumatized for a lifetime, coping with feelings of betrayal, guilt, worthlessness and rage, and sometimes with physical injury.

3. There can be a loss of trust and confidence in the work a ministry is trying to do. There can also be loss of faith in God if the person professing to be there "in the name of Jesus" is the abuser.

4. Accusations of sexual abuse can be a public-relations disaster for a ministry, damaging good work done in the past and raising questions about future effectiveness.

5. There may be financial implications that have the potential to destroy a ministry and consequently its work with children.

Setting a house in order

Risk-reduction measures will vary from organization to organization, depending on size and the scope of work, but basic steps are applicable in all situations:

1. Has the awareness of staff and volunteers been raised? (This can be accomplished by using both internal and external

resources, such as psychologists, police and child protection agency experts).

2. Are there organizational guidelines for the protection of children from sexual abuse? If so, have the guidelines been reviewed and approved by local legal counsel, are they being implemented and is there a mechanism in place to ensure they are being followed?

3. Are there behavior protocols for staff and volunteers about appropriate conduct in working and interacting with children? For example, a well-known behavior protocol for work with children is the "two-person" rule. Staff under most circumstances should not be working alone with children. As well as protecting children, the "two-person" rule can also protect staff members from false allegations of abuse.

4. Are there reporting procedures to follow if staff or volunteers ever encounter a suspected situation of sexual abuse, and have staff members been made aware of them?

5. Are careful staff selection procedures in place with persons trained to ensure interviews are structured and documented? There needs to be more than a "gut" feeling that the person is appropriate for the position. Gaps in work history need to be explained, as do reasons for leaving. Reference checking should be thorough and documented, especially circumstances surrounding the refusal by a former employer to provide a reference (some employers have a policy only to confirm employment dates and position held).

6. Are background checks carried out wherever local law allows? Although the arrest and conviction rate for child sex offenses is low, still, a background check may bring to light a previous conviction for child molestation. Background checks are also considered to have a deterrent effect.

7. Are there "exclusions" in the hiring process? The more well-known or respected a person is considered, the more reluctance there may be to conduct a background check, carry out an extensive interview process, and ask the "hard" questions. Some ministries insist on the same screening process for all potential employees, knowing that such a policy establishes credibility and reduces the risk of a mistake.

Getting started

A good starting-off point is finding out what information on protection of children from sexual exploitation is already available from many organizations. But who better to listen to than the children? The youth panel of the World Congress raised awareness of issues that the victimized children themselves see as important:

- Listen to and consult young persons concerning the campaign against sexual exploitation, to work for solutions;
- Punish those who commit violence against children;
- Establish juvenile courts;
- Offer protection centers day and night;
- Provide hot lines for help; and
- Forbid inhalants.[11]

While it may not be feasible to address all of these issues, each concern can be considered in conducting a self-assessment of a current or proposed ministry to children. Raising awareness can involve children in activities that prevent them being exploited. Just as the categories of exploitation are connected in many ways, efforts to alert children and raise their awareness to the dangers of sexual exploitation are also not carried out in isolation.

For example, at a recent Children's Congress in Bohol, Philippines, children were taught to distinguish between exploitative labor and the hard work and cooperation that are highly valued in the Filipino culture. They were also educated about child prostitution and how to avoid being victimized by sex syndicates or pedophiles, problems that children are increasingly facing in their own lives.

Other areas for consideration

Depending on the scope of a ministry, the following issues should also be considered:

The Donor/Sponsor Relationship

Increasingly, donors desire to have a closer connection with the ministry and/or individual children they are supporting financially. As the sexual abuse of children becomes more and more openly discussed, there is an increasing interest among supporters of ministries to children regarding how the issue is being addressed.

Raising awareness takes on a more important role. An openness about steps being taken to ensure children are protected also makes the necessity of protocols for visits much more acceptable to the donors.

If applicable, correspondence to children should be reviewed for sexual references and obscenity. Where local law allows, ministries should conduct background checks prior to a donor's visit.

Marketing and Communications

Work with exploited children requires finances. Increasingly, ministries of all sizes are plunging into the challenge of fundraising. How can the needs of hurting children be marketed in a way that does not do them further harm? The following issues should be considered:

- ♦ How are children presented? Are they portrayed as unduly vulnerable and helpless or pitiful?
- ♦ Does the language used to describe a relationship with children imply power or a sense of ownership? A word that has invoked much debate is *our*. The children that a ministry works with are not possessions.
- ♦ What style of photographs are used? Are they suggestive? Do they expose a child in an undignified way? Pedophiles use pictures and photographs in their fantasies about children. Is there a need for the ministry to review the style of photographs used?
- ♦ Many children, after being asked to share repeatedly the story of their abuse, must wonder how many times they have to tell it to be believed. For some children, an interview can be part of the healing process. For others, being asked to share their story one more time may be very painful and imply a lack of trust. Workers supervising such a situation need to be able to say with authority, "No more interviews."
- ♦ Identities may need to be protected. A child trying to start a new life can be hurt if pictures or stories about a past keep surfacing.
- ♦ Information about and pictures of children should be kept in a secure environment with limited access rights.

CONCLUSION

I have been involved in Christian ministry for many years. As a nurse and a public health professional I have seen much physical suffering, but the emotional and spiritual destruction of a child because of sexual abuse is particularly abhorrent. In a poem quoted in the powerful book of the same name, an anonymous pedophile describes himself as the *Slayer of the Soul!*[12] Ministries must protect the precious souls of children by including a deliberate focus on preventing sexual abuse.

Notes

[1] Thérèse Blanchet, *Lost Innocence, Stolen Childhoods* (Dhaka, Bangladesh: University Press Limited, Rädda Barnen, 1996), p. 111.

[2] 1959 United Nations World Declaration on the Survival, Protection and Development of Children, agreed to at the World Summit for Children on September 30, 1990.

[3] Maggie Black, *Children First: The Story of UNICEF, Past and Present* (London: Oxford University Press, 1996), p. 130.

[4] Ibid., p. 24.

[5] Article 34, Convention on the Rights of the Child, United Nations Resolution 44/25, November 20, 1989.

[6] UNICEF, *The State of the World's Children* (London: Oxford University Press, 1997), p. 32.

[7] Graça Machel, *UN Study on the Impact of Armed Conflict on Children* (1996) UN Document A/51/306, Section C/98.

[8] End Child Prostitution, Pornography and Trafficking, an ECPAT Resource (Melbourne, Australia, 1996).

[9] Richard R. Hammar, et al. (Church Law and Tax Report), *Reducing the Risk of Child Sexual Abuse in Your Church* (Mathews, N.C.: Christian Ministry Resources, 1993), p. 5.

[10] Teo van der Weele, *From Shame to Peace, Counseling and Caring for the Sexually Abused* (Crowborough, Great Britain: Monarch Publications, 1995), p. 294.

[11] Report of the Rapporteur General, Prof. Vitit Muntarbhorn, the World Congress Against Commercial Sexual Exploitation of Children, August 27–31, 1996, Stockholm, Sweden.

[12] L. M. Lothstein, "Psychological Theories of Pedophilia and Ephebophilia," in Stephen J. Rossetti, *Slayer of the Soul: Child Sexual Abuse and the Catholic Church* (Mystic, Conn.: Twenty-Third Publications, 1990), p. 19.

PART FIVE:

Caregivers' Concerns

20

Technical Skills

Laurence Gray

In September 1996 the U.S. television program "60 Minutes" aired a segment on sex tourism and child prostitution. The photographers had filmed children in Thailand, Cambodia and the United States. The photographs revealed some of the main players in the industry: victims, customers and stakeholders who are attracted to the girls or money. Cambodia's brothels featured prominently as the owners' involvement with children has been more visible than other countries in the region. One part of the program shows "60 Minutes" anchor Ed Bradley being offered the choice of two 14-year-old virgins for US$400. A month earlier the show's producer had visited this area with me while researching the story. He was shocked at what he saw and was confident that the outrage caused by coverage of the issue would bring about change. Unfortunately that change has been slow and the practice continues.

Factors that lead to the exploitation of girls as young as nine vary. Research prepared for the 1996 World Congress Against the Commercial Sexual Exploitation of Children[1] shows that young children are seen to be free from sexually transmitted diseases (STDs), are easily deceived and are more likely to be compliant, not resisting unprotected sex. Young girls are often traded as property and are displayed to attract customers. Others contribute to the financial support of their family and put those needs ahead of their own. Widespread poverty and lack of access to education or training opportunities also contribute to the vulnerability of children to exploitation. Understanding the story and influencing factors for individual children is vital in working to address resulting issues. Technical skills that aid this understanding will be highlighted through relating the experience of World Vision's work with street children and sexually exploited children in Cambodia.

The Cambodian context

Prostitution in Cambodia, as in many countries, has been practiced with varying degrees of openness under different governments. While the United Nations Transitional Authority in Cambodia (UNTAC) forces were in Cambodia (1991-93), commercial sex workers (CSWs) in Phnom Penh alone were estimated to number around 20,000. When UNTAC left, the numbers of CSWs fell, but studies by the Cambodian Women's Development Association (CWDA) and Human Rights Vigilance showed that in 1995 girls of 12 to 17 comprised 31 percent of the CSWs.[2] The estimate should be considered low, as it is often difficult to gain access to the very youngest girls in the brothels.

Boys on the street in Phnom Penh are also involved in offering sex to foreigners and Khmer men. Interviews with street boys show that their involvement is rarely cohesive and, once involved, they often viewed prostitution as a source of easy money.[3] In 1995 local authorities acted against the problem with the first prosecution of a foreigner. This led to the conviction of a British doctor in a case that highlighted the situation of street boys in Phnom Penh.

TECHNICAL SKILLS

The sexual exploitation of children is a social problem that exists on many levels. Skills required to effect change will vary depending on which aspect of the issue is being addressed. Contextual issues of politics, religion and cultural understanding of the social position of children are also considerations. Three

282

principle areas that require technical competence in direct work with victims of sexual exploitation are:

♦ Legal
♦ Health
♦ Psychosocial recovery

These areas are interrelated and require sensitivity in information gathering and recording technique. Action in any of these areas must draw from a broad view of the issues and resources available across organizations.

Legal response/child rights

The picture that the "60 Minutes" segment portrayed is one in which the interests and rights of children have no part. They are raw material for others' pleasure and profit. Basic rights of protection, development, participation and even survival are violated daily. Actions from any group that seeks to improve the plight of children are based on a position that opposes this exploitative view. Agencies are in conflict with the interests of profiteers and the customers who are threatened by exposure, prosecution or profit loss. This conflict requires an understanding of the risks and available resources.

A chief resource and a summary of principles that shape an effective response is the United Nations Convention on the Rights of the Child (CRC). This key international legal document outlines the obligations a state has to children. It has the signed endorsement of the vast majority of the world's countries, including Cambodia, and is the most supported international legal document. Thomas Hammarberg, the special advisor to the United Nations on human rights, says that the CRC can be summarized in four words: "Children should be respected."[4] He goes on to say that this means:

♦ children's survival protection and development should be given priority;
♦ their best interests should be a primary consideration whenever decisions are taken that affect them;
♦ their views should be heard and given due weight;
♦ these principles should be applied to all children without discrimination of any kind.

A visible framework reflecting these principles needs to be apparent in the working relationship we seek to build with children, their families and communities.

The CRC embodies these principles in measurable and enforceable terms. Article 32 recognizes "the right of children to be protected from economic exploitation." Article 34 requires countries to protect children from all forms of sexual abuse and exploitation. Article 39 directs countries to "take all appropriate measures to promote physical and psychological recovery and social reintegration of a child victim."[5] Children who have been victims of such crimes require support in adjusting to the effects of the crime. They also may be required to give a statement or evidence in a court case, which may be distressing for them. Agencies have a responsibility to ensure that the child's immediate and long-term best interests are considered throughout any legal process. Interview technique, information recording and links with specialist groups, where appropriate, all aid in ensuring that a child's legal rights are promoted and protected.

My purpose in identifying key articles is that they are invaluable in putting a legal context to issues of sexual exploitation. An understanding of the CRC and its application is a vital technical skill for Non-Government Organizations (NGOs) providing direct services to children. Further, the CRC is the best platform for advocacy or cooperation with government bodies. Governments that have made an international commitment to upholding the CRC are receptive to constructive comment on methods and partnership approaches. In this way agencies can have input on policy formation and preventive strategies to assist children. In Cambodia NGOs have had input on prevention, law enforcement and recovery responses as well as regional issues.

Health

Physical health is a primary consideration when working with children who have experienced difficult circumstances. Cambodia, like other developing countries, has very limited resources to respond to health needs. Gaining an understanding of medical histories is only possible through anecdotal means. Liaison with competent medical services that provide accurate medical

284

assessments and assistance has proved an important resource in responding to the needs of children. World Vision's service supports children who experience a variety of conditions requiring attention. These have included general afflictions, sexually transmitted diseases (STDs), pregnancy and psychosomatic illnesses. It is common for children who have a history of trauma to present physical symptoms of illness that are a reaction to their experience. Cambodia presents a great challenge in diagnosing illness as some medical services are not sufficiently discriminating in their treatment. An intravenous drip and antibiotics are often the preferred response for a wide range of ailments, even when such treatment is not necessary.

The constant issue of STDs is one that crosses the legal and recovery areas. Gynecological health is discussed with children and, where infections are active, appropriate medical treatment gained. HIV infection is a reality when working with such a vulnerable group. In Cambodia recent studies show that approximately 52 percent of commercial sex workers are HIV-positive. Appropriate policies that are sensitive to cultural context and laws need to be developed. In Cambodia, World Vision's policy is to allow children to make an informed choice about having an HIV test. We explain any questions they may have about the condition and serve as liaison with other groups on the HIV issue. We train staff on the need for confidentiality in many sensitive issues in working with children who have been sexually exploited. Some children are already aware of their HIV status before being in contact with our service. Further consideration to respond to need is included in the case plans of children who are HIV-positive. Sometimes this response is to involve them in peer-education activities, creative expression through drama, art or media. Health needs are monitored and responded to.

Psychosocial recovery of sexually abused children

I am reluctant to generalize the way such children present themselves, as each situation is different. Responses must focus on the best interests of the child and involve as much participation of the child in planning as possible. Issues that must be considered when addressing trauma center around the following areas identified by Wendy Freed. Dr. Freed is qualified in both medicine and psychology; she contributes some of her time to the Physicians for Human Rights, a U.S.–based organization of health professionals. The report, funded by World Vision, contains a valuable summary of the psychosocial effects of exploitation. These include:

- *Trauma:* Sexual trauma is the violation of the most intimate and personal aspects of the self. One's own body becomes the setting in which the atrocities are perpetrated. For the young women living in the brothel, the sexual violations take place inside the tiny cubicle that is their only private living space. There is no safe haven for them.[6]

- *Shame:* A powerful psychological reaction of shame is linked to the sexual nature of the trauma. Personal value falls sometimes to the point of seeing no other option than prostitution because they are worthless.

- *Betrayal of trust:* Approximately half the young women are sold to brothels by people they know. This betrayal has long-lasting effects and relationships develop slowly with children in recovery. Information is precious and sharing in it is earned.

- *Layers of truth:* The meaning of personal stories and their accuracy are not constant and reveal some of the coping mechanisms the girls may have used. Some girls need to re-create their identity, being given a new name and history every week by brothel owners wanting to control them and evade searches for a missing girl.

- *Self-blame:* Many girls blame their fate on themselves and have an exaggerated sense of their part in the interaction that led to such a circumstance.

- *Disruption in normal development:* Young women are forced into a role that separates them from the community. They cannot take part in many informal activities that are important in socialization for future roles as income earner, wife and mother.

- *Separation from family:* Important relationships suffer and many young women grieve the loss of contact, particularly with siblings.

- *Grief and depression:* A sense of hopelessness at the loss of freedom, relationships and innocence.

+ *Fear:* Beatings and punishment from brothel owners are common. Young women also fear contracting AIDS. However, they cannot refuse clients.
+ *Captivity:* Young women have been in captivity for weeks, months and sometimes years. Initially they often fight the brothel owners' demands for them to service clients. This response has resulted in being locked in a room for a week or being beaten until they modify their response to their circumstances. Control over one's fate has gone.
+ *Being a good daughter:* In the Cambodian context this crucial factor allows meaning to be given their circumstances by many young women. They see themselves as being in a position to help their family survive, giving context to their personal sacrifice.

CAREER SKILL DEVELOPMENT

The impact of these different aspects of trauma vary from individual to individual. Direct-care staff need training opportunities to build their understanding and skill in recognizing and responding to individual needs. Resources that have proved valuable in skill development include networking with other direct-care services, local trainers and external consultants. Commitment to training and support of staff development is vital in addressing recovery needs. This idea is especially true in the context of a developing country, where access to education (especially for women) and standards are limited.

Procedures for working with sexually abused children

To respond in the best interests of the children or young women, opportunity to allow the exploration of these issues is World Vision's aim. Our primary response is to ensure that they are in a safe, secure environment where it is possible for them to tell their stories. From this base we then discuss the meaning the child has given these experiences and explore possible alternative meanings. This communication will happen at the pace of the individual and as relationships between children and workers develop. Where possible, other family members will be contacted and may be involved separately in this process and then with the child. It depends on individual situations, what is in the child's best interest and what the child will support. The context of the contact we have with a child who has experienced trauma is significant as to which skills will assist in any movement toward recovery. The areas of distinction in our current work in this area are:

- ◆ *Referrals:* Young women who have been rescued from prostitution by Non-Government Organizations or the police.
- ◆ *Self-referral:* Girls may have escaped from a brothel, may have been raped while living on the street or may have left an exploitative domestic environment. Their experience and the meaning they give to it are significant factors in planning the most appropriate response.
- ◆ *On the street contacts:* Boys involve themselves in sexual exploitation as a means of earning income by receiving gifts and as the cost of a more attractive life or lifestyle. Contact is established with them through outreach activities, a drop-in center and a residential center. Boys' need for secure accommodation is not usually as great, and a different approach is required. Our focus is HIV prevention, supporting boys who may want to develop other skills and leave prostitution. Protection issues do emerge if the boys are involved in a legal action against a pimp or pedophile. Once again, understanding their experiences and the meaning they have for them is important in planning individual responses.

First contacts

The issues we handle in our initial contact help us gain basic biographical details about the child. This information includes family history, which province or district they have connection with and how they came to be in Phnom Penh. If they are forthcoming with details of their particular story, we will listen. At an early stage we focus on building a relationship with them and do not want to push too hard. We gain needed information through conversation. Recording the information being shared is kept to a minimum, as formal approaches inhibit some children. Further opportunities to gain or test information will emerge as relationships deepen.

Areas initially addressed include:

1. Survival needs including food, accommodation and health care. Health care includes immediate needs, such as wounds or infections needing attention. Sometimes the contact comes about because a child wants to gain medical assistance for an STD. Some children have presented themselves a number of times with syphilis, only to return to the street once their treatment is complete. With such children we strive to show concern while maintaining a non-condemning relationship that clearly demonstrates that our doors are open and assistance to move beyond the streets is always available.

2. Protection issues include threats posed to the child from pimps, gangs, customers and sometimes their family. This issue is constantly with children who have been exploited for profit. Children, staff and centers have been threatened. In one case a pimp felt threatened by our support of some boys in a legal case in which he was convicted of pimping for foreign pedophiles. He threatened to toss grenades into our center. It did not happen, although in Cambodia such a thing is very possible. Protection issues are sometimes linked to legal action to gain support from the authorities. Legal action requires clear record keeping and documentation. It also requires coordination and cooperation with other groups. It may require lobbying both formally and informally. It always requires much patience, diplomacy and perseverance.

3. Development issues begin with the end in mind, says management guru Steven Covey.[7] This premise holds true when considering outcomes for children who require support. The aim is to utilize all ways possible for them to achieve independence and integration with their families and community, where this action is in their interest. During the initial contact, early indications of key development areas that need further follow-up will emerge.

Longer term

Involvement moves from immediate survival issues to longer-term needs. At this point a case plan is developed. This plan will address any ongoing legal and health issues as well as skill training and educational needs, family reconciliation (where appropriate) or long-term alternative accommodation. Case plans are constantly reviewed as new information is shared or circumstances change. Children in residential care require longer-term alternatives. Planning these alternatives needs their input to be effective. Where possible, immediate and extended family and the community with which they have the greatest link also should have input into any planned solution.

Participation remains an important part of the case-plan approach, and children and sometimes families are involved in discussions and decision making.

CASE STUDY

The following story gives an account of a successful outcome for girls who were freed from prostitution. This story is discussed to provide examples of how technical skills from a variety of disciplines come into play in responding to particular needs of children.

On Thursday July 31, two Vietnamese children got on a plane at Pochentong Airport to go home. The 12-year-old girls, rescued in a brothel raid nearly a year ago in Phnom Penh, are the first trafficked children to be formally repatriated from Cambodia through a special arrangement with the Cambodian and Vietnamese governments, the International Organization for Migration, and World Vision.

The girls, who are twins, had been sold by relatives in Vietnam and smuggled across the border to work in a brothel in Svay Pak, a red-light district 11 km. outside the Cambodian capital. When they arrived in June of 1996, they were 11 years old and spoke no Khmer. They worked in a brothel where the owner openly entertained clients seeking girls as young as 10 years of age, administering painkillers and sedatives to "encourage" the children to receive their customers cheerfully.

In August 1996 Cambodian police and a detective working with the international organization ECPAT (End Child Prostitution, Abuse and Trafficking), raided the brothel where the girls were held. World Vision and a local NGO, the Center For the Protection of Children's Rights (CCPCR), then stepped in to provide care and protection for the girls. The CCPCR provided shelter while World Vision provided some funding and skilled case-workers to follow up options for their future.

The two girls expressed a wish to return home to Vietnam where they could be reunited with their grandmother. But having been trafficked across the border, they possessed no travel documents and were unable to return legally. The International Organization for Migration (IOM), a UN agency, then began the process of negotiation with the Cambodian and Vietnamese governments to allow the girls to return home. Meanwhile, World Vision accepted legal guardianship of the girls so their interests could be formally represented to all parties.[8]

According to local NGOs, estimates of children in prostitution in Phnom Penh alone run as high as 10,000 to 15,000. Provincial surveys have indicated that one-quarter to one-third of sex workers in the provinces are also underage.

Many ethnic Vietnamese are long-term Cambodia residents or even citizens. Therefore, establishing the case for these children to be returned was a difficult and lengthy process involving Vietnamese-speaking social workers, a local legal aid group and several visits to Ho Chi Minh City by World Vision and the IOM to meet and negotiate with Vietnamese officials.

It is the first time the IOM has worked in Cambodia with an NGO to organize such a repatriation. While the IOM negotiated with the relevant government departments to organize the necessary administration, NGOs that are specialists in care and protection provided the casework support.

When the girls landed on Vietnamese soil, World Vision's guardianship expired and they were handed over to the care of the National Committee for Protection and Care of Children (CPCC), a quasi-government body. They will initially stay at the CPCC's Educational and Vocational Center in Ho Chi Minh City, with one of their present caregivers staying on for the first week to help with the familiarization process.

The IOM will provide a small amount of funding to support the girls' initial care in Vietnam and to develop a long-term plan for them ultimately to return to a suitable family situation. World

Vision Vietnam will be in contact with the girls, and the Vietnamese authorities will continue the supportive role the NGOs in Cambodia have begun. This contact will be important in ensuring that future plans for the girls are responsive to their needs and that an active interest in this case is maintained.

The following is a brief summary of the steps that led to the girls' freedom, repatriation and reunification.

Investigation

In June 1996 a particular brothel in a red-light area had come to the attention of NGO workers as having very young girls in its employ. It is not unusual for underage girls to be available for clients. Underage girls, however, are usually screened away, making access to them, and obtaining information from them, difficult. Information received needs to be tested in ways that add to the overall picture and that do not place staff at unacceptable risk. Sharing the role of information collecting is sometimes necessary, as any action will partly depend on skills, resources and contacts available.

In this case the brothel in question was advertising that it specialized in children by having the girls wear clothes that emphasized their youth. The girls also would stand by the entrance of the brothel to be seen by as many potential clients as possible. Their availability was directed largely at expatriates, who comprised a more lucrative market than locals. The brothel owner, a woman in her 40s, had been quite successful in this strategy. Further investigation showed that there were four girls between 11 and 13 who were on display and available for clients. Two of the girls had arrived from Vietnam two months earlier and were visibly scared of the brothel owner and their situation. It was learned that another girl's mother was working as a cook in the area and had involved her daughter in this activity.

Networking

Representatives of World Vision, LICADHO (a human-rights organization) and End Child Prostitution Abuse and Trafficking (ECPAT) met to discuss the situation and explore possible responses. Information gathered confirmed the original reports and

292

showed that the girls clearly were being exploited in ways that contravened CRC Article 34, as well as a number of local laws. These laws included UNTAC Law S.42 regarding indecent assault on a minor; UNTAC Law S.33 regarding rape; and State of Cambodia Law on Unlawful Confinement. The difficulty now faced was to gain cooperation from the authorities to enforce the laws.

Technical skills required at this stage were understanding of the law, information-gathering ability and clear procedure on who needed to know and what their input could be. A risk to workers and the children could come from the injudicious use of information. Pimps and customers alike protect themselves, sometimes through force or bribery. Our main concern at this time was that the girls might be relocated or sold again. Issues following any course of action, such as the immediate accommodation and support needs for the children, were considered.

Cooperation with local authorities

An ECPAT trainer and legal adviser proved to be invaluable in gaining cooperation with the local authorities on law enforcement. Authorities are sometimes reluctant to take action against brothel owners because they pay protection to the police or have strong links with powerful figures. The ECPAT trainer worked with NGO representatives in gathering further information, which was used in legal proceedings. Recorded information ensures a greater degree of cooperation from the authorities, as one court prosecutor noted, saying, "lack of evidence obscures real prosecution of traffickers and brothel owners."[9] In August 1996 this information, along with details of the laws it related to, was presented to the district police. These facts assisted in gaining their cooperation in acting to rescue the girls and arrest the brothel owner.

Immediate needs

The rescue, while successful, did not result in the prosecution of the brothel owner, who was back in business within weeks, having been released from questioning after six hours. It was later revealed that a bribe was paid. Nevertheless, the main objective of freeing the four girls from sexual exploitation had been achieved. The girls were accommodated in a safe but temporary environment. They had suffered shock from the rescue; it took some time for them to trust the NGO workers involved. Bilingual Khmer and Vietnamese speakers were available to assist the girls. Working through three and sometimes four languages, however, is clumsy. During the first week the girls had access to counselors, medical treatment and activities. From this point on, the basic physical needs of shelter, food, medical and developmental requirements needed to be addressed. At the same time legal issues of the children's status and any local prosecutions needed to be pursued along with the issue of repatriation.

Ongoing legal needs

Two NGOs–World Vision and the Cambodian Center for the Protection of Child Rights (CCPCR)–were to address the temporary accommodation, support and counseling issues. The Cambodian Ministry of Social Affairs, Labor and Veteran Affairs granted World Vision legal custody of the children while efforts to repatriate them were pursued. LICADHO and Legal Aid of Cambodia ensured that the court received relevant documentation for the legal procedures to continue. The International Office of Migration was involved to follow up repatriation options with the Vietnamese and Cambodian authorities.

Repatriation and recovery issues for the girls became the task of four NGOs working cooperatively for a period of eleven months. Several trips to Vietnam to meet with organization and government representatives were required. A delegation from Vietnam made a visit to Cambodia as the issues of nationality of two girls were examined and a process of reintegration agreed upon. Although an estimated 35 percent of commercial sex workers in Phnom Penh alone are Vietnamese, this was the first case for legal repatriation of a trafficked child. The process would set precedents and needed to be correctly undertaken. This not only took time but considerable energy in prompting the machinery of two governments into action. It was a process requiring a knowledge of international law and diplomatic skill, as national pride was at risk for both countries. The International Office of Migration was the best placed of all agencies to fulfill this role.

Long-term development and recovery needs

World Vision and CCPCR cooperated in providing support and accommodation for the children, who were soon joined by others who had experienced a similar fate. The experiences of the four girls over the subsequent months contained joy and sorrow. Providing skills that enabled the children to understand, and sometimes redefine, the meaning they give to their experiences is a training area in which we constantly strive. The girls made great gains in their education and took pride in newfound skills. Their beliefs about acceptable standards of behavior and expectations changed. One outcome was that they experienced sorrow at the realization of how they had been exploited and had their trust betrayed. Two (whose mothers live in Cambodia) redefined their relationship with them and have since been reunited. Counseling staff have assisted the children and mothers in negotiating the relationship over a process of twelve months. The mothers have been assisted in starting and managing their own businesses, have moved away from the brothel area and are supporting their families. The girls are attending school and engaged in skill training. The girls want to be with their mothers and feel more secure receiving regular support. Both mothers and daughters have assisted in peer support of other children and families where daughters have been sold.

CONCLUSION

Direct service support to children who have been sexually exploited is labor-intensive, sometimes complicated and involves risk. However, such support also offers hope to the vulnerable and the innocent who are caught in a modern form of slavery. Technical skills are the tools that enable good intentions to bear fruit; these skills are resources to be developed and shared. In this way the capacity of services and individuals that serve as stepping stones to a brighter future is strengthened.

Notes

[1] Delia Paul, *Regaining Honor: Cambodian Children's Experience in Prostitution and After* (Cambodia: World Vision International, 1995).

[2] Cited in UNICEF, *The Trafficking and Prostitution of Children in Cambodia: A Situation Report* (Phnom Penh 1995).

[3] Paul, *Regaining Honor.*

[4] Cited in Standard's *Minimum Rules for the Treatment of Victims of Trafficking, Forced Labour and Slavery-Like Practices: Global Alliance Against Trafficking in Women* (Thailand, 1997).

[5] The Convention on the Rights of the Child (The United Nations, 1989).

[6] Wendy Freed, "Commercial Sexual Exploitation of Women and Children in Cambodia: Personal Narratives / A Psychological Perspective" (Boston: Physicians for Human Rights, 1997). The report is available from Physicians for Human Rights, 100 Boylston St., Suite 702, Boston, MA 02116 (or see www.phrusa.org)

[7] Steven Covey, *The Seven Habits of Highly Successful People* (New York: Simon and Schuster, 1990 ©1989).

[8] Delia Paul, "Repatriation of Rescued Child Sex Workers a First for Cambodia," World Vision International-Cambodia Newsletter, Phnom Penh, July 31, 1997.

[9] Annuska Derks, *Trafficking of Cambodian Women and Children to Thailand* (Phnom Penh: IOM [International Organization for Migration, a UN organization] and CAS, 1997).

21

Compassionate Care for Caregivers

Phyllis Kilbourn

A high emotional cost comes with caring for sexually exploited children. Listening to the children's stories of fear, pain, exploitation, suffering and hopelessness causes endless mixed and energy-sapping feelings: anger, fear, helplessness, powerlessness, vulnerability, sadness, pain and frustration.

Caregivers also grieve over the needless and senseless abuse of children who are so vulnerable—abuse that robs them of their childhood and innocence. Being containers for the children's painful feelings, plus coping with their own, is an overwhelming task for caregivers.

These many stresses, which daily confront people caring for traumatized children, result in a variety of psychological reactions that can cause secondary stress disorder and lead to secondary trauma. Such stress and trauma come from being exposed to a reality that is beyond ordinary comprehension and seem unbelievable, especially to caregivers who are new to the work. Providing care for caregivers suffering from secondary trauma, however, is often overlooked.

That people can be traumatized both directly or indirectly through a traumatic incident is well documented. The American Psychiatric Association's *Diagnostic and Statistical Manual of Mental Disorders*[1] describes what constitutes a traumatic experience:

> The essential feature of posttraumatic stress disorder is the development of characteristic symptoms following exposure to an extreme traumatic stressor involving direct personal experience of an event that involves threatened death, actual or threatened serious injury, or the threat to one's physical integrity; or *witnessing* an event that involves death, injury, or a threat to the physical integrity of another person.

With secondary traumatic stress (STS) comes a sense of helplessness and confusion and a sense of isolation from those who could support and help. Exposure to this kind of trauma is ongoing and threatening to caregivers' safety, health and well-being. It can produce long-term emotional consequences.

Thus intervention plans for sexually exploited children must provide not only for the care of the children but also for their caregivers. Emergency workers from all fields of trauma care report that they are most vulnerable to stress when dealing with the pain of children. If unresolved, the stress from secondary trauma can lead to burnout, rendering caregivers ineffective in helping children.

SECONDARY TRAUMATIC STRESS FACTORS

Secondary traumatic stress can flare up with little warning. Along with handling the children's pain, there is much frustration in working with sexually exploited children. Some of the chronic and long-term post-trauma symptoms that have been reported in crisis workers include a sense of alienation, isolation or withdrawal, delayed loss of confidence, guilt, feelings of insanity and loss of control and even suicidal thoughts. The following lists some of the realities caregivers confront that contribute to their stress and trauma.

Hearing children's stories

For most caregivers of sexually exploited children, the cruelty and sadistic atrocities enacted on innocent children are difficult to fathom, much less believe. The most powerful and shattering effect on caregivers is their sense of personal outrage and disillusionment. What they hear becomes a violent attack on their own sense of integrity and worldview. The exploitation can be so horrifying that it is practically impossible for counselors and caregivers to maintain the balance between empathy and objectivity necessary to facilitate working through the children's experiences.

Mistrust

One of the most difficult aspects in working with sexually exploited children is the children's mistrust of caregivers—those who so desperately long to make a difference in their lives. This mistrust stems from repeated experiences of broken trust; often their perpetrator has been someone known to or loved by the child. Therefore, attempts by caregivers to develop a caring and open relationship could be misinterpreted by the child as a lead-in to more abuse. Perhaps the children have experienced a similar method used by the abuser. Caregivers know they can offer constructive help, yet their attempts to intervene are met with rejection and silence. This can cause intense frustration.

Compassion issues

Webster's dictionary defines compassion as "a feeling of deep sympathy and sorrow for another who is stricken by suffering or misfortune, accompanied by a strong desire to alleviate the pain or remove its cause." Often caregivers become emotionally drained by caring so deeply for the children. We become emotionally vulnerable to the exploitation that has an impact on them. Because of our emotional connection with the children, we too can become "victims."

Longing for the children to be free from their exploitative situations so they can enjoy the happy, carefree childhood God intended is a piece of the idealism that caregivers often have to forfeit. Accepting this fact is painful.

Caregivers also struggle with their own deep disappointment and feelings of depression when children rescued from sexual exploitation leave the safety and care of concerned workers to return to their former lifestyles. To witness them being snatched away by family members who only intend to resell them for further profit causes deep grief and a sense of loss. The workers may even blame their own lack of faith or prayers for causing the children's failure to adjust to their new lifestyle or to experience yet further exploitation. When working from compassion-driven motives, caregivers of sexually exploited children have a greater tendency to hold unrealistic expectations.

Dilemma of confidentially
Often abused children who confide in a counselor or caregiver will not want the abuse reported. While caregivers want to respect a child's right to privacy, they realize that they are not dealing with a single child but also with other children who may have been abused in the past and those who could be abused in the future. This tension causes conflict when trying to establish trust with the child.

Safety issues
Safety factors that put children and caregivers at risk produce a lot of stress. Attacks can be expected from pimps and crimelords who have their own lucrative plans for exploiting the children. Exploiters will try any tactics to terrorize and abort efforts by caregivers to help the children. Their threats and attacks are not just empty words but are executed through violence and even murder.

Justice issues
Justice issues stir up strong emotions of anger, frustration, helplessness and sometimes feelings bordering on hatred. Knowing that the children will never receive justice for the offenses committed against them makes closure to their trauma a much more difficult task. Caregivers also know that perpetrators will likely never appear in court. Thus their hope for children to receive justice also is dashed.

Legal issues

When planning advocacy and care for children, you feel confident that governments and law officers will come to your aid in helping put an end to the senseless abuse of children. But all too soon you discover your voice is only met with stony silence from both the justice and legal systems. The resulting frustration only increases when it is evident that officials are knowledgeable about the children's plight but do not have the moral will to stand against this profitable business. Those who could help make a difference in the children's lives won't.

Ethical issues

When injustice and neglect of children are rampant, and law enforcement agencies do not provide a supportive forum for sexually abused children, caregivers are easily tempted to ignore local laws and requirements concerning their work. This thinking is particularly prominent when caregivers try to work from what they assume are the best interests of a child. They struggle with deciding upon morally right actions.

Isn't it better to provide inferior housing for the children than no housing? Should parents who abuse and sell their children have a right to "reclaim" them? Is it right to keep parents from knowing where their children are? When is it right to remove a child from his or her home because of abuse? Struggles are always imminent over how to decide which children to help when funds aren't sufficient to care for all who need help.

Ethical dilemmas also surface over injustice issues. Since the law does not take up prosecution of perpetrators, shouldn't we? Should we seek revenge on perpetrators when the opportunity arises? Or, is it right to expose callous governments and officials through the media? The painful choices are new and varied every day.

Cultural issues

When ministry takes caregivers across cultural borders, they face adjustments to many new geopolitical situations and ideologies. They are removed from the expectations and structure that their culture has provided and that make their environment "safe" and comfortable. Cultural differences, of course, can be experienced even in one's own country when, for example, caregivers are exposed to "foreign" inner-city environments.

Caregivers, however, also face yet another even more traumatic cultural shift. The world of the exploited child is truly as foreign to most caregivers as the normal customs and culture of their work area. Living in an unfamiliar culture and subculture can be a major source of stress.

Caregivers' issues

In helping sexually abused children, repressed memories may surface in caregivers who, themselves, have suffered sexual abuse. These memories, if not worked through and brought to closure, will not only intrude on every aspect of their lives but will also hinder the effectiveness of their care for children. Caregivers also could transfer their own conflicts and feelings onto the children, making their problems worse.

Spiritual warfare

Compounding all the above factors that tend to render caregivers ineffective is the issue of spiritual warfare. When actively engaged in ministry to children who are being exploited and abused for evil purposes, workers are on the front lines against evil. An intense spiritual warfare is waged to thwart rescue efforts. The enemy delights in the children's broken and crushed spirits, their deeply scarred lives, their dashed hopes and the cruel bondage they experienced through coercion to serve the base desires of humankind. An abundant measure of emotional and spiritual energy is required to confront the evils behind children's sexual abuse.

BURNOUT

Burnout, unlike secondary traumatic stress, emerges gradually; it occurs when stress has built up to an intolerable level. Emotional exhaustion is always the key factor in burnout, linking it closely to secondary traumatic stress. According to Pines and Aronson, burnout is "a state of physical, emotional and mental exhaustion caused by long-term involvement in emotionally demanding situations."[2] By physical exhaustion the authors mean feeling tired or rundown; emotional exhaustion includes feeling depressed and hopeless; and mental exhaustion is feeling disillusionment and resentment toward people.

In a comprehensive review of the empirical research on the symptoms of burnout, Kahill identified five categories of symptoms:

- *Physical symptoms:* Fatigue and physical depletion/exhaustion, sleep difficulties, specific somatic problems such as headaches, gastrointestinal disturbances, colds and flu.
- *Emotional symptoms:* Irritability, anxiety, depression, guilt, sense of helplessness.
- *Behavioral symptoms:* Aggression, callousness, pessimism, defensiveness, cynicism, substance abuse.
- *Work-related symptoms:* Quitting the job, poor work performance, absenteeism, tardiness, misuse of work breaks, thefts.
- *Interpersonal symptoms:* Perfunctory communication with inability to concentrate or focus, withdrawal from clients or coworkers, and then dehumanizing, intellectualizing clients.[3]

INTERVENTION

Because caregivers suffering from secondary trauma exhibit many of the same symptoms as traumatized children, some of the same treatment methods can be effective for their care. Caregivers need the same support that they provide for the children: emotional care, comfort, love and affection, encouragement, advice, companionship and practical help.

Caregivers also must be given time to leave their burdens for a while. Burnout can cause a loss of joy and effectiveness in ministry. Adequate time for renewal, reflection and restoration of hope will result in more effective caregiving for the children.

Caregivers are often reluctant to admit their need for help because they perceive it as an admission of their ineffectiveness in caregiving. Instead, burned out and wounded, they may choose to abandon the work. This possibility underlines yet another reason why prevention is a vital aspect of caregivers' care.

The first step in treating caregivers is to help them identify the basic elements of their multifaceted trauma. Once identified, these issues can be addressed and worked through. The following enumerates some issues that cause trauma-producing stress for caregivers. With keen observation, you will doubtless be alerted to others.

Recognize limitations

Caregivers must recognize that everyone has a limit to his or her natural resources of empathy and patient caring. They also face limitations in their expertise to meet the needs of deeply wounded children. The children's needs are always critical and always present. Yet no one can solve all the children's problems or fulfill all their needs. Caregivers also must recognize that the situations they are handling are very complex; they will make mistakes.

Caregivers' time, energy and strength also have limits, and the emotional investment adds significant intensity to their workloads. It is important for them to learn to say no to unreasonable or overloading demands. Flexibility and resiliency will stretch their coping powers when overwhelming needs must be attended to. Often overlooked is the fact that children, too, have their trauma-produced limitations in responding to caregivers. If this is recognized, caregivers can be more patient and understanding of the children who initially resist and reject their help.

Utilize support groups

From the onset of their work, caregivers should have a small support group to whom they can turn for counsel and times of fun and relaxation. Ideally this group should consist of those not working with traumatized children—trusted friends, significant persons in their lives and a minister or other spiritual leader. This group can more objectively interact with the caregiver on ministry issues and partner in special prayer concerns.

Caregivers also need a supervisory group with co-workers and ministry leaders. They must not be allowed to isolate themselves from the rest of the team. Definite times should be set for caregivers to meet for debriefing with supervisors and co-workers. Such sessions are vital for caregivers to express their feelings of pain or of guilt regarding their responsibilities. Sharing together with a peer support group of colleagues provides a deeper understanding of their feelings and helps them discover ways they can more effectively cope.

Group sharing at debriefing times has been found most beneficial. Caregivers not only realize that others share their same pain and frustration, but they also learn valuable ways of handling their feelings and gain insight into the needs of children with whom they are working.

Develop healthy relationships

Mutual and trusting relationships between children and caregivers and between involved caregivers lay the foundation for successful care for both children and workers. Trust is foundational to feeling secure enough to open one's hearts and share issues that threaten to destroy a caregiver's ability to cope with trauma and pain. Authentic sharing and learning from one another can only take place in the context of trusting relationships. Time and effort are required to develop and maintain such relationships, but the benefits are well worth the cost.

Negative criticism and fault-finding are natural reactions to stressed-out, weary caregivers. Developing supportive relationships will mean nipping negative criticism and fault-finding in the bud. Good relationships are crucial to effective debriefing.

Relationships with children also have to be properly maintained and guarded. Bonding too closely with a child can shut other potentially helpful co-workers out of the relationship. Caregivers may also experience difficulty in making objective decisions concerning the child's care. Vigilance must be kept to not cross boundaries or feel as though you are the only one capable of helping a child. While you may have the closest relationship to that child, God also can use others gifts and skills in the life of that child.

Maintain a balance in ministry and personal life

It is imperative for caregivers working with traumatized children to maintain a balance between their professional and personal

305

lives. When caregivers are overworked, tired and traumatized, their relationships with co-workers, family and friends are affected. Stressed caregivers become withdrawn and are not there in a meaningful way for others.

Maintaining a balance in one's personal life enables caregivers to have fun, to enjoy themselves alone or with others, to laugh and to retain their faith and hope. In the area of hurting children, it is difficult to find anything to laugh about, but in a group there are always things happening that allow for fun and laughter. Maintaining this balance in one's personal life also positively affects the children. As caregivers are enabled to approach their work with a renewed spirit, they will inspire hope in the children with whom they work.

Maintain physical and emotional health

Stress has a negative effect on physical health. People under stress have been shown to have reduced functioning of their immune systems and a litany of physical problems. Listening to children's problems day after day is not only emotionally draining, but strenuous work. Without stamina, caregivers cannot tolerate the stress that working with traumatized children entails, nor can they facilitate healing. Listening in a way that facilitates healing requires a stamina that can be maintained only by caregivers who are in good mental and physical health.

Staying healthy both emotionally and physically requires a regime of regular exercise and play, a balanced diet and sufficient rest. Time is needed for caregivers to nourish their physical needs, personal needs and professional needs. To maintain the boundaries necessary for good mental and physical health, caregivers may have to set priorities for their commitments and even terminate some of them.

Another area of emotional care, as mentioned earlier, is making sure caregivers have adequately dealt with their own trauma issues of past sexual abuse. It is important that such caregivers come through their own grief process to healing. If the counselor is stuck at a certain point in dealing with pain, loss, sorrow or grief, very often the children will not make progress past that same point.

SUMMARY

Caregivers need assurance that they will be provided with the necessary resources and supportive networks that will enable them to become involved with the issues affecting children deeply wounded through degrading sexual exploitation. These needs can be met through a carefully devised, ongoing care plan that supports and informs caregivers.

They also must be encouraged to take care of themselves physically and emotionally to ensure effectiveness in their caregiving. If personal care is ignored, the children will suffer not only directly through exploitation but also indirectly through the quality of care they receive.

Caregivers need to be empowered to use their skills, knowledge and strength as an investment in the children's future. Making a difference in the lives of the children they care for is a primary goal of caregivers. Helping them know how to set boundaries, or limits, on their energies, time, competency and resources will enable them to reach this goal and their expectations.

Notes

[1] American Psychiatric Association, (1994); *Diagnostic and Statistical Manual of Mental Disorders*, 4th ed., ed. Charles R. Figley (Washington, D.C., 1994), p. 424.

[2] A. M. Pines and E. Aronson, *Career Burnout: Causes and Cures* (New York: Free Press, 1988), p. 9.

[3] S. Kahill, "Interventions for Burnout in the Helping Professions: A Review of the Empirical Evidence, *Canadian Journal of Counseling Review* 22:3 (1988):310–42.

PART SIX:

Reflection

22

Mobilizing the Church for Action

Viju Abraham

Suppose 500 congregations from Bombay's churches had a tangible ministry among the city's more than five million shanty-town dwellers and 150,000 pavement dwellers, its 100,000 street children, its 150,000 prostitutes and innumerable drug addicts and alcoholics? What if they preached the gospel and saw spiritual transformation while they served the poor and the marginalized of the city? What if the churches' population got involved in Mother Teresa–type works of compassion to sexually exploited children? What if the AIDS epidemic hitting our city found Christian caregivers who would help sufferers in home care and in staffing counseling centers? What if Isaiah 61:1–6, the works describing the Messiah's mission, were fulfilled in his local body, the church?

I have asked these questions of church groups and leaders many times. The answer? If the churches responded in this way they would see the people of Bombay glorifying God as they witnessed the churches' shining lights. And yet this scenario is far from the real situation today. The majority of people in the local church are immobilized. They could aptly be called God's "frozen chosen."

It is almost a given that a local church emphasizes either the "word" or the "works" of the gospel, depending on its theological emphasis. I live in Mumbai (Bombay) where I am part of ACT (the Association for Christian Thoughtfulness), a ministry started in 1973 to get those involved in evangelism to respond to the suffering and poor of the city—men, women and children. We have been involved in a number of projects in the slums of the city since then. In 1992, however, we felt led to change our focus from doing our projects to helping Mumbai's churches as local congregations to develop their own outreaches to the poor and abused in the areas in which they are located. This strategy is getting more churches involved and expands the scope of the ministry.

Now, this plan may not represent God's calling every mission and parachurch body. We need to see continuing, well-managed ministries among the poor and exploited, but there is, today, a great need to thaw out God's people and release them into ministry to the suffering in our world, including sexually exploited children. The people in a church are God's great untapped resource.

Here are some reasons why the local church ought to be involved in mission to those who are hurting:

1. As a body they are inter-generational, not just a peer group, allowing for a greater variety of personnel available for different types of ministry.
2. Normally every church needs to be involved in holistic mission. Unfortunately, the local church has a greater emphasis on the Sunday service than on mission activities out of the local church, so most self-motivated individuals go outside their congregations for involvement.
3. The church has financial resources for its own work, and if each church had its own project it could easily involve its members, while also promoting a greater motivation for giving.
4. The most important factor, as I see it, is the calling of the church to preach the gospel as well as to demonstrate good works. There need not be a conflict between the word and the works of the gospel.

These are practical reasons for involvement based on a biblical mandate.

THE CHURCH'S BIBLICAL MANDATE

The great divorce, as one writer called it—the separation of social concern and evangelism in the evangelical church—came about as the "social gospel" emphasized that mission was only for the physical and social needs of humankind. This move was the result of a person-centered theology where the demythologizing of the German theological schools influenced a large section of theological institutions around the world in the beginning of the century. Along with it came a belief that Christ was not unique as the way of salvation but was only one of many ways. The reaction to this teaching that took place in many evangelical churches and groups around the world was to divorce the clear teaching of Scripture in its emphasis on both proclamation and doing good. In India in the 1950s and 1960s, during my school and college years, sermons in evangelical churches avoided whole portions of the Scriptures that taught about social concern and the mandate to get involved. I came from an evangelical generation in the 1960s in India that chose to ignore the biblical social mandate.

The salt and light metaphors in Matthew 5:13–16 should be more than enough reason for the local church to do good works to manifest the presence and character of God in its midst. The Lord also gave the story of the Samaritan caregiver to a Bible-thumping questioner after expounding Leviticus 19:18 to him in this parable. The caregiver in this case who fulfilled God's law was not a covenant-believing Jew but a heretical Samaritan. The Lord had a sense of humor and sarcasm. In their answer the critics did not even mention the accursed race by name (Luke 10:25–37). The common purse kept by the Lord's band and looked after by Judas, among other things, was meant for the poor. For that reason, apparently, Judas objected at Mary of Bethany's waste of expensive perfume in extravagant worship of the Lord (see Mark 14:5, John 12:4–6, John 13:29).

The New Testament church also had a priority for looking after the poor and the needy, and it is interesting that at the Jerusalem Council the three nonnegotiable practices common to both Jewish and Gentile believers were sexual morality, the dietary restriction (only kosher and Halal meat, please!) and the command to care for the poor (Gal. 2:10). James, who was part of the council, insistently

313

emphasized in his later epistle the working out of the believer's faith in practical good works. It was not that he was asking for a return to salvation by works but rather to challenge the church to fulfill God's purpose in living out the faith that demonstrated itself in good works. Paul would not have disagreed. Ephesians 2:8–10, Titus 2:14 and Philippians 2:12–13 give evidence of Paul's theology regarding the believers' demonstration of the life of God in the soul of man. James 1:27 quotes almost word for word the Old Testament commands to look after the widow, the stranger and the orphan—a command given regularly throughout the Old Testament. Though apostolic emphasis was on looking after the poor in their midst, the equal emphasis was on looking after the marginalized of society, which included the stranger and the alien.

ACT: A personal pilgrimage

I was a product of the anti–social gospel position of many evangelicals. My post-conversion years in college and the years on InterVarsity staff had no social involvement, especially with organized student groups. We left that to the more liberal Student Christian Movement. It was only after 1974 and the historic Lausanne Congress, called together by Billy Graham, that integration started. The Lausanne Covenant changed a rigid position held for many years by evangelical Christians. Holistic evangelism began to be talked about.

In 1973, while helping as an InterVarsity staff person in Bombay and working part time in a Christian book shop to help support myself, I was rudely shaken from my theological position of the need to concentrate only on proclamation. I was hurrying to work one day when I saw a man sprawled in a bundle of rags on the sidewalk with a small crowd around him. He was in a coma. Some people had put small coins, a glass of water and a banana in front of that limp body. I had previously picked up a person or two off the streets, but this time it was inconvenient and I hurried on to work. I began to feel like the priest in the story of the Good Samaritan, anxious to get to temple duties.

That morning two of my friends from the graduate wing of InterVarsity met me. They had had similar experiences and feelings. We shared our frustrations and decided that we must do

314

something. In subsequent weeks we met, studied the Scriptures, hammered out a biblical social involvement statement and decided to form ACT. Our members, like us, were evangelicals who, while sharing the message among youth and college students, were looking for a balance in their practice of discipleship, especially in their witness among the poor.

After starting in 1973 (about a year before Lausanne 1974) we went through a project emphasis period where our main focus was getting programs started in the slums. We were never more than 15 in the main group. Our aim was to get everyone among the founding members involved. We learned a lot initially from volunteering in one of Mother Teresa's homes, where we would cut fingernails and toenails and give haircuts and a shave to the patients after worship on Sunday. In those early projects we collected donations from individuals and funding agencies to help small slum communities with education, nutrition and micro-business enterprises. Finally we hired a local worker, as we found our commute time hampering to the project. Organizational needs in the locale required people on the spot.

Our most successful project was with 300 children in three preschools in the slums of Marol near the international airport. Something was missing, however. We were finding involvement at the grassroots level diminishing, and we were hiring only professionals. Apart from mission groups and individuals, we were not seeing the local churches involved. Moreover, the emphasis had shifted only to social needs; sharing of the Scriptures was increasingly less. In the early years the children and parents had seen some wonderful things happen as a result of prayer. They had even seen water come up in a dry slum well in the heat of summer after the children prayed with their Sunday school teacher.

From project emphasis to church involvement

In 1991 we made a major paradigm shift. While waiting on God together, our board unitedly felt that, as a ministry, we had to take the biblical mandate of involvement with the poor to the body of Christ in Bombay. They were the best multi-generational structure set up for holistic witness in a community. They also were resourced and funded—sometimes very generously—by their own

315

members. As a result we shifted from the very successful project to work primarily in mobilizing local churches in the city of Bombay to reach out to their poor neighbors. That conviction and action took ACT from being a parachurch social agency to a mobilizer of the immense task force in the local congregations of Bombay. It called on them to respond to the incredible, mind-boggling needs among the poor of the city.

The long-range vision was to see each of the city's more than 500 urban congregations have a viable ministry to the poor. The impact would be deep and wide in our pluralistic society, with its cafeteria of gods and philosophies yet, with all the religion, one of the most oppressive stratified social systems one can imagine.

Poverty here comes as a result of oppressive social systems. Millions in India's villages and cities are trapped in economic cul de sacs, and neither they nor their children's children will be able to escape in spite of all the laws written in our statute books banning discrimination on the basis of caste and religion. Millions of the country's tribal people live on a subsistence level in spite of scores of schemes for their upliftment.

The need to see the gospel preached to the poor is not only for the future afterlife existence. It is supposed to let the oppressed go free and liberate captives (Isaiah 61) *now*! This is the gospel we are to present. Biblical salvation has profit both in this life as well as the life to come (1 Tim. 4:8). What if this vision became a reality and both justice and right thinking were integrated in all 500 congregations and in the whole city? The impact of doing "something beautiful for God" (to use Malcolm Muggeridge's phrase for Mother Teresa's work) multiplied many times over in churches can only be imagined.

We must realize that Mother Teresa's sodality of 5,000 nuns and 500 consecrated brothers, along with more than four million lay volunteers, is doing what Jesus expects every church to do. As local congregations we have drifted in to playing at "church and pastors," instead of being dynamic leaders leading the church to costly involvement, are busy doing the routine. To use G. K. Chesterton's phrase, the clergy are busy mainly in "hatching, matching and dispatching." Instead of the church being released into mission we are "pew warmers," basically Sunday attendees anxious to get the ritual over and the pastor to end his ten-minute homily. The inspired lay volunteer often has to find a parachurch body to get her or his hands dirty for the Lord.

Is it possible for a local church to be unleashed into ministry with the poor, the exploited and the marginalized? I believe this ministry is biblically warranted and wherever done in today's world it has been a powerful statement for the effectiveness and relevance of the gospel, leading to transformation in mind, soul and spirit. ACT, in 1992, left the project in charge of the project manager and an aid agency and moved into a church-related development and AIDS awareness and care emphasis called PACE (Prevention of AIDS through Care and Education). We structured and rooted the new program in the local church. We aimed, instead of trying to do it alone, to recruit churches all over the city. In its AIDS program the churches of the city are the resource pool for setting up community centers for awareness and care. There are currently eight of them.

On the community development side we offered ourselves as empowerers to local congregations through the pastor to help quick-start a ministry to the poor. These were congregations that, because of a lack of initiative or lack of resources or know-how, had not begun such a ministry. Over five years ACT has now had fifteen churches as partners in what are local congregations' programs. ACT's involvement stops with limited financing (generally 25–60 percent for three years), supervision and monitoring of projects if needed and know-how to run anything from preschools, literacy programs and health programs to savings banks for women coupled with loans for micro-enterprises. These are all maintained through sustainable programs.

We would like to be a resource for housing in Bombay's abominable housing situation. Forty-five percent of our population of 15 million live in shacks, while 150,000 live in shanties literally built on the sidewalks. Ambitious government schemes often result in bulldozing the houses of the poor into the ground to get rid of the problem for a short time.

317

THE CHALLENGE

Our present plans call for a steady recruitment of local congregations into development and AIDS-related ministry. Our prayer is that we will see a large percentage of local congregations involved with the city's poor and needy in the next five years. The eventual goal: dare we envision 500 churches involved? These are goals and dreams for one city. What changes would we witness in our cities globally if all churches had this same vision for ministry to the poor, the exploited, the never-ending stream of suffering humanity that overflows city streets? How would the people's situations change—men, women and children? How great would be their joy in having hopelessness and despair turned to expectant hope! Such hope is God's plan for each of our lives:

> For surely I know the plans I have for you, says the LORD, plans for your welfare and not for harm, to give you a future with hope (Jer. 29:11, *NRSV*).

Many, including sexually exploited children, will never know God's hope-producing plans for their lives unless we compassionately respond to their cries of need and desperation. May we indeed allow God to use us as instruments of hope and healing.

APPENDIX:

Resources for
Ministry & Networking

Books

Blanc, C. S. *Urban Children in Distress: Global Predicaments and Innovative Strategies*. UNICEF, 1994.

Crewdson, John. *By Silence Betrayed, Sexual Abuse of Children in America*. Boston/Toronto: Little Brown & Company, 1988.

De Koster, Katie, editor. *Child Abuse, Opposing Viewpoints*. Greenhaven Press, Inc.: San Diego, 1994.

ECPAT. *Children in Prostitution: Victims of Tourism in Asia*. Bangkok: ECPAT, 1992. (ECPAT, 328 Phyathai Rd., Bangkok 10400 Thailand.)

Eisenberg, A., H. Murkoff and S. Hathaway. *What to Expect When You Are Expecting*. New York: Workman, 1991.

Ennew, J. *The Sexual Exploitation of Children*. New York: St. Martin's Press, 1986.

Garbarino, James. *Raising Children in a Socially Toxic Environment*. San Francisco: Jossey-Bass Publishers, 1995.

Garbarino, James, Nancy Dubrow, Kathleen Kostelny and Carole Pardo. *Children in Danger: Coping with the Consequences of Community Violence*. San Francisco: Jossey-Bass Publishers, 1992.

Garbarino, James, E. Guttman and J. Seeley. *The Psychologically Battered Child*. San Francisco: Jossey-Bass Publishers, 1992.

Jurkovic, Gregory J., Ph.D. *Lost Childhoods: The Plight of the Parentified Child*. Bristol, Pa.: Brunner/Mazel Publishers, 1997.

Kilbourn, Phyllis. *Healing the Children of War: A Handbook for Ministry to Children Who Have Suffered Deep Traumas*. Monrovia, Calif.: MARC Publications, 1995.

Magid, Ken, and Carole A. McKelvey. *High Risk: Children Without a Conscience*. New York: Bantam Books, 1989.

Malchiodi, Cathy A. *Breaking the Silence: Art Therapy with Children from Violent Homes*, 2d edition (includes child sexual abuse). Bristol, Pa.: Brunner/Mazel Publishers, 1997.

McFarlane, K., and J. Waterman. *Sexual Abuse of Young Children*. New York: Guilford Press, 1986.

Monahon, Cynthia. *Children and Trauma: A Parent's Guide to Helping Children Heal*. New York: Lexington Books, 1993.

Oates, R. Kim, M.D. *The Spectrum of Child Abuse: Assessment, Treatment and Prevention*. Bristol, Pa.: Brunner/Mazel Publishers, 1996.

O'Grady, Ron. *The Rape of the Innocent*. Bangkok: ECPAT, 1994.

———. *The Child and the Tourist*. Bangkok: ECPAT, 1992.

Rushford, Patricia H. *The Jack and Jill Syndrome: Healing for Broken Children*. Chicago: Fleming H. Revell, 1996.

Weisberg, K. *Children of the Night: A Study of Adolescent Prostitution*. New York: Lexington Books, 1985.

Wharton, J., and M. T. Camacho de la Cruz. *Right to Happiness: Approaches to Prevention and Psycho-social Recovery of Child Victims of Commercial Sexual Exploitation*. NGO Group for the Convention on the Rights of the Child, 1966. (Available from the NGO Group, c/o DCI, PO Box 88, 1211 Geneva 20, Switzerland.)

Journals

First Call for Children
A quarterly publication of the Division of Information, UNICEF, New York.
First Call for Children,
UNICEF,
3 UN Plaza, H-9F,
New York, NY 10017

Journal of Child Sexual Abuse
Editorial Office
The Hawthorne Press
10 Alice Street
Binghamton, NY 13904

Child Abuse and Neglect: The International Journal [a professional journal]
The Journal of the International Society for the Prevention of Child Abuse and Neglect
Editorial Office
1205 Oneida Street
Denver, Colorado 80220

Network

Viva Network has a forum catering for the unique needs of Christians working with sexually exploited children. World Vision UK, as part of the network, serves as the facilitator of this forum. The forum's goals include:

1. Serving as a point of contact and support for Christians working specifically with sexually exploited children.

2. Helping meet the information needs of organizations working in this field by establishing a forum for the sharing of information and ideas, and for discussion of issues.

3. Identifying and sharing educational and training materials which will help resource those working with sexually exploited children.

For more information on joining this network, contact David Westwood at Viva/Box 633/Oxford OX1 4YP/UK or Internet: david.westwood@worldvision.org.uk.

Counseling Resource

Life After Assault League, Inc.
1336 West Lindbergh
Appleton, Wisconsin 54914 USA
920-739-4489 Telephone
920-739-1990 FAX

Life After Assault League (LAAL) is a unique ministry founded by Kay Zibolsky, a licensed minister. LAAL, a non-profit organization, seeks to reach out to people who have been sexually abused. Free Christian counseling is offered to assist sexually abused adults and children. LAAL is a resource for many ministries, including Focus on the Family. Send a self-addressed, stamped envelope to the above address for further information and a listing of available booklets. *Healing Hidden Hurts*, a book featuring Rev. Zibolsky's story of healing from sexual abuse, also can be purchased from the above address.

 **MARC**

Bringing you key resources on the world mission of the church

MARC books and other publications support the work of MARC (Mission Advanced Research and Communications Center), which is to inspire vision and empower Christian mission among those who extend the whole gospel to the whole world.

Other books by Phyllis Kilbourn:

▶ *Street Children: A Guide to Effective Ministry.* Equips Christians for service to children who are struggling to survive on the streets. Explains who street children are, where they can be found, why they are on the streets and the nature and extent of their trauma. Ideal for those working directly with children or in urban ministry.

264 pp. $23.95

▶ *Children in Crisis: A New Commitment.* Moves you to a biblical response to children who are facing various crises around the world, such as AIDS, abandonment, sexual abuse, forced labor, war, urban violence and girl-child discrimination. 304 pp. $21.95

▶ *Healing the Children of War: A Handbook for Ministry to Children Who Have Suffered Deep Traumas.* Children are the most innocent and helpless victims of war. This volume is designed to give practical guidance to those who desire to be of service. Equally applicable to those working with victims of national wars or urban violence.

330 pp. $21.95

Recent MARC titles:

▶ *Choosing a Future for U.S. Missions*, by Paul McKaughan, Dellanna O'Brien and William O'Brien. Helps your organization project itself into the future in order to begin strategically planning today.

128 pp. $11.95

▶ *Together Again: Kinship of Word and Deed*, by Roger S. Greenway. Concisely and creatively reunites evangelism and social action under the banner of evangelical missions. 40 pp. $5.95

▶ *Symbol and Ceremony: Making Disciples Across Cultures*, by A.H. Mathias Zahniser. Shows how the rites, symbols and ceremonies of many cultures can be given a Christian meaning and used for discipleship. Ideal for Western Christians seeking to avoid syncretism while discipling Christians from other cultures.　　183 pp.　$11.95

▶ *Beyond Duty: A Passion for Christ, a Heart for Mission*, by Tim Dearborn. Designed for group or individual study, this guide restores the joy to mission by showing that it is not a duty, but a privilege that flows from our personal relationship with the God of mission.

Study guide　88 pp. . . . . $ 8.95
Leader's guide . . . . $ 2.95
Video $15.95
Complete set $19.95

▶ *Mission Handbook 1998-2000*, John A. Siewert and Edna G. Valdez, editors. Brings you key information about mission agencies in North America. Listings include all contact information to help you network effectively. Contains new research and analyses of emerging mission trends and addresses today's paramount mission concerns.

528 pp.　$49.95

▶ *The New Context of World Mission*, by Bryant L. Myers. A thorough yet concise visual portrayal of the entire sweep of Christian mission. Full-color graphics and up-to-date statistics show the history of mission and reveal its future challenges.

Book . . . . 60 pp. $　8.95
Slides . . . . 49 pp. $149.95
Overheads . . . . .49 pp. $149.95
Presentation Set *(one book, slides, overheads)* $249.00

Contact us toll free in the U.S.: 1-800-777-7752
Direct: (626) 301-7720

 MARC A division of World Vision
800 W. Chestnut Ave. • Monrovia, CA • 91016-3198 • USA

Ask for the MARC Newsletter and complete publications list